CATHOLIC EDUCATION
FACES ITS FUTURE

NEIL G. McCLUSKEY, S.J.

Catholic Education
Faces its Future

Foreword by
THEODORE M. HESBURGH, C.S.C.

DOUBLEDAY & COMPANY, INC.
GARDEN CITY, NEW YORK

Library of Congress Catalog Card Number: 68–10544
Copyright © 1968, 1969 by Doubleday & Company, Inc.
All Rights Reserved
Printed in the United States of America
First Edition

Contents

861065

What paralyzes life is not to dream and not to dare. The difficulty is not in resolving problems but in posing them.

Today something is happening to the whole structure of human consciousness. A fresh kind of life is starting.
Pierre Teilhard de Chardin, S.J.

This book is for John Courtney Murray, S.J.,
and the others who stayed under the cloud, like Teilhard,
because they believed in the Son.

Acknowledgments

How does a writer do a complete job of acknowledging ideas and of thanking the people who encouraged and helped? Many seeds of thought in this book were planted by individuals, groups, and audiences during visits to a score of states over the past several years. How does one properly acknowledge the intellectual osmosis that takes place through daily association with faculty colleagues and friends on a vibrant campus? How does a professor tell his graduate students how much their exchange in seminars means in refining his ideas?

Special note of gratitude must go to friends who were kind enough to read the manuscript: George N. Shuster, James M. Lee, Robert Hassenger, J. Philip Gleason, C. Albert Koob, Vincent P. Lannie, John E. Walsh, Didier Piveteau, and Bishop William F. McManus. The manuscript was typed and duplicated by Eloise Mihills, Carolyn Pietrzak, and Eileen Davitt. This book would still be in preparation without generous help from my students: Sister Eileen Kelly, Sister Marilyn Rose Ginder, Sister Clara Jordan, Larry Bright, and Ed Ziegler. To my long-suffering editor and patient friend, John J. Delaney, I say with a sigh: "Thanks, John, for keeping me at it!"

The Author

Foreword

Ten years ago Father McCluskey wrote *Catholic Viewpoint on Education,* which the *New York Times* called "a concise, well-documented book . . . about Catholic education within the total spectrum of American education." Once more in his new book he has attempted to situate, analyze, and suggest approaches to the major problems facing Catholic education within the full spectrum of American education. Comparing the two books, one recalls with amazement how very much has happened during the past ten years.

Beyond doubt the problem that looms largest in people's minds in 1969 is the justification for the separate Catholic institution. What precisely is a *Catholic* school? What is a *Catholic* university? The present volume contributes richly to the answers. Father McCluskey argues that there is—or at least can be—something truly distinctive about the Catholic educational enterprise. He writes of a quality, a climate, an atmosphere—something that does more than "protect" the faith, something that brings life, something that shines as a beacon before all men, something that makes the school a Christian community.

The age of apologetics is over. In his early chapters, Father shows how the protectionist function of the Catholic school mirrored the siege mentality of the church which extended almost to the middle of the present century. In such a beleaguered atmosphere, it was natural that the separate Catholic school should be accepted without question by most Catholics, all the more since it was under periodic attack from the non-Catholic world. The current reappraisal of Catholic education is part of the general re-evaluation of the means the church uses to achieve her goals. The Catholic school, as is brought out by the author, is no longer viewed as an absolute institution but as one way of introducing the young into the Christian community. With this fresh perspective many thoughtful Catholics have come to realize that they are much less clear than they thought they were about the purpose of the Catholic school. Aware of the increasingly heavy cost in manpower and money to support a system that provides for a minority of Catholic youth, some argue against having any Catholic schools. Probably the majority of Catholics are still convinced of the necessity of the Catholic school. Both camps will find in this book ammunition for and against their positions. Nor is this strange. The school issue is frightfully complex and it really cannot be intelligently discussed, as Father's final chapter tells us, in the old terms and concepts.

It is expected that university educators would have a bias in favor of higher education. Accordingly, Chapter Seven is for a Catholic university president the best reading in the book. Having worked on several projects with Notre Dame's professor of education, I know of his efforts to rouse the leadership in the Catholic college and university world to pool their efforts and build significantly for tomorrow. His temporary loan to Notre Dame is part of the new cooperative spirit of which he writes. And I know of no one who is better qualified than Father McCluskey to write this book at this time. He has both wisdom and courage, a rare combination.

Our new open society calls for a new and open Christian. He will have to be trained in a different and an even better way than his parents and grandparents. An essential characteristic of the Catholic school of the future—on any level—must be its openness to truth and charity. The Vatican Council called the Catholic school important because "it can contribute so substantially to fulfilling the mission of God's people, and can further the dialogue between the church and the family of man to their mutual benefit."

In their own 1967 statement the American bishops repeated the tone of the Vatican II statement: "Our schools must be an expression of what is meant by being a Christian in today's world. If they are, there will come a time, and not in the too distant future, when the trials and troubles of the present moment will be seen for what they really are, steps toward a new era for Catholic education."

As Catholic education faces its future, those of us involved therein will need to have the qualities of the pioneer: vision, courage, confidence, and a great hope inspired by faith and freshened by love. The present book challenges its readers to take up the work of tomorrow with this kind of intelligent optimism. We are grateful to Father Neil McCluskey for the stimulus his book will bring to what deserves to be a wide and varied audience.

Theodore M. Hesburgh, c.s.c.

December 8, 1968
Notre Dame, Indiana

CATHOLIC EDUCATION
FACES ITS FUTURE

CHAPTER ONE

The Idea: Time and Eternity

The explosive forces unloosed by the Second Vatican Council are forcing a complete reappraisal of Catholic education in the United States on every level. As in all other areas of Catholicism, traditional patterns and forms are being scrutinized to determine their relevancy to contemporary life. In theory, and perhaps ideally, such an *autocritique* should take place within an atmosphere of great calm and deliberateness. However, history instructs us that such a thing seldom happens, because man inclines more toward revolution than evolution, and, as his dissatisfaction with the shortcomings of his social institutions increases, so his patience decreases. In fact, it can be argued that revolutions take place, not because social change is not occurring but because it is not taking place rapidly enough. In other words, the teased man can quickly turn into the man of fury who strikes out wildly to seize what he wants.

To find a period similar to the present, one must search back to the early sixteenth century when the medieval structure of Christendom broke up into fragments. Then, too, traditional ideas, customs, and relationships underwent far-reaching change. Then, too, the Western world had to revise much of its understanding of man and his relations to his fellows, to the universe, and to his Maker. Then, too, man was forced to re-examine the school and clarify its objectives.

* * *

For several decades the American Catholic community has been lulled by a false sense of security. We had taken pride in the massive growth of Catholic education—the number of schools, the millions enrolled, the impressive buildings. Behind the statistical façade there was security, and with confidence we looked ahead to more and more of the same. Today the Catholic community is widely aware that all does not go well within its schools, and this awareness is in addition to the general concern of society that all is not well with America's whole school structure. Yet Catholic education hovers on the brink of its greatest challenge. This statement might seem anomalous, given the fact that in many dioceses school enrollments are falling off, the ranks of religious faculty are thinning, schools are being closed, and many colleges and universities are in a financial crisis. Last year's total of full-time pupils in the elementary and secondary schools dropped by 218,840 from the 1966–67 school year and by 108,748 from the preceding year. Though the downward trend seems to have been arrested with this year's leveling off of enrollment (Catholic secondary school enrollment by itself is at an all-time high of an estimated 1,116,395), the decline from 1964's peak of 5,662,328 amounts to a drop of over 400,000 pupils.[1]

The times call for neither Cassandras nor Pollyannas but for hard-nosed realists with clarity of vision and conviction of principle. An example of this balance is found in the 1967 address of the Bishop of Manchester, New Hampshire, Ernest J. Primeau, to the National Catholic Educational Association (NCEA) annual convention:

We should neither fear change nor should we seek it for its own sake. Both are dangers as the renewal of the church proceeds. Sometimes indeed it seems as if Catholics were on the brink of dividing themselves into two polarized camps: on the one hand, those who fear and resist every hint of departure from the old ways of doing things, and on the other those who feel that radical uprooting is the only road to renewal.[2]

The gift of prophecy is not required to predict that the Catholic school of the 1970's, like America's schools generally, is going to differ dramatically from its predecessors, each of which has reflected the constantly changing society of which it is part. It can likewise be predicted that the question of the relation of the publicly-supported school to religion and religious education, along with the correlative question of the role of the church-related school in the total scheme of things, will be approached in a more sophisticated and socially realistic manner. The college scene will also shift radically.

[1] See appended table.
[2] National Catholic Educational Association, *Proceedings and Addresses of the National Catholic Educational Association* (Atlantic City, N.J., 1967), p. 17.

School leadership in the American church is beginning to come to grips with the new social realities. Awareness is coming that the "business-as-usual" attitude must go, for "the church is, essentially, not an instrument for the preservation of the status quo, but rather a dynamic agent for bringing about change." The disciplined, respectable, conformist product of yesterday's parochial school does not fit into the world of tomorrow. The new house of Catholic education is going to be more compact and will be put to better use. The new emphasis with be upon Catholic *education* (with an ecumenical coloring) rather than on formal Catholic *schooling*. Priorities are already shifting. The new allocation of personnel and resources will give a better opportunity to the disadvantaged.

On what are these predictions based? There is a growing awareness that an "inner city" with schools that are impoverished, declining, and racially unbalanced, has emerged in almost every one of our large urban areas. In some metropolitan areas, like New York and Chicago, the only extensive reservoirs of non-Negro pupils left in the inner city are in Catholic parochial schools. Nor is this simply a problem for New York and Chicago, whose predicted Negro population in 2000 A.D. will respectively be 50 and 55 per cent of the total population. The same prediction gives for that year these percentages: Washington, 75; Cleveland, 67; Newark, 63; Baltimore, 56; Philadelphia, Detroit, and St. Louis, 50 per cent.[3] Obviously whatever general scholarship and aid programs are devised to assist Negro pupils to move into schools of lesser racial concentration will have to include proportionate places in private and church-related elementary and secondary schools.

Catholic schools come in for a fair share of the blame with the public schools for not combating more vigorously the educational pattern which, given the decline of the cities, has inexorably evolved and locked the Negro family in the urban ghetto. In fact, in some neighborhoods the parochial schools lie open to the charge that they are a barrier and a handicap to racial integration. But the generalization made by spokesmen for the American Jewish Congress and the American Civil Liberties Union during the heated debate over

[3] White House Conference "To Fulfill These Rights," *Council's Report and Recommendations to the Conference,* Washington, D.C., June 1–2, 1966 (Washington, D.C.: Government Printing Office, 1966), p. 37. See also Herman Kahn and Anthony J. Wiener, *The Year 2000* (New York: The Macmillan Company, 1967).

dropping the "Blaine Amendment" from the 1967 revised New York State constitution was errant nonsense. They charged that white upper- and lower-middle-class families put their children in parochial schools in order to keep them out of the public schools, with the result that the public schools in America's cities are fast becoming educational hovels mainly for the Negro poor. As one long-time critic of Catholic schools has phrased it:

> The bare, unadulterated truth of the matter is that the private school is a major instrument of segregation. It is not, except in the South, purposefully racially segregated. Indeed, it is becoming less religiously purposefully segregated. Racial segregation in the private schools, and increasingly religious segregation, is a function of economic segregation. The private school is becoming the home of middle and upper classes. Negroes don't go to private schools, not because of the blackness of their skin but because of the emptiness of their pockets.
>
> The public school is fast becoming the dumping ground for society's rejects. And for some reason or other, those rejects almost all have black skins.[4]

The element of truth in this allegation is unfortunately obfuscated by exaggeration. True, there is a regrettable pattern of segregation in both the public and parochial schools of most of the large American cities, principally because the inner city neighborhoods are *de facto* segregated. It is an unfortunate reality that the public school in an all-black neighborhood ends up as an all-black school. However, it is also a matter of record that many church-related schools in the inner city of the large metropolitan areas have at great sacrifice made provision in classrooms for thousands of pupils from the ghetto who do not belong to the religious faith of the sponsoring group. Though the Catholic Negro population of the United States is less than 2 per cent, in the Catholic schools of New York City there is an impressively higher Negro enrollment. In fact, the Negro and Spanish-speaking elementary-school enrollment of the borough of Manhattan is 46.7 per cent and the figure for Manhattan and the Bronx is 30 per cent nonwhite.[5]

---

[4] Leo Pfeffer, "Freedom and Control in Education," *Public Controls for Non-Public Schools,* Donald A. Erickson, ed., University of Chicago Press (in press) 1969.

[5] 1966–67 figures supplied by the Superintendent of the Archdiocesan Schools of New York and the Superintendent's Office of the Brooklyn Diocese. Virgil C. Blum writes: "There are 35 racially mixed neighborhoods in Man-

Every one of the ninety Catholic high schools in the two counties making up the Archdiocese of Chicago has a policy of open enrollment, and over two-thirds of them have both white and Negro pupils. The proportion of students from the inner city parishes of Chicago going on to Catholic high schools is considerably higher than in the suburbs, not uncommonly as high as 90 per cent.[6] Yet as the move to the suburbs continues, open enrollment invariably results in blacker and blacker schools.

Though some dioceses and certain Catholic educational leaders have from the beginning consistently applied the church's concern in schooling to the economically underprivileged of urban America, in the years immediately ahead this concern will have to be much more universal. Awareness has certainly become widespread that the Christian witness of the religiously-inspired school for the poor must be more emphasized. No one has put the issue more bluntly than Philadelphia's superintendent of Catholic schools, Edward T. Hughes, in stating, "If we abandon the poor and underprivileged, if we cease to reach out to the Negro child, if we become more and more suburban and less and less inner city, then we ought to get out of the educational business."[7] In the Philadelphia Catholic schools there are proportionately more Negroes than there are in the Catholic schools of any other city in the nation.

It was the former U. S. Commissioner of Education, Harold Howe II, speaking to the Easter 1968 convention of the NCEA in San Francisco, who touched on the three characteristics of the Catholic school system that fit it for leadership in the job of integrating America's schools.

1. The Catholic system is mainly metropolitan and hence well suited to dealing with the problems of the city.

2. Catholic schools are free from the political considerations that so regularly clog the administration of public systems.

---

hattan and the Bronx in which the Catholic elementary school is better integrated than the neighborhoods themselves. The Nativity School with an enrollment of 766 pupils has 325 white children who are bussed in from 31 white middle-class neighborhoods. And in Harlem the Irish Christian Brothers operate Rice High School with 913 students, of whom 589 are whites who come from middle-class neighborhoods into the ghetto and into an integrated school." *Education: Freedom and Competition* (Chicago: Argus Communications Co., 1967).

[6] Figures supplied by the Catholic School Board Office, Archdiocese of Chicago.

[7] *Washington Perspective*, II (April, 1968), 8.

3. The diocesan boundaries of the Catholic school system include both cities and suburbs, a factor that makes for a regional approach to integration.

His words merit quotation:

> By refusing to abandon the inner cities as your traditional clientele moves to the suburbs, you can serve an American society that has not yet overcome the political fragmentation and economic myopia which make our cities powerless to help themselves.
>
> Indeed, you can seek new adventures of cooperation with public schools, if you can locate school leaders who are unafraid to challenge some of the unconstructive assumptions of traditional church-state separation. Leaders of this character are emerging in at least a few cities.[8]

Moreover, the commissioner gently reminded his Catholic audience that "if the Christian message in our time seems increasingly to go unheard, if organized religion seems to evoke as much cynicism as enthusiasm from those under thirty, it is because the churches —while preaching a denial of worldliness—have too often embraced it, have profited from it, have accepted the American way of life in its most superficial, materialistic sense."[9]

Costly as it may prove in terms of dollars and cents, the church's vocation of witness and service must, like its Founder's, be to the weak and the poor. It is good to be reminded of this bedrock truth from the voice of one technically an outsider. The last reason for closing down a Catholic school should be that the neighborhood can no longer support it. At their spring meeting last year in St. Louis, the Catholic bishops of the United States publicly addressed themselves to the issue. They stated:

> The educational resources of the church should be activated to assist in improving the education of black people and other minority groups handicapped by underprivilege, and in attacking the evil of segregationalist attitudes.
>
> Over 200 Catholic schools located in the ghettoes have closed their doors in the last two years. Not only must this trend be reversed but the church must make every effort to provide the highest quality of education in such schools. Her limited resources of money and personnel prohibit

[8] National Catholic Educational Association, *Proceedings and Addresses of the National Catholic Educational Association Convention* (San Francisco, April 18, 1968).

[9] *Ibid.*

mass education in these areas; however, model schools should be developed and maintained.

While the dioceses and the teaching congregations in the church are making new commitments to education of the underprivileged, there is still a limit to what private resources can do. As the federal and state governments address themselves to these same handicapped areas, it should be clearly in the national purpose for them to find appropriate ways to work with private educational agencies and even through them. Again it should be clear that teaching aids created to educate for new social attitudes or to sharpen mathematical and scientific skills can never be fully successful if they are not made easily available to the private and church-related institutions. The same things can be said of almost any new pattern, like the proposed "educational parks." Without some provision to include all types of schools in such a complex, the original intent is thwarted. These remarks are made with the full consciousness that the American philosophy of separation between church and state does not always allow *identical* treatment of church-oriented and tax-supported schools but does call for the appropriate *equivalence*. In other words, even though the ways and means available to the federal and state governments to make use of the resources of the private and church-related schools in confronting the racial problem in American education are constitutionally limited, they must be studied and, where feasible, employed so that these schools may serve as full partners with the public schools in the struggle for improved education for all. In a later chapter this point will be more fully developed.

* * *

There is widespread concern over the increase of religious illiteracy among American youth and its influence upon public morality. The presence of the church-related schools is a reminder that the deepest values traditionally cherished in America are rooted in the religious and ethical traditions of Western culture. As presently structured the American public school is unable to assist its pupils to take a stand on, or perhaps even to confront, the central questions which come to grips with the meaning of man: his origin, his purpose, his destiny. Even with good will and personal commitment, public-school teachers and advisers are generally not permitted to answer or to raise the great questions that transcend the secular order but must speak in muted voice about God, duty, rights, and the future life.

In these sophisticated years it still seems ironic that the religiously-sponsored schools are almost expected in some quarters to apologize for their existence. Yet they were America's pioneer schools. They have played a critical role in transmitting the American heritage and in enriching our society. In furnishing healthy competition, they often have been a stimulus to the public schools.

On the other hand, there have always been those who have not been content to let the public school sell itself on its own merits but have tried to establish a public school monopoly in education, based on the assumption that national unity required the bringing together of all American children into a single school system. This thesis, which still crops up from time to time, grew out of the historic Protestant-Catholic tensions of the last century.[10] For people of this mentality the public school has somehow been officially elevated to the status of the establishment, and, as the guardian and interpreter of the American way of life, is the unique teaching arm of the great New World (once Protestant, now secular) republic. The uneasiness of some public-school leaders was heightened during the two decades after World War II because of the explosive expansion of Catholic schools. While in 1940, there were 2,580,000 pupils in Catholic elementary and secondary schools, 9.2 per cent of the total school population, in the peak year of 1964 the total had increased to 5,660,000 or 12 per cent of America's school population. Dire warnings were heard that the end of public education was in sight.

Yet many of these critics were sufficiently astute to see the inconsistency of their position with the liberal avowal of freedom of choice. Here was their dilemma. If the common good of the nation so hinged on a uniform type of school system, then no competing system should be tolerated. Then the real question would be not the growth of the Catholic schools but the propriety of their existing at all. But to forbid religious schools or to place a quota upon their number would be to ape the pattern of certain countries where things

10 Though most often motivated by anti-Catholicism, the fundamentalist urge to suppress all nonpublic schools has been propelled by fear of both the immigrant class and the privileged class. These are the tight-lipped folk who enacted prohibition and put the "monkey laws" on the books.

like personal freedom and individual dignity have pretty well gone by the board.

Obviously the growth and expansion of rival schools did to some extent take place at the expense of the public schools, just about in the same way that Standard Oil grew at the expense of Shell Oil. The good of American society, however, has never been identical nor coextensive with the good of the public schools. It must be immediately added that the public schools have served American society well—and service is precisely their function. That so many millions of American parents decided that the publicly-supported schools were not fulfilling an educational need of their children and so felt constrained to build their own schools should, however, give pause. The state clearly has rights in education, but the school belongs to the nation, not the state. Pluralism should be an essential note of the school world lest the nation lose the beauty and richness of diversity. Nationalization of the schools would be a betrayal of the national culture.

The independent church-related school has already performed—and is performing—a considerable service to American society simply by preserving a link to an earlier era when the state's hand rested less heavy on education, and parents were more aware of their freedom to choose the kind of school they wanted for their children. Despite the assumption of some people, the state-established secular school has no prior claim on the allegiance of all citizens, and no parent is in the slightest degree "disloyal" when he exercises his natural right to patronize his own school. If there is a primacy of spiritual values over the purely secular, there is a valid choice of a religious over a secular school—at least this has been the tradition of Western civilization.

*   *   *

As already stated, the Catholic schools share in the penetrating criticism of education which has been rocking the school world. The same pressures that have forced a reappraisal of public-school education are at work on the Catholic schools from a society demanding more particularized care of the pupil, more professionalism in handling the learning process itself, better techniques in the use of teaching aids and machines, more efficiency in the expenditure of the school dollar, and more accountability to the public paying the bill.

Understandably enough, these pressures have evoked strong reaction from Catholic school people. One can easily appreciate the frustration and anger of those who have labored long and hard to strengthen the Catholic school and who find their successes passed over by critics who see only the many things that remain to be done. Yet criticism is necessary and healthy. In fact, it can be argued that the impressive improvements in the staffing and administration of so many Catholic schools in recent years have come about precisely because of it.

On this general subject we can listen with profit to one of the giants of the church of the nineteenth century. Orestes A. Brownson penned these words over a hundred years ago:

> . . . the subject of Catholic education itself cannot be prudently withdrawn from discussion, either private or public; nor can its discussion be confined to the prelates and clergy alone. The laity have, to say the least, as deep an interest in it as have the ecclesiastics or the religious, and they have in regard to it the common right of all men to judge for themselves.[11]

Brownson noted that "parents have certain duties growing out of their relation as parents which they cannot throw upon others, and they must themselves discharge them according to the best of their ability. They are bound by the law of God to give their children, as far as in their power, a truly Catholic education, and they are free to criticize and to refuse to support schools, though professing to be Catholic, in which such education is not and cannot be expected to be given."[12] His point is still true. The qualification "Catholic" does not render a school immune from criticism nor sacred from investigation.

It is unfortunately true that irresponsible critics at times utter foolish remarks and these may be temporarily damaging. But the alternative is far worse. Good can rarely emerge from an imposed silence or from party-line conformity or from fear of scrutiny or from rigid defense mechanisms. As we face the challenges of the

---

[11] Henry F. Brownson, ed., XII, *The Works of Orestes A. Brownson* (Detroit: Thorndike Nourse, 1884), 496–514; reprinted from *Brownson's Quarterly Review*, Third New York Series, III (January, 1862), 66–84.

[12] *Ibid.*

years ahead, the Catholic school will be the stronger and the healthier for not seeking refuge behind a clerical curtain.

* * *

No field is so crowded with authorities and experts as is education. Nor is any subject so difficult to define. Definition is difficult because of the broad nature of education and its instant reflection of the kaleidoscopic changes in society itself. In the large meaning of the term, education is any learning experience—a cognitive or affective or emotional influence that is formative of man as a person. In society there is a host of factors that continually play on man's relationship to his environment. The popular media, for example, television and newspapers, contribute largely to man's continuing education. The presence of traffic police and street signals establish order for man's walking or driving and as such are educational influences. Living with others at home, associating with people with whom one shares the same religious views—these are all educative factors forming man.

Assuming man to be a dependent social being, the most elemental understanding of the term "education" is as the introduction of the young into a society. The elders of the community, particularly the parents or immediate family, take upon themselves the responsibility for initiating the generation behind them into the culture of the group—the lore, the skills, the traditions of that society. Again, in its simplest form, education consists of a value system or hierarchy of assumptions against which the community measures worth of ideas and deeds. This is the group value system or philosophy of life or *Weltanschauung*. Some things are to be sacrificed in favor of other things because they are esteemed more highly. Good, better, and best are decided in relation to the community's total system of values. The process of acquiring a set of values is in large part an indirect one, involving as it does commitments and loyalties not always susceptible to logical analysis but absorbed within an atmosphere. Yet these become so firmly enmeshed in one's life that there have always been individuals and groups in society which have suffered material loss, social ostracism, and even death rather than abandon or compromise their ideals.

Nor can the learning process be completely separated from the acquisition of values. In studying the words and deeds of preceding generations, the young are attracted to the ideals of those who have gone before and, by living in a somewhat controlled environment, they tend to absorb in some degree these same attitudes. In fact, the elders purposefully structure the initiation process so that the young will view favorably and begin to identify with the group values. Before anyone arches a critical eye, let it be recalled that this is an ancient process of which every country has always made use to build patriots. We older Americans teach our young to respect our flag, to sing our songs, to learn our legends, to honor our great men, to be prepared even to die for America because of pride in its traditions. We value our country and so we are biased in favor of the American idea and train our children to the same bias. Nor are things different in Canada, China, or the Congo.

In searching for a definition of religious education, we must keep two principles clearly in sight. The first is, to paraphrase Gabriel Cardinal Garrone, that initiation to God does not follow the laws of any learning, for God is not an object among the objects of knowledge. A person does not learn to love God, no more than he learns to know Him as something outside the rest of one's learning. Hence, we cannot exclude God from our knowledge or from our love or from our education. The second is that the family is the first and ideal cadre for initiation to God, and any other artificially constructed cadre must adjust to the family, and not vice versa.[13]

Religious education is an ambiguous phrase. In a restricted sense religious education is instruction in the beliefs and practices of a systematized or institutionalized religion in order to achieve knowledge and understanding. However, since the sponsoring group usually undertakes religious education because it aims to strengthen commitment among its members and to introduce a new generation to its religious heritage, loyalty and service to the faith community are also goals of religious education. When all these are combined, i.e., understanding and commitment with loyalty and service, religious education is perhaps more accurately called religious formation. Both of these latter should be distinguished from theology. The science of theology, a venerable academic discipline, has traditionally held a respected place among humanistic studies. Man's experience with the transcendental or the divine is woven largely into

[13] *Documentation Catholique,* LXIII (1966), col. 819–25.

his total culture, and man's attempts to analyze and synthesize religious experience, utilizing the same principles as used in other academic disciplines, are the bases of scientific theology.

Because the distinction between Catholic formal education or *schooling* and Catholic education in the larger sense of formation is often blurred in people's minds, discussion becomes difficult, if not impossible. In fact, it can become fruitless, even bitter. It has always been accepted that Catholic parents are conscience-bound to provide for the Catholic education of their children. Does this mean that parents fail in their obligation if they do not send their children to Catholic schools? Not necessarily, because the separate Catholic school is not the only way of giving a Catholic education. At a given time and place it might well be the best way. But most Catholic children even in affluent America have not gone to separate Catholic schools and are not attending them now. Catholic communities in few other countries have even attempted separate Catholic schools on the scale America has, and yet the obligation to give a Catholic education has always and everywhere been present. The separate school then may be the ideal way but it obviously cannot be the exclusive way.

When Christ urged His disciples to "go and teach," more accurately translated, "go and make followers of," He hardly had in mind arithmetic or phonetics. Teaching the rudiments to impressionable young minds may be an excellent way to indirectly present Christ and His message to potential followers. In fact, founding a Catholic institute of thermonuclear physics or applied mathematics may be an excellent way to make keen minds indirectly aware of Christian ethics. Yet the "education" intended by Christ is not immediately and directly related to profane learning or secular knowledge. Christ did not come to found schools. Formal education was not His mission. If anything, He was concerned with adult education.

The most contemporary of the new catechisms reminds us that "the gospel says little about culture. Jesus does not reject art or science. Neither does He counsel them. He refers to the flowers by the wayside, which He finds more beautiful than the magnificent clothes worn by Solomon. When His disciples admired the architecture of the temple, He had its destruction before His mind's eye. But on the other hand, His parables are so simple and telling that

He must be counted among the greatest wielders of the word among mankind."[14]

As a man, Christ was one of the greatest forces in human culture. However, continues the catechism, "He did not explicitly devote Himself to science or to art, and He did not give any instructions on the subject. The one thing that dominates His mind is the lordship of God, the leaven of the world which is for its peace. He accepted so fully God's preference for poverty and service that He gave His whole life to these things. They were the greatest beauty and the greatest truth that He knew. It is a vocation and a privilege to share with Him this passionate single-mindedness."[15] With similar single-mindedness the church pursues its essential teaching objective: to bring Christ to men—and formal schooling is simply one of the ways.

* * *

In discussing the necessity for separate Catholic schools, proponents often cite as an argument the words of Pius XI, from his encyclical letter on education. In describing the nature of education, the late pontiff writes:

Since education consists essentially in preparing man for what he must be and for what he must do here below, in order to attain the sublime end for which he was created, it is clear that there can be no true education which is not wholly directed to man's last end. . . .[16]

And again in speaking of the goal of all education, he says:

The proper and immediate end of Christian education is to co-operate with divine grace in forming the true and perfect Christian, that is, to form Christ Himself in those regenerated by baptism. . . .[17]

These quotations are then supposed to triumphantly terminate discussion. There is no more to be said.

However, there is a great deal more to be said. The pope is here

14 Higher Catechetical Institute at Nijmegen, *A New Catechism, Catholic Faith for Adults* (New York: Herder and Herder, 1967), p. 440.

15 *Ibid.*

16 "The Christian Education of Youth" (*Divini Illius Magistri*), in *Education,* ed. by the Benedictine Monks of Solesmes, trans. by Rev. Aldo Rebeschini (Boston: The Daughters of St. Paul, 1960), p. 203.

17 *Ibid.,* p. 243.

giving a description of the ultimate and general purpose of all education and by no stretch of the imagination is he attempting to give a definition of the *specifying* end of the school as such. In other words, the pope is discussing Catholic education in the broad sense, a concern shared by many agencies.

The Catholic apologist who explains the rationale of the Catholic school with the neat statement that it exists "to save souls" is giving only the general explanation of the school's purpose. It does not indicate the specific objective, the factor which tells us the purpose of the school as such, in distinction to the purpose of the hospital or the asylum or the retreat house or the summer camp. Each one of these activities has its proper objective that specifies it or makes it what it is. Since "to save souls" is also a purpose of each of these other activities, it can only be a description of the school's ultimate purpose—a purpose the school must, of necessity, share in the absolute order with all human undertakings. Lamentably, this view of formal education as an almost exclusively or predominantly moral undertaking has justified some rather dismal pedagogical practices and policies. Maybe it cannot be different. There will always be good people who will tolerate and defend incompetent and ill-prepared teachers, creaky and irrelevant curriculum, undermanned staff and "over-childrened" classrooms, and, in general, ignore sound educational principles because of a fervent conviction that all that really matters is a cross atop the building. Their minds seem impervious to the point that before you can have a *Catholic* school, you must have a *school*. Apropos of this pietistic attitude, Notre Dame's Leo Ward once commented: "In some circumstances, an inherently lower end must rate highest; for instance, it is better to give a starving man some soup than to pray for him; and good as it is to pray for him, we should not let the praying get in the way of the soup."[18]

Similar to the "saving-of-souls" explanation of the purpose of the Catholic school is the "teaching-of-catechism" theory of the Catholic school; i.e., it exists to teach Christian doctrine. Contrary to a widespread misconception (frequently among Catholics themselves), a Catholic school does not exist primarily to teach the catechism. Were this the purpose, there would truly be no necessity for the separate Catholic school. Why not? Because if this were its *raison d'être*, it would mean there could be no other way of teach-

[18] *New Life in Catholic Schools* (St. Louis: Herder and Herder, 1958), p. 15.

ing religious truths except by means of the separate school. Yet
there have been many other ways in the church, some long in use
by other religious groups as well. Bible or catechetical instruction
can be given in special classes either before or after a Sunday religious
service, by the parents in the home, by home visits of a teacher,
by instruction during Mass, and by a rich variety of released-time
and dismissed-time programs. Any one of these or a combination
could fulfill the objective of imparting adequate religious knowledge.
The teaching of Catholic doctrine, therefore, cannot be either the
exclusive or even the principal function of the Catholic school, let
alone its reason for existence.

That so many people continue to regard the separate school either
as the only valid form of Catholic education or as an instrument
designed chiefly to preserve the faith or as an enterprise undertaken
primarily to save souls becomes more understandable in the light
of the history of the Catholic Church in America. This important
subject will be treated in the following chapters but here it might
be pointed out that the papal and episcopal documents written to
encourage American Catholics to fulfill the obligation to protect
the faith of their children through separate schools are framed within
a special historical context.

There has not yet been a carefully thought-through philosophy of
contemporary Catholic education. Those who point to authoritative
declarations on education by church leadership, papal or episcopal,
to justify the nothing-but-parochial-schools position miss the thrust
of these pastoral documents. Invariably the statements insist that all
school activities, including the strictly academic, are means to an
ultimate end: the student's Christian formation. It can be readily
admitted, though, that much Catholic writing over the past fifty
years has stressed to an extreme the moralist approach to formal
education, a factor which has unquestionably been of profound influence in the thinking of pastors and bishops. Nonetheless, the
moralist approach to formal education is incomplete and can never
substitute for an authentic philosophy of Catholic or Christian
education. Need it be added that it would be equally wrong and, in
the long run, more disastrous, to ignore or slight the moral dimension
of education which, in effect, is what secularist educators do.

It is evident, moreover, that by and large the religious men and
women of the teaching congregations which staff the Catholic schools
have regarded their work as essentially moral and religious. The

query is regularly posed by outsiders: Is it not true that in conducting schools the Roman Catholic Church is simply seeking to make loyal partisans, and that the priests and brothers and sisters who teach in the schools are agents promoting the strictly sectarian aims of the Catholic Church?

The argument seems unassailable at first sight. In reality, it is based on a confusion between the purpose of the work (*finis operis*) with the purpose or motive of the worker (*finis operantis*).[19] Failure to make the distinction between the motivation or reason why an agent engages in an activity and the formality of the activity itself gives rise to the contrived dilemma, wherein one is confronted with the stark choice of the flag or the cross, country or faith—and ultimately Caesar or God! But must loyal Catholics or Protestants make a "guts" choice between a secular public school established to produce a citizen and a religiously-oriented school established to turn out Christian partisans?

In its most basic terms the choice really hinges on the compatibility of membership in the Catholic Church with citizenship in the American democracy. There are Christian groups who recognize a basic incompatibility here and carry out the logic of this decision in their lives. One thinks immediately of the Amish Church of the Mennonites. These people do not consider themselves in the mainstream of contemporary American life. They are striving deliberately to reject all worldly concerns while living the Christianity of apostolic times. The bearing of arms, contact with those outside their communion, knowledge of the world, and any formal education beyond the rudiments are anathemas to the Amish folk. There is an admirable, if misguided (from the point of view of other Christian bodies), consistency here. Periodically the Amish philosophy of life clashes with the draft laws and the compulsory school attendance laws but the Amish seem serenely unperturbed as they move closer to the heavenly Jerusalem.

On the other hand, the traditional Christian philosophy of education sees no antagonism between the two goals of fully active citizenship and deep religious commitment but conceives them as perfectly compatible and complementary. Why? Because the primary purpose of the school is neither one. The school as such possesses its own reason for being: it exists primarily—"formally" is the time-

[19] For a fuller treatment see author's *Catholic Viewpoint on Education* (Garden City, N.Y.: Hanover House, 1959).

honored philosophical term—to develop the morally intelligent person.

There are several agencies in society that share concern for the education and formation of the child in attempting to attain their appropriate social objectives, but in the process *the school* does not alter its nature. In other words, the school retains its own identity and basic purpose regardless of the reasons or motives different societies, natural or supernatural, may have in sponsoring formal education. The state engages in education because it must have a citizenry informed of its civic duties and rights, and possessed of a certain level of physical, intellectual, and moral culture commensurate with the common good. The state's motive does not substantially alter the nature of the school itself. On the other hand, the church sponsors schools so that her communicants will better acquire the supreme integrating principle of supernatural wisdom in ordering the knowledge, skills, and attitudes they learn. Nor should the church's motive essentially modify the nature of the school.

The same thing can be said about the motives of teachers in the schools. A person may take up teaching as a career for many reasons. He may love to be with young people. He may simply enjoy the school atmosphere. He may have soaring ambitions to become a famous and influential teacher. He may be following a four-generations-old family tradition. He may simply need the money or be moved by some other consideration. Any single one of these motives, or a combination, can be his purpose in teaching, but the nature or intrinsic idea of the teaching process does not change with differing or even conflicting motives among those who teach. Nor is the religious teacher—priest, brother or sister—somehow outside this reasoning. He or she may enter the classroom impelled by one of the motives just mentioned, but the principal motive most often will be to spread Christ's message among men or "to save souls." Nor should this startle. By definition that is what following a vocation has always meant.

The danger is, however, that the sense of "mission" arising from the formal commitment to a religious congregation or group may turn the nun or priest into a "missionary" in the classroom. No matter how apostolically committed the becassocked teacher is, the formal duty of *teaching* remains to be discharged, and the same holds true for men and women with enthusiastic attachments to a political party, a patriotic organization, or a social philosophy.

Nor is the above intended to play down the role of the teacher as a *person*. It is precisely at this point that the formal process of teaching is colored by the cross-play of other legitimate aims. In a somewhat different context, George Klubertanz has given brilliant expression to this idea. He writes:

> In all of this, we must single out the role of the teacher as a person. True, what the teacher says constitutes the formal part of his instruction. But the teacher is a person, and being a teacher is a personal activity in relation to other persons. This interpersonal (intersubjective) relation is in the order of what is *real* for the students, at the level of humanistic teaching as well as of philosophy and theology. A teacher who does not appreciate literature will not bring many of his students to like poetry, no matter what he says about it.[20]

With all this said, however, there still remains an *ideal* of Catholic education. And what has just been stated about the influence of the teacher upon the young is one important reason why Catholics will continue to support Catholic schools wherever and at whatever levels they are feasible. Catholics are in general agreement that the objectives of religious education can be best realized in an atmosphere wherein spiritual and supernatural realities hold their proper place in the hierarchy of values. Perhaps the key words here are *atmosphere* and *values,* for outside of these factors and formal instruction in religion, the Catholic school and the public school seem to be substantially identical. In much or even most of their educational objectives, organization, curriculum, activities, standards, and educational results there is little to differentiate the average parochial and public school.

Yet, at least in theory, they are miles apart. One is practically constrained to operate within a context limiting knowledge and wisdom to the merely temporal order. The other can call upon the total spectrum of man's experience including his insights and revelations of the transcendent order. Christianity is not merely cult and belief. Christianity offers a *life* which envelops the whole person. Christian education, accordingly, is not confined to a series of concepts or a table of precepts. It is rather a conception of life that inspires and leads to Christian living. In the ideal order, the Catholic school serves as a primary conduit of Christian culture—a way of

[20] "Knowledge and Action," in *Christian Wisdom and Christian Formation,* ed. by Barry McGannon, Bernard J. Cooke, and George P. Klubertanz (New York: Sheed and Ward, 1964), pp. 60–61.

looking at total reality. Even though our world is a pluralistic society, there will always be a Christian way of regarding it.

Even the systematic study of religious doctrine can be better achieved in a separate religiously-oriented school, for a person learns religion in somewhat the same way that he acquires a language. If he is raised in the country where the tongue is spoken, almost always he will have a surer grasp of the language than he would through self-instruction or private tutoring or enrollment in a special class.

The atmosphere of a religiously-oriented school psychologically reinforces and facilitates the learning process. Above all, in a thousand ways that defy strict definition, this atmosphere strengthens and completes the influence of home and church. No one has perfectly analyzed or described it. Exaggerated claims have been made for it. Unfriendly critics have at times labeled it brainwashing. To some extent it is a conditioning process but then so is the similar conditioning process that results in love of country, home, and family. Within a Catholic school there is more likelihood that a youngster will acquire a Catholic attitude or outlook on life—and for this no apology is needed. Americans regard it a duty and a privilege to transmit the American heritage to the younger generation. A similar pride and responsibility lead American Catholics to hand on to their children the riches of the Christian heritage.

*   *   *

Psychologically man is an "ordering" creature; that is, he classifies his experiences and relates them to one another. Moreover, man's ordering depends on his premises and assumptions. Formal Catholic education is built on definite premises and assumptions of which the principal ones might be listed as follows:

1. There is a transcendent Deity who has revealed to man that the nature of divinity is a Trinity of persons.
2. Man is a "person," that is, a rational free being whose perfection consists in knowing and possessing truth, beauty, and goodness, in limited fashion during his life upon earth, in an unlimited way for eternity.
3. Though man's material body gives him a continuity with nature, his soul or life principle marks him for a destiny beyond the purely material order.

4. God created man with an added gift or "supernature" by means of which he would be enabled to participate in the divine life after suitable probation.
5. In some mysterious way man has lost original integrity so that perfect order is missing in his life.
6. The Eternal Son of God became incarnate to be mankind's Messiah and to restore man to God's full friendship and the supernatural life.
7. Since this restoration can only take place through some kind of incorporation into Christ, church-sponsored education in its broadest and richest sense aims to build Christ in its members.

This, then, is the meaning of the statement that the starting point in the Catholic philosophy of education is the reality of the supernatural as revealed through and in Jesus Christ. The Catholic belief that man is a creature of God destined to share in the divine life answers the two chief questions upon which every philosophy of education must take a stand: What is man? What is his purpose?

It is true that these principles also permeate the truly Christian home, but the separate Catholic school is admirably suited to complement the work of the home. In the last analysis, the Catholic philosophy of education acknowledges the primacy of the supernatural in the total scheme of things. The values, goals, and ideals of the natural order—important and worthy of pursuit as these may be—are subordinate in Catholic eyes to those of the supernatural order. Actually, the dichotomy is more in terms than in reality. Contemporary theology is emphasizing the truth that the order created by God was never a purely natural order, but from its inception was elevated to the supernatural. The lapse of Adam from grace did not destroy this fundamental ordering; it did give rise to an antagonism between the material and spiritual orders, particularly within man himself—as personal reflection at times makes one painfully aware.

Nor is the Fall of man one of those medieval legends or quaint sectarian beliefs which can be dismissed as not really relevant to the large questions in education. Every philosophy of education has to address itself to the nature of man, the educand, and thereby, albeit by way of assumption, accepts or denies the dogma of original sin. Somehow man's inhumanity to man is hard to explain simply in terms of insufficient education or deficient chromosomal patterns. The humbling reality of original sin does help explain the twisted tragedies of Dachau and Buchenwald, Hiroshima and Hué, to say nothing of the mass murderer, extortioner, assassin, and the child-rapist in our modern civilization.

Again the Catholic school shares with the home and parish church the responsibility of teaching the child that "his chief significance comes from the fact that he is created by God and is destined for life with God in eternity." Amidst the moral and intellectual confusion of our contemporary society, the person is indeed blessed whose life is ordered by a grasp of total reality, who has a grip on perspective and proportion, to whom life has a completely rational meaning. Some call it religion.

Needless to mention, Catholics and Catholic schools hold no monopoly on these things. There are millions of American non-Catholics who are as deeply committed to these truths as are any Catholics. Yet neither Catholic nor Protestant family can count upon the public school as an ally in helping to pass on to their children even as primary a truth as the existence of a personal God or the reality of the supernatural order. In the inevitable process of acquiring a more secular and profane orientation, American society has watched this basic philosophy of Christian education being replaced by an allegedly neutral philosophy of secularism.

In any event, these principles are not taught in a Catholic school day by day by means of blackboard diagrams and class exercises. In a gentle imperceptible manner, however, their meaning is absorbed and they become quietly operative in the life of the child in the Catholic school.

Though formal religion classes are only a small portion of the day's instructional total, religion has an indirect influence that enters normally and naturally into many areas of the curriculum. Religious ideas and subjects receive proportionate treatment in other courses when they are germane to the subject. Although at times this can be overdone in a Catholic school, most of the time it is underdone in the public school. This would be especially true in literature, history, and social studies. It is axiomatic that we receive new knowledge through the filter of what already has become part of a basic philosophy. For example, if a man believes that human kind is nothing more than a freak accident of the impersonal forces of nature, his evaluation of man's story upon earth will differ markedly from that of a believer in the God of Genesis.[21]

The complete religious formation comes about through the joint efforts of home, school, and parish. Hence the liturgical life of the Church into which the child is initiated is lived in all three spheres of influence. The encyclical letter on "The Christian Education of Youth" speaks of the educational environment of the church as embracing "the sacraments, divinely efficacious means of grace, the sacred ritual, so wonderfully instructive and the material fabric of her churches, whose liturgy and art have an immense educational value."

Ordinarily the Catholic school is situated near the church, and this proximity makes for close cooperation in religious education and formation. During his parochial-school days a Catholic youngster is closer to the liturgy than at any other period in his life. From September to June he acquires a familiarity in his daily living with the saints and seasons of the church. Along with his knowledge of the heroes of the profane world, the youngster meets the great men and women of the church world. He observes Advent in preparation for Christ's birthday at Christmas and the season of Lent in preparation for Christ's resurrection at Easter. The boys learn to assist at Mass and other liturgical functions, and the girls learn to sing the sacred chants and music that accompany these ceremonies.

The Catholic school shares with the home and church the responsibility of teaching the child that his chief significance comes from the fact that he is created by God and is destined for life with God in eternity. In a modern society where the old religiously-based value system is under constant attack, the young follower of Christ acquires the powerful integrating force of religion.

The role of the Catholic school is not the simple one of teaching a set of formulas but in a thousand imperceptible ways to impart an attitude toward life as a whole. It is Catholicism as a culture, not as a conflicting creed, which is at odds with the spirit of the modern world and in a sense makes Catholics a people apart. Christian or Christ-centered culture is the supreme integrating principle from which proceeds all activity within a truly Catholic school. Christianity cannot be reduced to a series of propositions or a moral code that is apart from a man's life, for it is in essence the light

[21] See page 172. Justice Douglas' dissent in the *Allen* case is based on the assumption that secularism is not sectarian.

and life that illumines and vitalizes all his activity. From this point of view—and, *in the ideal order*—schooling and formation, which are distinct, are inseparable. True, the individual can himself realize the synthesis but it is much more natural for a child or adolescent to grow in Christian culture within a Christian atmosphere under the guidance of those who share it with him.

What has been loosely styled *a* or *the* Catholic philosophy of education is more accurately a viewpoint or a position. The differences are important. A viewpoint or a position on education is as much the result of social adaptation and compromise as it is of principle. Like controverted issues in the world of global politics that can present honest arguments in conflict because of national presuppositions or traditions, school policies are most often arrived at through patient diplomacy. On the other hand, a philosophy of education is pre-eminently of the ideal order. We need both a position and a philosophy. It might here serve a purpose to rehearse some of the points which the American Catholic community have generally worked for in the realm of education.

There has always been insistence at least on these points: secular education ideally should be integrated with religious education; a weekly catechism lesson in Sunday school is at best an inadequate substitute; attendance at public schools, because of a historic Protestant and currently secular orientation, can prove spiritually harmful to Catholic youngsters; ideally, Catholic children should be educated in Catholic schools.

While the Catholic Church may not have a carefully articulated philosophy of education, it definitely possesses a reasoned philosophy of society which colors its approach to formal schooling. One can style that involved process by which a man arrives at adult maturity as *education*. But since education is as extensive as human life itself, different agencies in society share rights and responsibilities in this broad field. The traditional church understanding of this division is that man is born into three institutions of the large society: the family, the state and the church. In theory, the rights of each are divided so as to avoid any clash; in practice, history records alternating periods of battle and uneasy truce, with most often the child the pawn of ecclesiastical or political policies in the battlefield of the classroom.

Only the absolute statist denies that the family into which a child is born has the primary right and obligation to educate. The familial right is prior to the rights of civil and ecclesiastical society because it springs from the natural relation of parents to their offspring, the most fundamental in nature. Common sense, a venerable tradition in Western free society, and a series of important U. S. Supreme Court decisions would seem to have placed the priority of family right beyond dispute. The gargantuan presence of the modern state in the classroom, however, does furnish grounds for some concern in our own country. There are public-school apologists and philosophers of education who operate on the assumption that since the supreme goal for mankind is enlightened membership in a free democratic society, the state has the paramount right to educate. Because public education is now under the immediate control of the state and more and more the function of the state, the rights of parents are derived from those of the state, they argue.

It seems in place from time to time to recall that the U. S. Supreme Court has unqualifiedly reaffirmed the principle that "the child is not the mere creature of the state" (*Pierce* v. *Society of Sisters,* 1925); and that "the custody, care and nurture of the child reside first in the parents" (*Prince* v. *Massachusetts,* 1944). The recent commemoration of the anniversary of the Universal Declaration of Human Rights, proclaimed by the General Assembly of the United Nations on December 10, 1948, brings to mind the words uttered on parental right in education:

Article 16 (3) The family is the natural and fundamental group unit of society and is entitled to protection by society and the State.

Article 26 (3) Parents have a prior right to choose the kind of education that shall be given to their children.[22]

Though at times handle has been given to the charge that the church itself operates schools without real consideration of family rights, the familial prerogative has been defended consistently. In "The Christian Education of Youth," Pius XI states: "So jealous is she [the church] of the family's inviolable natural right to educate the children that she never consents, save under peculiar circumstances and with special cautions, to baptize the children of infidels, or provide for their education against the will of the parents,

---

[22] To commemorate the twentieth anniversary of the Universal Declaration of the Rights of Man, the International Federation of Catholic Universities has published a volume of essays ed. by Robert F. Drinan, *The Right to Be Educated* (New York: Corpus Instrumentorum, 1968).

till such time as the children can choose for themselves and freely embrace the faith."

Nevertheless, the family right in education is not an absolute and despotic one, he says, but is "dependent on the natural and divine law, and therefore subject alike to the authority and jurisdiction of the church, and to the vigilance and administrative care of the state in view of the common good." Because familial society is not self-sufficient but achieves its development in unison with other family units of civil society, the common good takes precedence over individual good. It is in this sense that the state or political society does have a superior right. Those who can see no place for the valid concern of the church in education have consciously or unconsciously adopted a monist or secularist philosophy of life. In other words, they look upon man's earthly life as the be-all and end-all of human purposes. Since their perspectives are limited to the world of time, they have no sympathy for any institution which claims to transcend time and hence pay no heed to the church's claims in education.

The crux of the church-state problem is simply how to coordinate the rights of both societies for the benefit of man. The problem arises because, in establishing the supernatural society of the church, God did not destroy or lessen the natural ordering of human life which is the valid concern of the state. However, the natural, being of a lower order, respects the primacy of the supernatural. So even though church and state are independent and sovereign in their own spheres, these spheres are, as in the spiritual and material aspects of man's own nature, of unequal dignity and importance. The spiritual concerns of man, which, according to religious belief, God has entrusted to His church, are of a higher order than those concerns entrusted to the state. To keep "first things first" in the order God has created, the entire temporal order, including the state, must be in some wise subordinated to man's eternal destiny. And all this is simply a rephrasing of what is traditionally called "the primacy of the spiritual."

Those who look upon the primacy of the spiritual as something sectarian or peculiarly Catholic might reflect that this is a venerable tradition of Western wisdom. Without it, protest and defiance of unjust legislation is meaningless. As the U. S. Supreme Court has stated:

The victories for freedom of thought recorded in our Bill of Rights recognize that in the domain of conscience there is a moral power higher than the state. Throughout the ages men have suffered death rather than subordinate their allegiance to God to the authority of the state. Freedom of religion guaranteed by the First Amendment is the product of that struggle.[23]

The child's status as a member of a family, as we have seen, takes priority generally over his status as a citizen of the state. At the same time, however, the state has its own valid rights in the field of education. The state has a right, in fact an obligation, to make sure that its young citizens acquire such civic education as they need in order to help promote the common welfare in the temporal order. To this end,

. . . the state can exact, and take measures to secure, that all its citizens have the necessary knowledge of their civic and political duties, and a certain degree of physical, intellectual and moral culture, which, considering the conditions of our times, is really necessary for the common good.[24]

The state is acting fully within its right when it requires that children possess basic knowledge and skills, so that they may not become a burden to the community or fall short of the standard of good citizenship. For years this has been one of the most used arguments for federal aid: certain of the individual states just do not have the taxable income to provide good education for all their children. This is also the reasoning behind state-required courses in history and government. It is a concern of the state that its youthful citizens will come to understand and love the traditions of the nation and will be prepared to discharge the duties of citizenship.

The state has an obligation to protect and foster the prior rights of the family in education. The parental right is given for the sake of the child. In turn, the state is bound to protect the right of the child itself, when the parents are delinquent. The state promotes education by encouraging and assisting the initiative and activity of the family. The sophistication and complexity of modern living has made it impossible, except under the most unusual circumstances, for a single family to provide within the home an adequate formal education for its children. When the state steps in and mobilizes the

[23] *Girouard* v. *U.S.*, 1946.
[24] "The Christian Education of Youth," *op. cit.*, p. 219.

resources of the whole community to make up what is wanting in the resources of its members as individuals and family groups, it is assisting the parents to fulfill their natural obligation. It is not replacing them. The rights of the state in education—and the point bears repetition—are secondary and derived from parental delegation, as are the rights of the church.

So much then for the theory—whose principles are rooted in eternity and whose applications are continually subject to the play of time and space. Have the Catholic schools in America been a failure or a success? The first answer is a retort: Has any human institution been an unqualified failure or success? One could as easily ask: Is any marriage an unqualified failure or success? Perhaps in all fairness, we should let each generation return its own answer. In general, however, it can be readily said that in many important ways, as shall be seen, the Catholic school has been and is an outstanding success. Frankly, where it may have fallen short of its demanding ideal, a portion of the blame can be laid at the door of government whose policies on support have made the burden of financing the Catholic school such a heavy one. In any event, the Catholic school has tried to keep troth with the transcendent character of its Master's mission.

Novelist James T. Farrell once remarked how he had been a very intense critic of parochial schools. "I was wrong," he said. In explanation he listed valuable things he had learned and absorbed in these schools. He learned that a person can think of the world in terms of order, that truth is important, and that there are things important enough to die for. And fourthly, the creator of *Studs Lonigan* concluded,

I got a sense that there was something before me and something after me, that there was depth of experience, and that I was living in a continuity where there was an idea of greatness and grandeur and also mystery and reality. Where you face tragedy, you face yourself. You ask yourself if you sin or not. That can have the effect of making you see rather realistically.[25]

Another product of Catholic schools, writer Mary McCarthy, touched upon the same basic point: "If you are born and brought up a Catholic, you have absorbed a good deal of world history and the history of ideas before you are twelve, and it is like learning a lan-

[25] "Minds at Work," *Catholic Mind,* LXII (September, 1964), 32.

guage early; effect is indelible. Nobody else in America, no other group, is in this fortunate position."[26]

In America the idea and the ideal have survived for well-nigh three hundred years.[27] They have proved their hardihood—come what may, come what will.

Elementary-Secondary School Enrollment in the U.S., 1900–67

Year	Total Enrollment	Catholic School Enrollment	Percentage of Total
1900	16,357,633	854,523	5.2
1910	19,050,798	1,236,946	6.4
1920	23,404,529	1,826,213	7.8
1930	28,147,047	2,469,032	8.8
1940	28,016,138	2,581,596	9.2
1950	28,191,593	3,080,166	10.9
1960	41,375,576	5,288,705	12.7
1961	42,901,868	5,397,678	12.5
1962	44,450,566	5,613,956	12.6
1963	45,842,255	5,625,040	12.2
1964	47,078,617	5,662,328	12.0
1965	48,637,354	5,582,354	11.4
1966	48,625,606	5,473,606	11.2
1967	49,154,766	5,254,766	10.7

SOURCES: *Official Catholic Directory* (New York: P. J. Kenedy and Sons); *Biennial Survey of Education and School Life,* U. S. Office of Education, 1968.

[26] *Memories of a Catholic Girlhood* (New York: Harcourt, Brace, and Company, 1957).

[27] The first Catholic school in the colonies was established by the Jesuits at St. Mary's City, Maryland, probably around 1640. The next recorded foundation was probably in 1673 at Newton, a center of underground Catholic activity in the Maryland colony.

CHAPTER TWO

The Old Context: The Rise
of the Immigrant Church

The social institutions that man devises to meet his needs represent a continuity of thought and experience. Schools no less than styles of dress and food are largely influenced by preceding patterns. When the colonists from Europe came to the shores of the New World, they brought with them the social patterns and basic institutions of the countries they left behind. These were the models they then strove to re-create on the shores of *New* Orleans, *New* Amsterdam, or *New* England. The schools they built were closely modeled after what they had experienced. In erecting schools the first colonial generations sought the same purposes, followed the same curriculum, and served the same class of people as in the old countries. Yet, whenever a social institution is transplanted it begins to take on the coloring of the new environment. The same powerful process which by stages transformed Europeans into Americans, turned European schools into distinctively American ones. Though characteristics of one generation need not necessarily be carried across to a later generation, nevertheless, it is helpful to know what those earlier traits were and, when possible, to understand why they changed. "Nothing is comprehensible," Teilhard de Chardin reminds us, "except through its history."

In tracing the origins of the American public school one characterization stands out. Early Americans looked upon the schools as "the children of the church." Nowhere was this description more accurate than in the colonies of New England. When the colonist of the seventeenth century built a school in the pioneer commonwealth of Massachusetts, he was little bothered over the niceties of church-state relations, which in our more sophisticated day have complicated the dual problems of support for the religious school and of religion in publicly-supported education. For him and his fellows, schools were a public concern, and few folk were troubled over a dividing line between secular and religious authority. The school was simply considered the normal means for inculcating loyalty to the sponsoring confessional group. Literacy was virtue for it gave a person access to the word of God, thereby binding him to the Scripture-inspired community covenant. The oldest piece of public legislation on schools is the famous "Old Deluder" Act of 1647, tightly linking the school and religious formation.

It being one cheife piect of ye ould deluder, Satan, to keepe men from the knowledge of ye Scriptures, as in formr times by keeping ym in an unknown tongue, so in these lattr times by pswading from ye use of tongues. . . .[1]

So the Act would thwart him by requiring each township of fifty householders or more to appoint a teacher and set up a school.

During the century and a half of the colonial period, the religious tensions of the colonies were a faithful mirror of the social situation in the European mother countries, notably England. While there were a few Roman Catholic families of prominence and affluence, Catholics generally lived their lives outside the cultural and political activities of the community. The church as such existed in the shadows with next to no organization and without strong leadership. A rigid penal code laid heavy disabilities upon Catholics, depriving them of freedom to worship together, to take part in public life, and to educate their children. The Catholic child was an undesirable alien in the colonial school, and yet his parents were liable to a heavy fine if they sent him out of the colonies for his education. Catholics themselves were barred from teaching or establishing schools. By 1704 even Catholic-founded Maryland had passed "An Act to Prevent the Growth of Popery," among whose bristling provisions was one which threatened to deport any Catholic who should keep school, board students, or instruct children.

The Revolution and its successful outcome eased many of the more onerous disabilities upon Catholics, but only four states in their constitutional conventions gave them political equality with Protestants. As the established Protestant churches began to lose, at least *de jure,* their privileged status, distinctive articles of belief and particular features of church organization were de-emphasized, and believers of divided allegiance discovered more and more in common. This development was a decisive factor in the success of the

---

[1] *Colony Records:* Massachusetts Law of 1647.

public-school movement by making a common endeavor possible among Protestant factions.

Since the community-sponsored schools belonged to everyone, any pattern of education, especially in its moral and spiritual aspects, could become a socially divisive issue. Some doctrinal common ground had to be found which would satisfy a spectrum of religious beliefs, ranging from liberal Unitarian to the most doughty Congregationalist. It took imagination and diplomacy to bring off the necessary compromise which would unite the community in supporting a common school. The movement found its most influential leader in Horace Mann.

However, during the first struggling years of the public-school movement in Massachusetts, religious traditionalists and conservatives alike turned their anger on Mann, who held the position of secretary to the Board of Education of the commonwealth between 1837 and 1848. They charged that he was reducing the place of religion in the school, divorcing religion and education, and creating godless institutions. Throughout his career he had to defend himself repeatedly against such charges. His stock reply was to point out to his critics that he had always acted upon the principle that in a Christian nation Christianity should hold an honored place in the schools. Admittedly his own idea of Christianity was vague and almost indistinguishable from Unitarianism. In any event, he developed a point that gave many observers pause. Children should be given "so much religious instruction as is compatible with the rights of others and with the genius of our government."[2] However, it was the responsibility of parents, he said, to give children "any special and peculiar instruction with respect both to politics and theology," and "at last, when the children arrive at years of maturity . . . commend them to that inviolable prerogative of private judgment and of self-direction, which in a Protestant and a Republican country, is the acknowledged birthright of every human being."[3]

Mann's program called then for a kind of Christian religion that should not be identifiable with the distinctive tenets of Congregationalist or Methodist or Episcopal or Baptist faith. It should be nonsectarian, not favoring any one sect or church. The cornerstone of Mann's religion was the Bible, the great symbol and source of Protestant Christianity. Though "our Public Schools are not theological

[2] *Life and Works*, II, 289–90.
[3] *Ibid.*, p. 290.

seminaries, is admitted," he wrote in his final *Annual Report,* yet "our system . . . welcomes the religion of the Bible, and in receiving the Bible, it allows it to do what it is allowed to do in no other system—to speak for itself."[4] As long as the Bible remained in the school, the school was Christian. Granted the times, any other approach but Mann's nonsectarian, biblically-based compromise would probably have meant the end of the common-school movement.

In agreement with philosophers of education from Plato to Dewey, the American people have looked upon the schools as the main channel for the transmission of the national ethos or public philosophy undergirding their society. It has always been assumed that the common school had a large, if not the largest, part in the development of the American character, in inculcating moral and spiritual values, in laying the ethical basis of character in the child. The social context of early America lent itself to an operative consensus regarding the religious roots of the nation's political patrimony. Even after this consensus no longer held, the United States of America considered itself a Christian nation, not in the sense that any general or specific understanding of Christianity was the established religion, but rather that the overwhelming bulk of the citizenry continued to profess some formal or nominal allegiance to the Christian tradition.

Provided the public school did not favor any special church or sect, it remained pretty well free to inculcate the generally-agreed-upon moral and religious truths found in the common Bible. Despite creedal differences, people agreed that moral and spiritual values were rooted in some kind of transcendent value system. American democracy was presumed to be drawing its strength from a collective awareness that there was a divine value stamped upon man, and that the ultimate guarantee of the rights of man defined in America's first political documents was the Almighty Creator of mankind.

In the historic working out of Horace Mann's compromise, the unavoidable became the inevitable. In the effort to remain "neutral," at first among warring Protestant sects and later between Protestant and Catholic, the educational process in the schools turned

---

[4] Twelfth Annual Report, facsimile ed., pp. 116–17. Quoted in Neil G. McCluskey, *Public Schools and Moral Education* (New York: Columbia University Press, 1958), p. 91. This book contains an extended discussion on the historic issue.

"secular" at least officially, for the compromise approach bore the seeds of its own dissolution. The area of agreed-upon tenets contracted inexorably, leaving almost nobody happy with the state of things. The only group that seemed to benefit was that which held a minimum of positive doctrine or none at all.

*   *   *

Historically the American public school descended from the common schools of New England without reference to non-Protestant groups, but in time these too had to be reckoned with. In the first decades of the nineteenth century, the total number of Catholics, while not negligible, was certainly not significant.[5] Consequently, each Catholic family had to face the dilemma of placing its children in a religiously hostile environment or of depriving them of the educational preparation essential to economic and social advancement. There was no American Civil Liberties Union around to fight what today would be judged a blatant infringement of religious liberty—nor did that public think such an organization necessary. As Robert D. Cross has put it: "To the eighteenth-century American, the Roman Catholic Church was pure evil—an affront against God and an international conspiracy against legitimate government. To the gilded age, it was an object of distrust because of its startling growth, of dislike because of its religious error, and of distaste because of the cultural backwardness with which it was usually associated."[6]

As the American public increasingly accepted and then enthusiastically supported the public-school movement, the Catholic community was torn. Heretofore, the church's commitment to formal education had been slight. Before the nineteenth century, society generally regarded education beyond the rudiments as the preroga-

---

[5] By 1820 the estimated Catholic population was 195,000; a decade later it was 318,000; in 1840 it was 663,000; and in 1850, 1,606,000. On the eve of the Civil War, it had doubled, and doubled again in both the census of 1880 and 1900. Estimates of today's Catholic population vary between 45,000,000 and 50,000,000, or 23–25 per cent of the total population. See John L. Thomas, *The American Catholic Family* (Englewood Cliffs, N.J.: Prentice-Hall, Inc., 1956), p. 108, for the earlier figures. *The Official Catholic Directory* for 1968 gives 47,468,333, a conservative figure.

[6] "The Changing Image of Catholicism in America," *Yale Review*, XLVIII (June, 1959), 575.

tive of the upper classes or the gateway to the professions. When in 1785 Bishop John Carroll wrote to Rome, mentioning a new college in Philadelphia and two other proposed schools in Maryland to which Catholics could be admitted, he was talking about classical academies not under church control. In fact, he expressed the hope "that some educated there will embrace the ecclesiastical state. We think accordingly of establishing a Seminary in which they can be trained to the life of learning suited to that state."[7] He wrote in another letter that the object dearest to his heart was "the establishment of a school, and afterwards of a seminary for young clergymen."[8]

At the same time Carroll was working with the Jesuits to establish "George-Town College," 1786, he was cooperating with Patrick Allison and William West, both Protestant ministers, to establish a nonsectarian college in Baltimore to prepare young men for the learned professions. That no general program for Catholic education was intended is clear from the pioneer bishop's pastoral letter of 1792 to the Catholic people of the United States. Referring to the opening of Georgetown, he writes:

I earnestly wish, dear brethren, that as many of you, as are able, would send your sons to this school of letters and virtue. I know and lament, that the expense will be too great for many families, and that their children must be deprived of the immediate benefit of this institution. . . .[9]

And in 1829, the Catholic bishops spoke of the luxury of a Catholic schooling in the same vein:

How well would it be, if your means and opportunities permitted, were you at this period to commit your children to the care of those whom we have for their special fitness, placed over our seminaries and our female religious institutions.[10]

The public school of those turbulent years, however, was not only Protestant-oriented but most often belligerently so. The textbooks were shot through and through with derogatory references to things Catholic. The widely-used *New England Primer* with its

[7] John Gilmary Shea, *History of the Catholic Church in the United States*, (New York: J. G. Shea, 1886), p. 260.

[8] Shea, *A History of Georgetown College* (New York: Collier, 1891), p. 9.

[9] Peter Guilday, ed., *The National Pastorals of the American Hierarchy*, 1792–1919 (Washington, D.C.: National Catholic Welfare Council, 1923), p. 4.

[10] *Ibid.*, p. 26.

stern injunction: "Child, behold that Man of Sin, the *Pope,* worthy of thy utmost hatred," is simply a graphic case in point.[11]

Catholic leaders were forced into a defensive posture. The school question and other long-accumulated problems brought the seven bishops of the United States together in 1829 for the first of the seven Provincial Councils of Baltimore, covering the interval between that year and 1849. Their joint letter to American Catholics urged the necessity for Catholic schools to preserve the faith of Catholic boys and girls, particularly from poor families. The textbooks were a sore point. "The schoolboy can scarcely find a book," the bishops said, "in which some one or more of our institutions or practices is not exhibited for otherwise than it really is, and greatly to our disadvantage."[12]

Nor had things improved by 1840, the year of the Fourth Council. The bishops put it baldly: "Since it is evident that the nature of public education in many of these provinces is so developed that it serves heresy, [and] the minds of Catholic youth are little by little imbued with false principles of sects, we warn pastors that they must see to the Christian and Catholic education of Catholic youths with all the zeal they have. . . ."[13] They urged pastors to protest what were still widespread practices: Catholic pupils in the public schools were required to join in reading the Protestant Bible, in reciting Protestant prayers, and in singing Protestant hymns. The bishops' letter again singled out the textbooks, saying: "We can scarcely point out a book in general use in the ordinary schools, or even in higher seminaries, wherein covert and insidious efforts are not made to misrepresent our principles, to distort our tenets, to vilify our practices and to bring contempt upon our church and its members."[14]

They voiced concern over the plight of parents for whom it is

[11] The *New England Primer* was a children's version of the Calvinist catechism. No textbook was more widely used. Between 1700 and 1850 the *Primer* sold three million copies.

[12] *National Pastorals,* p. 28.

[13] 6th Decree, Fourth Provincial Council, 1840. Burns estimates that in 1838 there were two hundred Catholic parochial schools. J. A. Burns, *The Principles, Origin and Establishment of the Catholic School System in the United States* (New York: Benziger Brothers, 1912), p. 386. Cross makes much of the fact that the first *Catholic Almanac,* appearing in 1833, failed to mention the few parochial schools in existence. It did, but they were lumped into the category of "charitable institutions."

[14] *National Pastorals,* p. 134.

"no easy matter to preserve the faith of your children in the midst of so many difficulties." The letter tries to explain why Catholics wanted their own schools:

> It is not then because of any unkind feeling to our fellow-citizens, it is not through any reluctance on our part, to contribute whatever little we can to the prosperity of what are called the common institutions of the country, that we are always better pleased to have a separate system of education for the children of our communion. . . .[15]

But attempts at compromise or conciliation by Catholics resulted in the "painful experience that in any common effort it was always expected that our distinctive principles of religious belief and practice should be yielded to the demands of those who thought proper to charge us with error. . . ."[16] The dismay of the Old World-oriented bishops, uneasy and torn over certain liberal assumptions underlying the public-school movement, is voiced in their next words:

> and because we saw with great pain the differences which an attempt to combine and conciliate principles, which we have never been able to reconcile, has produced in a distant church which has always been found faithful.[17]

The Catholic community sought to remedy the situation in several ways. They asked that the offending passages be deleted from the common textbooks; they asked that Catholic children be excused from the daily prescribed reading of the King James Bible. They asked that a fair portion of their own school tax money be returned to help support separate Catholic schools.

The textbook situation did slowly improve and by stages the more abusive references disappeared. The Bible, however, was looked upon by most Americans as the moral Gibraltar of the Republic, and it was simply inconceivable that the schools of a God-fearing nation could exist without it. In fact, powerful legal support for the retention of reading from the Protestant Bible was supplied

---

[15] *Ibid.*

[16] *Ibid.* One student of the period traces to this council the real beginnings of the Catholic drive for separate schools. (James E. Diffley, "Catholic Reaction to American Public Education, 1792–1852." Unpublished doctoral dissertation, University of Notre Dame, 1959.) This is extremely doubtful though it is true that by 1840 the clash between certain liberal assumptions underlying public education and certain traditional Catholic principles was under way.

[17] *Ibid.*

by an 1854 decision of the Maine Supreme Court, affirming the right of a school district to require the practice.[18] In a number of cities there was tension and strife consequent upon the caning or expulsion of Catholic pupils who refused to take part in what they steadfastly believed to be a Protestant religious exercise. It was only in 1890 that the Wisconsin Supreme Court in the much agitated Edgerton Bible case reversed the earlier precedent, and ruled the Bible a sectarian book.

In today's more open and sophisticated society we find it hard to conceive of this fanaticism on the part of numbers of Catholics and bigotry on the part of many Protestants over an issue which our generation would consider trifling. After all, it is still the Bible whether garbed in the English of King James or of Douay College. Yet it is easy to forget that during the centuries of religious conflict following the breakup of Western Christian unity, things of small significance in themselves grew into towering symbols of division—like the vernacular versus Latin, or a right-left or a left-right axis in making the sign of the cross, or even down to the inclusion or deletion in the Lord's Prayer of the words: "For thine is the kingdom, and the power, and the glory"!

Quarrels over different translations of the Bible were serious enough, but a larger bone of contention was in the unguided reading of the Scriptures themselves. In 1840 a spokesman for Archbishop John Hughes of New York voiced the Catholic objection:

> The Holy Scriptures are read every day, with the restriction that no specific tenets are to be inculcated. Here we find the great demarcating principles between the Catholic Church and the Sectaries introduced silently. The Catholic Church tells her children they must be taught by *authority*. The Sectaries say, read the Bible, judge for yourselves. The Protestant principle is therefore acted upon, slyly inculcated, and the schools are sectarian.[19]

As the traditional Protestant coloring of the public school faded under both Catholic and Protestant pressures, a new kind of criti-

---

[18] *Donahue* v. *Richards* (38 Maine, 376). The court ruled that the school board had "the legal and constitutional right to expel a child from school for refusing to read the Bible used by the school even though the child or its parents had religious scruples against doing so."

[19] The New York *Freeman's Journal*, July 11, 1840. Cited in Edward M. Connors, *Church-State Relationships in Education in the State of New York* (Washington, D.C.: Catholic University Press, 1951), p. 56.

cism arose: the public schools were irreligious if not downright antireligious. Archbishop John Hughes, never distinguished for his tact and embittered over his failure to win tax support for the New York parochial schools, was one of the most hostile critics. His remark in 1852 that education as perpetrated in America was "Socialism, Red Republicanism, Universalism, Deism, Atheism, and Pantheism—anything, everything, but religionism and patriotism" was scarcely calculated to ease Protestant-Catholic tensions.[20]

On the other hand, Catholic leaders in many localities did try to take the hand extended them in good will by public-school and community leaders. Occasionally a Catholic priest was even invited to serve on a local school board. An increasing number of Catholic young women became teachers in the public schools. However, until the deep Protestant animus toward the Roman Church, prevailing between 1830 and 1860, had been pretty well dissipated, rapport on any large scale was impossible. Bishops like John Ireland of St. Paul (1838–1918), John Lancaster Spalding of Peoria (1840–1916), and James Gibbons of Richmond and Baltimore (1834–1921) could and did exercise their social statesmanship only after Appomattox.

The unabashedly Protestant orientation of the public schools, though generally diminishing as the nineteenth century closed, was then the principal reason that led the Catholic community to establish separate schools. However, a second reason, by no means exclusively Catholic, was a philosophy that judged formal schooling a subject beyond the competence of the state. We of today are so used to the state's preponderant role in education that it is not easy to understand the strong feelings to the contrary entertained a century ago by many people. Yet, given the drastic shifting within the social strata, the state's full-scale entry into the school business was inevitable.

Education beyond the bare rudiments for the peasantry and working classes was hardly imaginable before the early decades of the nineteenth century. The cultivated aristocracy that had led the struggle of the colonists and established the American commonwealth retained a class outlook on education. The attitude of even such an enlightened leader as Thomas Jefferson was not a rarity. Writing in his *Notes on the State of Virginia* (1781; published 1785), he pro-

[20] Quoted in Vincent P. Lannie, *Public Money and Parochial Education* (Cleveland: Case Western Reserve University Press, 1968), p. 253.

posed a chain of widely dispersed elementary schools in order to diffuse knowledge more generally among the people. "The boy of best genius" in each would be given further education at one of twenty grammar schools. From each of these, a student would be selected after a one- or two-year trial, to continue for another six years, and "by this means twenty of the best geniuses will be raked from the rubbish annually, and be instructed, at the public expense, so far as the grammar schools go."[21]

To their credit, however, Jefferson and other leaders saw that the only solid basis for a republican form of government with broad suffrage was an informed and literate citizenry. Once the monarchical and aristocratic forms of Old World government were rejected, the new democratic form based on the consent of the governed could not long endure unless the people were educated to the level where they could participate intelligently in political and social decisions. Such was the incessant theme of Horace Mann, Henry Barnard, Calvin Stowe, and other leaders of the common-school movement. Moreover, the conviction was growing that the state should use its own resources to educate more of the people. True, the churches and other private groups were sponsoring schools but were clearly unable to provide education on the scale demanded by the times.

On the other hand, a large and influential cross section of American society refused to see any direct role for the state in education. They could point for support to men like the British philosopher Herbert Spencer, who wrote: "In the same way that our definition of state duty forbids the state to administer religion or charity, so likewise does it forbid the state to administer education."[22] In our modern industrialized and urbanized society we have grown accustomed to the shadow of the state over our lives. It could be argued that, given the conditions of modern life, an individual or a family of the mid-twentieth century has had to surrender certain areas of life to minute state regulation. Yet even seventy-five years ago, the attitude of American society toward control of education differed largely from today's.

If one argues that formal education is essentially a moral under-

---

[21] Saul K. Padover, ed., *The Complete Jefferson* (New York: Tudor Publishing Co., 1943), p. 667.

[22] Quoted in a pamphlet, *The Public School Question* (Boston: Duffy & Co., 1876), p. 9.

taking, and that morality must have a religious basis, education would seem to be the more proper business of the churches, and mistrust of Caesar in the classroom becomes entirely understandable. It is against this background that some of the statements made by church leaders of past generations about state-controlled education should be interpreted. Bernard McQuaid, the fiery Bishop of Rochester, stated: "The Catholic is unwilling to transfer the responsibility of the education of his children to the state. His conscience informs him that the state is an incompetent agent to fulfil his parental duties."[23] A Jesuit educator, writing in 1877, had this to say: "The state has the right and the duty to encourage good education; but its right to educate is but a Masonic invention."[24] Another critic went all the way with the bewildering charge "that the idea that the state has a right to teach . . . is not a Christian idea. It is a pagan one. . . ."[25]

*   *   *

Were these men right? What rights does the state truly have with reference to the education of its young citizens? The case for the state was spelled out baldly by Thomas Bouquillon, Belgian-born professor of moral science at the Catholic University of America. His pamphlet, *Education: To Whom Does It Belong?* was a somewhat tardy explication of a principle implicit in Catholic dogma, namely, that within reasonable limits, every state has the right to make use of the necessary means to achieve its legitimate ends in any stage of society. Still the pamphlet's appearance in 1891 caused consternation and drew heated rejoinders.

Bouquillon's adversaries could point to the long series of pastoral letters issued jointly by the American bishops in the discharge of their teaching office, not one of which gave the slightest hint that the state had any direct right in education. The most prestigious of these episcopal gatherings, the Third Plenary Council of Baltimore, at which sat fourteen archbishops and sixty bishops, wrote: "The three great educational agencies are the home, the church, and the school"—with no mention of the state.

23 *Ibid.*
24 Joseph Bayma, "The Liberalistic View of the School Question," *The American Catholic Quarterly Review*, II, 17.
25 *The Public School Question*, p. 9.

This traditional philosophy, which permitted the state merely to substitute for parents delinquent in their duty of educating the child, had hardened, no doubt, because of certain social changes that were remaking Western society. Social values, sanctions, even institutions themselves were perceptibly and imperceptibly shifting from the sacral to the secular order.

One radical departure was the state's encroachment on the regulation of marriage. For centuries the church had had sole jurisdiction over the "sacred" bond of matrimony. Though marriage was considered simultaneously a contract and a sacrament, both were regulated within the sacral order. The state's jurisdiction extended simply to the civil aspects of marriage, for example, to the regulation of dowries, inheritances, legitimacy of succession, etc. Even following the sixteenth-century breakup of Christian unity, the new churches and sects generally continued this division of ecclesiastical and civil jurisdictions. Luther alone of the major Protestant theologians parted company on the question and argued that the regulation of marriage was proper to the state, because it was *"ein weltlich Geschäft," "ein weltlich Ding"*—a secular business.

However, during the final years of the eighteenth century, the secularization of marriage was partially or wholly effected in every major country of the West. Church authority was set aside, and nations operated on the principle that the state had the principal if not the sole competence in marriage. The extreme occurred in the France of the 1790's. There the men of the Revolution organized a republican liturgy to replace the Catholic nuptial ceremonies. Robespierre pushed through the Convention a law which established the "Feast of Conjugal Love," upon which day marital unions could be solemnized by the state.

The wonder is not small then, that men who recoiled from these changes would likewise entertain grave fears regarding education, once it came under control of the state. Education and marriage are, in the nature of things, inseparably linked.

* * *

Catholic efforts to obtain tax funds for separate schools as a solution to the school problem failed. Swollen with the newly arrived immigrant population, New York City was the scene of the first important struggle by Catholics to obtain a proportionate share of the common-school fund, and the outcome here went a long way toward establishing a national policy that has endured to the present day. Between 1795 and 1825, the state of New York had given financial aid to every educational institution in the city, practically all of which were operated by the churches. In 1805 the Free School Society was founded "for the education of such poor children as do not belong to, or are not provided for by any religious society." Shortly, it adopted another title, the "Public School Society," and soon became the dominant educational force in New York City. In 1825, a bill passed the state legislature authorizing the city council to determine which schools should receive tax money. The next year the council decided that henceforth New York City's share of the state school fund should go exclusively to the nonsectarian Public School Society, except for minor grants to orphanages and mission schools.

Led by their colorful and combative Bishop (later Archbishop) John Hughes, the New York Catholics repeatedly urged the justice of their claims. 1840 was one of the peak years of Catholic activity abetted by the support of Governor William H. Seward, who proposed that state money be used to establish schools under church auspices for immigrant children. A public petition was put before the board of aldermen. Speaking of his fellow citizens, the spokesman informed the board that as Catholics

they bear, and are willing to bear, their portion of every common burden; and feel themselves entitled to a participation in every common benefit. This participation, they regret to say, has been denied them for years back, in reference to common school education in the City of New York, except on conditions with which their conscience, and as they believe their duty to God, did not, and do not leave them at liberty to comply.[26]

It was not that local communities did not attempt to come to terms with the school problem. An early effort at compromise took place in Lowell, Massachusetts, which must have had some approval from the secretary of the State Board of Education, none other than Horace Mann himself. Between 1831 and 1852, Mann writes in a letter, a "very intelligent committee," consisting of clergymen and laymen, entered into an arrangement with the Catholic priests and

[26] The full text of the document, "Petition of the Catholics of New York for a Portion of the Common-School Fund" is to be found in Neil G. McCluskey, ed., *Catholic Education in America* (New York: Teachers College Bureau of Publications, 1964), pp. 65–77.

parents, "by which it was agreed that the teachers of their children should be Catholics."[27] These schools were part of the public-school system and, as such, regulated by the district school committee like any other schools belonging to their jurisdiction. The plan was called "eminently successful" in 1837 by the school committee. By 1839 there were five schools enrolling 752 pupils under this arrangement.[28]

Similar arrangements were entered into in communities in at least ten states before the outbreak of the Civil War: Connecticut, Illinois, Indiana, Kentucky, Michigan, Mississippi, New Jersey, New York, Ohio, and Pennsylvania.[29] The objective was generally the same: to combine public and parochial schooling within a single institution. Actually, at one time or another, nearly every state in the Union has had some such plan in operation, at least briefly, for the benefit not merely of Catholic children but for those of Presbyterian, Quaker, Lutheran, Mormon, and other groups as well.[30]

The most notable pattern of compromise after the Civil War was at Poughkeepsie in New York, and the towns of Faribault and Stillwater in Minnesota, part of John Ireland's Archdiocese of St. Paul. The key provisions of the plan were: (1) an existing parochial school in a heavily populated Catholic area is leased to the public-school district; (2) the school board operates a "public" school in the parish-owned building, paying upkeep and salary costs; (3) all religious instruction or exercises are scheduled before or after the standard school hours; (4) with the Catholic pastor's approval, the school board appoints teachers and provides textbooks; (5) the school board retains complete control over examinations, promotions, and general policies.

The arrangement at Poughkeepsie worked smoothly for twenty-five years, beginning with 1873. It had the approval of the Archbishop of New York, John Cardinal McCloskey, and might have continued indefinitely but, as will be seen later, in the aftermath of the school controversy of 1890–92, it fell a delayed casualty. The

[27] Mary Peabody Mann, *Life of Horace Mann,* centennial ed. in facsimile (Washington, D.C.: National Education Association, 1937), p. 262.

[28] Robert H. Lord, John E. Sexton and Edward T. Harrington, *History of the Archdiocese of Boston,* II (New York: Sheed and Ward, 1944), 313–20.

[29] Richard J. Gabel, *Public Funds for Church and Private Schools* (Washington, D.C.: Catholic University Press, 1937), pp. 305–6.

[30] *Ibid.,* p. 493.

Faribault-Stillwater arrangement was short-lived and was likewise a victim of the controversy which so closely involved its sponsor, Archbishop Ireland.

*   *   *

During the middle decades of the century, the Catholic Church expanded rapidly. From the original ecclesiastical province of Baltimore, which was coterminous with the limits of the United States itself, were formed the Province of Oregon City (1846) and the Province of St. Louis (1847). By 1852, date of the First Plenary Council of Baltimore, Rome had erected three additional provinces: New Orleans, Cincinnati, and New York. From this council the six archbishops and thirty-five suffragan bishops published a national pastoral, treating mainly of church authority and education.

The document is hortatory in tone and betrays the anxiety of the pastors for their people. The Catholic Church felt itself under siege. Each of the preceding decades had had its ugly incidents which sent shock waves far and wide to frighten, to separate, to harden attitudes among American neighbors. The 1830's had seen the burning of the Charleston convent and the *Awful Disclosures* of Maria Monk. In the 1840's the Native American party had provoked bloody riots in the streets of Philadelphia over Bible-reading in the schools. The 1850's were to see the birth of the Know-Nothing party, the antipapal demonstrations which greeted the pope's first representative, Archbishop Bedini, the tarring and feathering of the Jesuit John Bapst, the Massachusetts law for the inspection of convents, and the riots of Louisville's "Bloody Monday."[31]

The bishops urged fathers and mothers to watch over the purity of their children's faith and morals with jealous vigilance, and to instill into their hearts principles of virtue and perfection. The lax parent is warned of the "terrible expectation of judgment that will fill his soul, should his children perish through his criminal neglect, or his obstinate refusal to be guided in the discharge of his paternal duties by the authority of God's church."[32]

To avert such an evil, parents are to give children a Christian education, "that is an education based on religious principles, accom-

---

[31] The most competent treatment of these troubled years is still Ray A. Billington's *The Protestant Crusade, 1800–1860* (New York: Macmillan, 1938).
[32] *National Pastorals*, p. 190.

panied by religious practices and always subordinate to religious influence." The faithful are warned against "false and delusive theories which are so prevalent, and which leave youth without religion." These educational philosophies leave youth "without anything to control the passions, promote the real happiness of the individual, and make society find in the increase of its members, a source of security and prosperity. Listen not to those who would persuade you that religion can be separated from secular instruction."[33]

Catholics are encouraged to establish and support Catholic schools. This worthy object will prevent Catholic children becoming "involved in all the evils of an uncatholic education, evils too multiplied and too obvious to require that we should do more than raise our voices in solemn protest against the system from which they spring." In urging this duty, they affirm that they are following out the suggestion of Pope Pius IX in his encyclical letter of the preceding year, which urged bishops throughout the world to provide for the religious education of youth.[34]

The Civil War brought a lull to anti-Catholic activity and effectively broke the political power of the Know-Nothing movement. Within a year of the war's end, 1866, the American Catholic bishops again gathered in plenary session at Baltimore to do their part in binding the nation's wounds. Two chapters of their pastoral letter were devoted to education. They repeated the admonition to establish and support parochial schools. They again expressed the conviction that "religious teaching and religious training should form part of every system of school education." The letter stated:

> Every day's experience renders it evident, that to develop the intellect and store it with knowledge, while the heart and its affections are left without the control of religious principle, sustained by religious practices, is to mistake the nature and object of education. . . .[35]

Here then was an attempt at a philosophy or, perhaps more accurately, a theology of education which, beginning in mid-nineteenth century, has long enjoyed almost official standing in the Catholic Church of the U.S.A. It was in sharp disagreement with the general philosophy of education that was beginning to change the nonsectarian Protestant orientation of the early public schools. The public

[33] *Ibid.*
[34] *Ibid.*, p. 191.
[35] *Ibid.*, p. 215.

school still felt itself responsible for the basic religious principles common to all creeds, that is, religious beliefs whose character was presumably not distinctive of any single Protestant sect. The public schools increasingly emphasized a knowledge and love of the great ethical principles which govern man's ideal relation to his fellows, and which came out of the great Judaeo-Christian tradition. The Bible retained its privileged place, for Bible-reading would inspire students to a veneration of these principles and ideals. Increasingly public-school leaders used the phrase "moral and spiritual values," in place of "religious values." They were puzzled and annoyed at charges that the public schools were responsible for the increase in crime and delinquency. Whatever breakdown there might be in community morals, they argued, should be considered the responsibility more of the churches and homes than of the schools. The Catholic bishops indirectly owned up to this responsibility in the same pastoral letter of their Second Plenary Council in a special chapter on "Catholic Protectories and Industrial Schools."

"It is a melancholy fact, and a very humiliating avowal for us to make," they begin, "that a very large proportion of the idle and vicious youth of our principal cities are the children of Catholic parents."[36] The reason might be poverty or simply neglect but there is an appalling ignorance by parents of "the true nature of education, and of their duties as Christian parents." A large number of Catholic parents are neglecting their duty of "providing for the moral training of their offspring," or doing it in such an imperfect manner that

day after day these unhappy children are caught in the commission of petty crimes . . . and day after day, are they transferred by hundreds from the sectarian reformatories in which they have been placed by the courts, to distant localities, where they are brought up in ignorance of, and most common hostility to, the religion in which they had been baptized.[37]

Once again pastoral concern by Catholic leadership missed the critical issue. Is proper discipline of headstrong and wild youth within the family the "true nature of education"? Does moral training under devout Christian auspices within the home exhaust parental responsibility in education? Or hopefully, now, does a Catholic reformatory

---

[36] *Ibid.*, p. 216.
[37] *Ibid.*

take over from inadequate parents (and pastors) to lead the errant sheep into the paths of gospel righteousness? Apparently these good men of 1866 thought so.

What is their solution? The bishops want to have *"Catholic* Protectories or Industrial Schools" established wherein "the youthful culprit may cease to do evil and learn to do good." They are happy that some dioceses have already begun to do this good work, and exhort the clergy

to bring this matter before their respective flocks, to endeavor to impress on Christian parents the duty of guarding their children from the evils above referred to, and to invite them to make persevering and effectual efforts for the establishment of institutions, wherein, under the influence of religious teachers, the waywardness of youth may be corrected, and good seed planted in the soil in which, while men slept, the enemy had sowed tares.[38]

There is here an exaggerated faith in the Catholic school as the great sacrament of salvation, which was only matched by Protestant faith in the public school as the panacea for all of America's woes. Just how the "Catholic Protectories and Industrial Schools" were to become the solution to the staggering problems the nation faced in its first year after the bloodiest and bitterest war of its history, their excellencies did not detail. One can be excused for reflecting that there might have been more practical measures called for to combat the unemployment and violence and squalor and corruption in the urban America of 1866. True, it would be two more decades before a conscience-stricken public would respond to the prophetic voice of a Jacob Riis or Jane Addams or Ellen Gates Starr and begin to face the ills of the industrial civilization whose grinding tenement misery was crushing the hopes and dreams of millions of new American Catholics. Largely cut off from the total community effort to cope with these problems, Catholic leadership no doubt felt that it had its own solution to the problem: protectories or industrial schools under Catholic direction. The slender resources of the immigrant church were courageously, if somewhat imprudently, expended in the cause of "true education." Perhaps though the letter also served as a bit of solace to the war-sick struggling Catholic community with the reminder of the rewards and

[38] *Ibid.,* p. 217.

punishments of the afterlife, guaranteed through loyal adherence to the one true church.

On the other hand, these bishops and pastors deserve great credit for the unrelieved struggle they carried on to achieve the unachievable goal of establishing a Catholic environment for the bewildered immigrant. We can hasten to make our own the sentiment of the dean of American church historians:

And if they sometimes stumbled as they went forward along their uncharted course, they attained their principal goal in preserving for the majority of their impoverished charges the essentials of their religious faith. It must ever remain, therefore, one of our prime duties as Catholics of this age of affluence to enshrine the names and achievements of the relatively few leaders who reached a measure of fame, and of their countless and nameless followers, in our grateful memory. Without them, many of us would not so much as own the faith today, and for that alone they are entitled to an enduring remembrance.[39]

After the Civil War popular education began to take wide hold, but it was only in 1880 that the public-school enrollment reached one million. Meanwhile the Catholic dilemma was not easing. The bishops were divided over the school question, and remained so throughout the final three decades of the century. Historians are beginning to think that too great an influence has been attributed to the Third Plenary Council of Baltimore in shaping the parochial-school system. In the sense that this last and greatest of the national councils did formalize a firm policy concerning the rejection of the public school on confessional grounds and commitment to the separate religious school, the council's influence was paramount. Moreover, where the earlier councils had been content to exhort priests and people to erect schools, this council laid down orders, a timetable, and sanctions. Nevertheless there were earlier factors at work, none of them larger than the 1875 *Instruction of the Roman Congregation of the Propaganda* to the American bishops, which provided the essential material for the Baltimore school legislation of 1884.

Recent studies have made clearer the role played in eliciting this document from Rome by a small group of all-out opponents of

[39] John Tracy Ellis, "American Catholicism in 1960," *The American Benedictine Review* (March–June, 1960), p. 3.

public education.[40] Their leader was James A. McMaster, a convert and able writer, who edited the influential New York *Freeman's Journal* between 1847 and 1886. As an editor he had few peers but his acid-dipped pen and strong prejudices left him few friends. In theological and political matters he was ultraconservative, even reactionary. Just what prompted his crusade to keep Catholic children out of the public schools has not yet been satisfactorily explained. Thomas T. McAvoy speculates that it was his brooding over events in France after the Franco-Prussian War, in particular his reaction to the senseless violence of the Paris Commune against the church in 1871.[41]

In an editorial that July, McMaster declared war on the state school:

> Then we propose opening on the promoters of non-sectarian, non-dogmatic schooling, in this country. We will show all who follow us most rigorously, that they are working towards bringing on our country the calamities France has been suffering, and preparing torches for American cities such as have laid nearly one third *of Paris in ashes.*[42]

The next week he defended his "declaration of war" with an astonishing claim which, if only partly true, indicates the deep division over the school question among the American bishops. He states that for twenty-three years he had fought for independent Catholic schools without tax support from the state and that his position had been *"deprecated"* by nearly all the bishops and by most of the priests then in office as "an idle theory of exclusive Catholic edu-

---

[40] See especially Thomas T. McAvoy, C.S.C., "Public Schools vs. Catholic Schools and James McMaster," *The Review of Politics,* Vol. 28, No. 1 (January, 1966), 19–46. No area was more bitterly fought over in the conservative-liberal struggle within the Catholic Church of the latter nineteenth century than the state school. Father McAvoy's work is vital background here: *The Great Crisis in American Catholic History: 1895–1900* (Chicago: Henry Regnery, 1957).

[41] After Napoleon III's surrender at Sedan, a republic was proclaimed which continued the war with Prussia. Paris underwent a three-months' siege and was at length occupied. The Parisians became more bitter over the peace terms accepted by the National Assembly, largely made up of conservatives and traditionalists, and seized control of the city. Extreme radicals gained control and proclaimed a municipal council or *Commune.* After a series of desperate fights, troops of the National Assembly retook Paris. During the last days of the struggle, "Bloody Week" (May 21–28, 1871), the Communards executed many distinguished hostages including the archbishop.

[42] New York *Freeman's Journal,* July 1, 1871.

cation, that cannot be realized in this country &c. &c." The sole prelate he excepted was Bishop Ignatius Reynolds of Charleston.[43]

Writing under the date of February 17, 1872, McMaster presented his position in full. The editorial was entitled "Thesis on Catholic Duties toward Catholic Children," and reads in part:

> The *law* of the Catholic Church, promulgated and reiterated, in the Encyclicals of the Vicar of Christ—in which he has spoken to the Universal Church is not obscure. It condemns any, and every system of mental training for Catholic children, that is not under the supervision of approved Catholic teachers; or in which the continual influence of Catholic instruction is not exerted.
>
> . . . The *conclusion* which we propose is that, considering the teaching of the Vicar of Christ, and of the general body of the Hierarchy believing with him, and teaching with him, the time has come for enforcing *everywhere,* the general law of the Catholic Church, that Catholics must not send their children to any schools except Catholic schools!

Intermittently but with unflagging fervor, the editor pursued the battle. He gave fulsome praise and complete coverage to the pastorals of bishops who called for the building of schools and never hesitated even to scold the many bishops who were, he thought, dragging their feet on the issue. He urged that parents sending children to the public school be denied absolution. He bitterly attacked the Poughkeepsie Plan and other kinds of school compromise. Over and over he thundered editorially that the school question was no longer open, "for Rome has spoken!" All that remained was to obey:

> The argument about the evils, and the dangers of godless schools, has been ended, long since. The question is now, solely, about obeying the law of the Catholic Church!
>
> The *law of the Catholic Church* is, now, that it is *forbidden* to Catholics to send their children to any "schools from which the authority (that is the Priesthood in its teaching capacity) of the Catholic Church is excluded.

Nor was he about to accept the so-called Sunday schools, which he contemptuously dismissed as "lazy pastors' soothing plasters." Mc-Master would settle for no less than "parochial day schools, under pious teachers."

Rome had spoken all right. In a strong letter to the Archbishop of Freiburg im Breisgau dated July 14, 1864, Pius IX protested the

43 *Ibid.,* July 8, 1871.

transfer of control of the public schools in the Grand Duchy of Baden from church to state. McMaster was certain that what was bad for a Europe whose moral strength was being drained away by Freemasons, socialists, and liberals was equally bad for the United States of America. Twice McMaster printed the translated text of the pope's letter. He reminded his readers that the very propositions condemning public education in the *Syllabus of Errors* of 1864 had been drawn from this source.[44]

American Catholics, the bishops included, were too slow to accept the promulgated law of the church, so the New York crusader would appeal directly to Pio Nono to speed things along. Appeal he did. Through his strategically situated correspondent in Rome, Ella B. Edes, and a priest friend visiting there, Edmund DePauw of the Diocese of Ogdensburg, McMaster presented a letter of petition and formal *Memorandum,* under date of February 20, 1874, to the Sacred Congregation of Propaganda Fide.[45] The

[44] *Ibid.* Here are the three propositions condemned by Pope Pius IX as errors:

A. The entire government of the public schools in which the youth of any state is instructed, episcopal seminaries being excepted for some reason, can and should be assigned to the civil authority; and assigned in such a way, indeed, that for no other authority is the right recognized to interfere in the discipline of the schools, in the system of studies, in the conferring of degrees, in the choice or approval of teachers.

B. The best state of civil society demands that the peoples' schools which are open to all children of any class of people, and the public institutions in general which are destined for the teaching of literature and the more exact studies, and for caring for the education of youth, should be exempted from all authority, control, and power of the church; and be subjected to the full authority of the civil and political power, exactly according to the pleasure of the rulers and the standard of current public opinion.

C. Catholic men can approve that method of instructing youth which has been divorced from Catholic Faith and the power of the church, and which regards only, or at least primarily, the natural sciences and the purposes of social life on earth alone. *The Sources of Catholic Dogma,* trans. by Roy J. Deferrari from the thirtieth edition of Denzinger's *Enchiridion Symbolorum,* printed in the U.S.A. by Vail-Ballou Press, Inc., Binghamton, N.Y. (St. Louis, Mo.: B. Herder Book Co., 1957).

[45] The influence of Miss Edes exerted in Rome on American church affairs throughout the final thirty years of the nineteenth century was uncanny. Like McMaster a convert, she worked in Rome for the prefect of the Propaganda as a secretary, and for several newspapers as a correspondent. Her instincts were all conservative. Her knowledge of Rome and her sense of *"Romanità"* made her an invaluable pipeline.

Memorandum asked two questions: (1) May Catholic parents send their children to non-Catholic state schools which have rejected the surveillance of the Catholic clergy? (2) Does Pius IX's letter to the Archbishop of Freiburg apply to the United States? It then added fifteen points to help clarify the issue, which in the grimmest possible terms depicted what was taking place in the American church and especially what was happening to Catholic children in the public schools.

McMaster viewed the school issue in stark black and white. Writing to Miss Edes, he stated:

My thesis has always been that parents cannot *in any case whatever,* without violating their consciences as Catholics, send their children to *primary* school, in which the rudiments of intellectual development are imparted by non-Catholic teachers, or by Catholic teachers in schools which refuse the supervision of a Catholic priest.[46]

And the basis for this sweeping statement? "I rest my argument formally," he wrote, "on the decretal letter, dated July 14, 1864, and addressed by the Holy Father to the Archbishop of Freiburg."

To reinforce the information sent to the cardinals of the Holy Office through Miss Edes, McMaster supplied Italian translations of news and articles from the *Freeman's Journal.* For example, one nightmarish article was "The Morality of the Public Schools in America."[47]

Action was speedily forthcoming. April 10, 1874, seven weeks after the date of the McMaster petition, Cardinal Allesandro Franchi, prefect of the Congregation, wrote to the archbishops of the United States. The letter opens with a summary of the situation, obviously colored by the harsh picture presented by the McMaster group:

It has been reported to this Sacred Congregation that so serious are the evils which befall Catholic youth in the United States of North America as a result of their attendance at public schools which are not subject to

[46] The original letter and *Memorandum,* quoted by McAvoy, "Public Schools," p. 28, is in the archives of the Sacred Congregation of Propaganda Fide.

[47] Lacking today's more highly developed journalistic ethics and libel laws, the journals and newspapers of the time were much more free-swinging than we are accustomed to today. Moreover, there was little church control over these media, which generally were in private hands.

the vigilance and inspection of ecclesiastical authority, that it can safely be said that there are in number more who thereafter fall into indifferentism and so lose their faith, than there are who every year, by virtue of the zealous work of our missionaries, renounce the false religion that they used to practice and are received into the bosom of the church.[48]

The money factor is then touched upon. "It has furthermore been reported that parents send their children to the aforesaid schools for reasons of small consequence, among which this one is cited—that their Catholic schools demand some small sum of money annually from the young people for their education, whereas in the public schools the instruction is provided at no cost whatsoever." This casual passing over of what was certainly a crucial factor in the whole question must have dismayed some of the bishops contemplating their impoverished immigrant flocks.

Cardinal Franchi went on to list five questions which the congregation wanted answered:

1. Precisely for what reasons do the faithful permit their children to attend non-Catholic schools?
2. What sort of means are there whereby young people can more easily be kept away from schools of this sort?
3. What are the reasons why some up to now hold that sacramental absolution must be denied to Catholic parents who send their children to non-Catholic schools, whereas others think that absolution should be granted?
4. Whether by the denial of the sacraments it can be easily brought about that parents will not allow their children to attend such schools?
5. Finally, whether, and with what difficulties, could a remedy of this sort be harmful, with due regard to the circumstances of places and persons?

In early May a group of prelates, including most of the archbishops, was assembled by Archbishop James Roosevelt Bayley of Baltimore to prepare a reply. They agreed to inform their suffragans of the content of the joint answer, leaving each bishop who might disagree with the group free to send his own answer to the Congregation. Archbishop Bayley edited the final draft, which represented

[48] Archives of the Sacred Congregation of the Propagation of the Faith, Rome, *Lettere della S. Congregazione Anno 1874*, Vol. 370, fol. 147, 148. Copy in the University of Notre Dame Archives.

an official position, considerably more moderate than that of the McMaster group.[49]

The bishops' answer began:

First of all, it is to be noted that these public schools are not non-Catholic in the sense that they have in their very nature something which is directly and purposely opposed to the Catholic religion but are properly secular in which, to be sure, are handed down the elements of secular knowledge with the omission of all religious education.

The letter reviewed the efforts made by "all provincial councils and especially in the Baltimore Plenary Council held in 1866" to urge clergy and laity to build schools. It would be highly desirable that all Catholic children could be taught in their own schools, "for although secular schools are not opposed directly and purposely to the Catholic religion, and as a matter of fact Catholic teachers are often employed in them, nevertheless it must be admitted that not infrequently they are operated by their directors in a frame of mind opposed to the Catholic religion."

They doubted the wisdom of denying absolution to parents sending their children to public schools, even when such schools are available. There could be valid reasons as would be explained in the body of the letter. They flatly denied that "there is always present in the public schools a serious and proximate danger of perversion, particularly in an area where Catholics live with non-Catholics in a mingled consortium of life."

The bishops then take up each of Cardinal Franchi's questions.

Why do Catholic parents patronize the public schools? A Catholic school is not always available, especially in rural areas and elsewhere where there is a scarcity of Catholics or a thin Catholic purse. Often the Catholic schools in the cities are too small to accommodate all the children. The next reason is an honest admission that "the literary instruction or training which has customarily been given in public schools sometimes—rather more often than not—surpassed the instruction which is given in Catholic schools, where sometimes at least the parents would desire more refined facilities." Moreover, "most Catholic schools, in fact, are considered somewhat inferior in rank, by reason of the impossibility of securing for them competent teachers. . . ." These are among the "serious

---

[49] Quoted in McAvoy, "Public Schools," pp. 33–35. Original in the Baltimore Cathedral archives.

considerations which persuade even devoted Catholics to prefer public schools to Catholic schools and in this manner make provision for the future of their children."

The first answer also takes care of the second question of the cardinal. The only remedy which can be safely employed to keep Catholic children from non-Catholic schools is to multiply the number of schools and get "the very best teachers for them." The bishops then bring up a point which has a contemporary ring:

> From the public treasury, the public schools have the wherewithal to offer far higher salaries to teachers than the directors of Catholic schools can provide, and as a consequence the directors of Catholic schools are unable to find any but less suitable teachers. Catholics indeed, who as a rule are poor, have to pay the government common taxes for the public schools, and in addition the funds necessary to maintain their own parochial schools must be provided by them.

To the third query, why there is a difference of opinion about the denial of absolution, the American bishops indicate that the point was met in the introductory statement. However, they add the warning "that absolution would have to be denied not only to parents, but also to Catholic members of the legislative assemblies by which public schools are established and supported in the individual states, and that it would forbid devout Catholics from taking part in assemblies of this sort to the considerable detriment of and even danger to religion." Accordingly, they do not approve of indiscriminate denial of absolution to parents sending children to the public school, "but think that the decision should be made in individual cases in accordance with circumstances, with a special investigation of the care of the parents regarding the religious education of their children."

Their reply to the fourth query concerning the efficacy of denying absolution is pointed:

> . . . We have already set forth the only means of achieving the end which we ought to have in view. Denial of the sacraments would only serve to exasperate feeling and stir up hatred against the Catholic religion among our non-Catholic fellow citizens.

The fifth and final point of the Franchi letter, about the harm of denying the sacraments, they felt had been answered.

It took another year and a half before Rome sent its definitive decision to the American church regarding the public-school question. Incredibly enough, the Roman cardinals who framed the policy were far more influenced by the lurid socioreligious picture presented them by McMaster than by the balanced answer of the archbishops of the United States to Cardinal Franchi's letter. Some inkling of the episcopal feeling here can be conjectured from a line in a letter of reply from Bayley to Bishop Bernard McQuaid of Rochester who was concerned lest too strict a policy be laid down from Rome, denying absolution to parents. The Baltimore archbishop assured McQuaid that strong representation against such a policy would be in the joint letter, and then indicated his awareness of where the pressure on Rome was originating. "McMaster is growing more & more dogmatic about this as well as other matters," he wrote. "He may abuse presbyterians [sic], but Presbyterianism is very deep in him. But before they send us any of their Procrustean rules from Rome, they had better inform us how it happens, that they absolve parents who send their children to the *present* Roman public schools."[50]

The tone of the "Instruction" was set by its opening sentence:

The Sacred Congregation of Propaganda has been many times assured that for the Catholic children of the United States of America evils of the greatest kind are likely to result from the so-called public schools.[51]

The "Instruction," confirmed by Pius IX on November 24, 1875, contained eight points. The whole idea of the public school which excluded religious instruction was condemned as "most dangerous and opposed to Catholicity." Because then the children "can neither learn the rudiments of the faith nor be taught the precepts of the Church; hence they will lack that knowledge, of all else, necessary to man without which there is no leading a Christian life." This almost blind belief in the magical power of the school is astonishingly brought out in the reason their eminences advance: "For children are sent to these schools from their earliest years, almost from their cradle; at which age, it is admitted, the seeds sown of virtue or of vice take root. To allow this tender age to pass without re-

[50] Quoted in McAvoy, "Public Schools," pp. 35–36. Original in Rochester Diocesan archives, McQuaid Papers, Bayley to McQuaid, Baltimore, June 25, 1874.

[51] "Instruction of the Congregation of Propaganda de Fide concerning Catholic Children Attending American Public Schools, November 24, 1875," printed in *Catholic Education in America,* pp. 121–22.

ligion is surely a great evil." One can honestly wonder if, in this philosophy of education, mother and father and pastor and everyone else outside the classroom are left any room to sow seeds of virtue and vice.

The nineteenth-century defensive mentality of the Catholic Church, which moved it so far out of the mainstream of culture and civilization, dominates the next point of the "Instruction."

> Again, these schools being under no control of the church, the teachers are selected from every sect indiscriminately; and this, while no proper precaution is taken to prevent them injuring the children, so that there is nothing to stop them from infusing into the young minds the seeds of error and vice. Then evil results are certainly to be dreaded from the fact that in these schools, or at least in very many of them, children of both sexes must be in the same class and class-room and must sit side by side at the same desk. Every circumstance mentioned goes to show that the children are fearfully exposed to the danger of losing their faith and that their morals are not properly safeguarded.[52]

James McMaster had done his job well.

Now followed the third point: "Unless this danger of perversion can be rendered remote, instead of proximate, such schools cannot in conscience be used." An appropriate reference is here made to Pius IX's letter to the Archbishop of Freiburg, which had so well served McMaster, to the effect that what is here enjoined is simply a dictate of the natural as well as the divine law.

"It only remains then," continued the document, "for the prelates to use every means in their power to keep the flocks committed to their care from all contact with the public schools." So, Catholic schools were needed, and every effort must go toward multiplying and improving them. Teaching brotherhoods and sisterhoods are to be established. The obligation to support Catholic schools "should be especially brought to the attention of the more wealthy and influential Catholics and members of the legislature."

Point five simply reminds American Catholics that since there is no law preventing them from having their own schools, "it is therefore in the power of Catholics themselves to avert, with God's help, the dangers with which Catholicity is threatened from the public school system." The next item treated is the exception to the rule. Circumstances may sometimes permit parents conscientiously

---

[52] *Ibid.*, pp. 122–23.

to send their children to the public schools. Whether there be sufficient cause in any particular case is to be left to the conscience and judgment of the local bishop. In general, if no school exists or there is an inferior school unsuited to the social condition of the family, public-school attendance may be condoned.

The old social strata were still very much a part of the America of 1875. Several times the American bishops had cautioned ambitious parents against educating their children for stations in life they could never assume. Nor were the bishops the only Catholics who weren't ready to adopt the Catholic school indiscriminately for all. One chancery official is quoted as observing that "when a pastor undertakes to erect a parochial school he meets with three classes of persons in his parish: the upper class which he cannot force, the middle class which he is able to force, and the poor people who are in favor of it."[53]

Christian training and instruction out of school hours is the burden of the seventh section. Pastors and parents are admonished to "spare no labor to give children thorough catechetical instructions, dwelling particularly on those truths of faith and morals which are called most in question by Protestants and unbelievers. . . ." Particularly must they "keep them from freedom and familiarity with those of the other school children whose company might be dangerous to their faith and morals, and absolutely away from the corrupt."

The final point, treating of the denial of absolution to parents, is diplomatically evasive, and is the one issue where McMaster lost out.

Parents who neglect to give this necessary Christian training and instruction to their children, or who permit them to go to schools in which the ruin of their souls is inevitable, or finally, who send them to the public school without sufficient cause and without taking the necessary precautions to render the danger of perversion remote, and do so while there is a good and well-equipped Catholic school in the place, or the parents have the means to send them elsewhere to be educated,—that such parents, if obstinate, cannot be absolved, is evident from the moral teaching of the church.[54]

Perspicacious non-Catholic observers of the time can be pardoned

[53] Quoted in *The School Controversy* (1891–93), p. 286.
[54] "Instruction," p. 126.

if, after learning of documents like this one, they became more convinced that the Roman Catholic Church by definition was opposed to just about everything the vigorous young republic was striving for. The less perspicacious became the mobs whipped up by nativist demagogues, ready to march and take action to destroy the foreign menace in their midst.

The "Instruction" of 1875 must remain one of the most curious documents in the history of the American church. That it resulted from the initiative of the laity and assumed a reactionary and rigorous character despite the modifying representation of what was a fair consensus of the American bishops are two unusual facts. The most remarkable circumstance surrounding this document, however, is the silent reception it got from the American hierarchy. For most of them it was an embarrassment. There was no announcement of it. Little action immediately followed. Naturally, it displeased most of all, those bishops who had pooled their thought in the letter sent to Rome by Archbishop Bayley. The "Instruction" seems to have been quietly buried until the preparations began for the Third Plenary Council of Baltimore.

* * *

In addition to the national assemblies of the bishops from which they had jointly addressed themselves to the school situation and other concerns, individual bishops and regional meetings of bishops had long been doing the same thing. Many dioceses had drawn up statutes ordering pastors to establish parish schools, and parents to send their children to these institutions. Nowhere was this done with more exactness than in the Midwest, most particularly in dioceses where there was a heavy concentration of German Catholics. The German immigrant tended to lump together his language, his culture, and his religion. Moreover, he was suspicious and resentful of attempts to dilute his *Deutschtum,* whether by Americanizing bishops or Americanizing public schools.

Differing from his Irish brother, the German Catholic immigrant had not been forced from his homeland by grinding poverty and the specter of starvation. He was usually better educated, notably in the possession of trade or farming skills, and had a more developed culture. Whereas the Irish who were crowded into the slum districts of Boston, New York, and Philadelphia had no affluent middle class upon which the burden of supporting schools might fall, the Germans of St. Louis, Milwaukee, and Cincinnati did. Moreover, the German immigrant had far less poignant memories of hunger and oppression from the old country. He tended to regard his parish church and parish school as his closest ties to *die alte Heimat*. The flourishing German language press fostered this love as did the numerous cultural and fraternal societies dedicated to keeping his traditions fresh and green in the frequently hostile American environment. In large measure, these differences explain why the parochial-school movement was pursued with greater *élan* among the German immigrant group in the Midwest, and later for pretty much the same reasons, among the Polish Catholic community there than in the Mid-Atlantic or New England areas.

The Second Provincial Council of Cincinnati had already ordered that all pastors of souls "under pain of mortal sin" were "to provide a Catholic school in every parish or congregation subject to them, where this can be done." The bishops of this region had much to do with the vigor of the decrees on the Catholic school of the Third Plenary Council of Baltimore, which at last opened on November 9, 1884.

CHAPTER THREE

The New Context: From Third Baltimore to Vatican II

This last of the plenary councils differed from its two predecessors, most notably in that the principal pressure to convoke the council came from Rome, and in that the schema of topics was controlled by the Congregation of the Propaganda. Rome's idea was to bring the "missionary" American church into conformity with the discipline and structure of the older European churches. Had the American bishops been more free to resolve the problems of the American Catholic community within a New World context, there would have been another history of the school question. In any event, one year prior to the opening of the Baltimore meeting, eleven archbishops and bishops were invited to Rome to plan the council's agenda with the advice and assistance of the Congregation of the Propaganda.

The 1875 "Instruction" and earlier published directives on mixed schools were among the "Principal Topics" in the center of the conference table around which the planning committee sat.[1] The Italian prelate, serving as secretary, dutifully recorded in the minutes for the session of November 29, 1883:

> The Most Reverend Archbishop of Baltimore [Gibbons] declared to be most admirable both what was now proposed with regard to parochial schools and what had been previously prescribed by the Sacred Congregation in the Instruction already issued, and he agreed that complete obedience was due in their fulfillment; he added that all difficulties in re-

[1] *Capita praecipua quae Emi. Cardinales S.C. de Propaganda Fide censuerunt a Romis Archiepiscopis et Episcopis Foederatorum Statuum A.S. Romae congregatis praeparanda esse pro futuro Concilio.* Copy in Boston Archdiocesan archives. These were the American prelates: Gibbons of Baltimore, Williams of Boston, Feehan of Chicago, Heiss of Milwaukee, Fitzgerald of Little Rock, Ryan of St. Louis, Corrigan of New York, Seghers of Oregon City, O'Hara of Scranton, Salpointe of Arizona, and Chatard of Vincennes.

gard to those schools would be readily solved if the provisions of the Holy See would be observed.[2]

The minutes further record that the Archbishop of Oregon City, Charles J. Seghers, expressed concern over the insistence by some American prelates "that the council should enact a decree which would require, under penalty, that missioners should build parochial schools within a brief interval of time to be specified by the Holy See." In view of the difficulties, the cardinals replied that this measure did not seem expedient but "that bishops should insist on the building of schools with appropriate attention to missioners who prove themselves culpably negligent." When Archbishop Michael Heiss of Milwaukee inquired "whether bishops could prohibit attendance at the public schools in order to prevent harm from coming to the parochial school," he received what he undoubtedly judged a surprising reply. Their eminences said "that if this was the sole reason involved the bishops could not attach a penalty to their prohibition." Heiss wanted to hear, it can be safely conjectured, that it was entirely appropriate for a bishop to use the power of command to guarantee that all the seats in the parish school were filled.

The penultimate step in preparing the council's agenda was to submit the different topics prepared by the Roman committee to committees comprising the archbishop and the suffragan bishops of a given province. The province of Chicago was given the chapter on schools.[3] Having accepted the suggestions from Rome, they added that parish schools should be established wherever possible but that they should be equal in quality to the public schools. Finally, a group of theologians drafted the legislation on education, laying down four rules which in substance, but after modification, were voted by the council itself.

1. Near every church, when it does not already exist, a parochial school is to be erected within two years from the promulgation of

[2] See "Minutes of the Roman Meeting Preparatory to the III Plenary Council of Baltimore," trans. in *The Jurist* (1951), pp. 121–31, 302–12, 417–24, 538–47. The school question is discussed on pp. 422–24.

[3] Chicago's Archbishop Feehan was chairman; the others were: Bishops Cosgrove of Davenport, Flasch of La Crosse, and Spalding of Peoria. The eminently diplomatic Gibbons balanced this group against a special deputation of bishops which reported to the council on Title VI; Heiss of Milwaukee, McNeirny of Albany, Gilmour of Cleveland, and O'Farrell of Trenton.

this council, and to be kept up in the future, unless in the judgment of the bishop the erection and maintenance of the school is impossible.

2. A priest who is gravely negligent in erecting the school within the time or is gravely negligent in its maintenance after it is erected can and must be removed from that church.

3. The mission or parish which so neglects to aid the priest in erecting or maintaining the school, that on account of this supine negligence, the school cannot exist, is to be reprimanded by the bishop, and if it shall have been contumacious, it is to be given spiritual punishments.

4. All Catholic parents are bound to send their children to parochial schools, unless at home or in other Catholic schools, they provide sufficiently and fully for their Christian education, or on account of a good reason approved by the bishop, using meanwhile the necessary precautions and remedies, they are permitted to send them to other schools.[4]

The final wording of the decrees eliminated the threat of spiritual penalties, so America escaped the nightmare of an entire parish sometime being placed under interdict or excommunication because a local bishop judged it seriously remiss in supporting the parish school. It likewise softened the wording of the disposition of the negligent priest, substituting "deserves to be removed" for "can and must be removed."[5]

The warmest debate was over the degree of parental obligation: Should parents be exhorted or commanded to send their children to the Catholic school?

McQuaid of Rochester and the "German" bishops of the Midwest led one side of the debate. On the opposite side was Edward Fitzgerald of Little Rock. He did not see the public schools as the evil and dangerous places many of his confreres did, and so he was in total opposition to the entire decree. The priest's obligation extends only to the teaching of religion, he insisted. Once the children have been taught their catechism, the pastor's duty is done. No law

[4] Printed in Francis P. Cassidy, "Catholic Education in the Third Plenary Council of Baltimore," *Catholic Historical Review,* XXXIV (1948), 257–305 and 414–36.

[5] *Interdict* bars the faithful from certain sacred acts, e.g., the bishop could order that no further Masses are to be offered in a parish church. *Excommunication* is a sentence cutting a member off from association with the rest of the faithful.

binds parents to send a child to school to learn secular subjects. Here Fitzgerald was a minority voice. However, when it came to a proposal which would have denied absolution to parents remiss in their duty, the vote defeating the proposition was 37 to 32. The majority drew back no doubt because not even the "Instruction" of 1875 had gone so far, except that it did underscore the *natural* law obligation of parents not to seriously risk the spiritual well-being of their offspring by placing them in a serious and proximate occasion of moral harm. Whether placing a child in any given public school was to run this risk and incur the penalty, Rome never got around to ruling.

But what was meant by a "Catholic" school? Two bishops argued that it was one "which is subject to the authority of the bishop and to ecclesiastical inspection through the bishop." But would this definition not wipe out the private schools of the Christian Brothers or the Ursuline Sisters? The Archbishop of Philadelphia affirmed that a school was Catholic if, in addition to profane letters, Christian doctrine were also "taught by professing and practicing Catholics." But professing and practicing to what degree? And would every other subject also have to be taught by professing and practicing Catholics? Michael A. Corrigan of New York gave the Roman understanding of the Catholic school as one wherein Christian doctrine was taught. It was Bishop Francis Chatard's ingenious definition which finally came to be adopted, namely, that a Catholic school is one which the bishop has judged to be such.[6]

Whatever misgivings might have been in the minds of those bishops who remained unconvinced that their people could support the burden of what actually amounted to a second public-school system for Catholic children, or who felt that some kind of compromise with the state schools could have been entered into, the Third Council of Baltimore voted out these four decrees in Title VI. "After full consideration of these matters," said the prelates, "we conclude and decree:

I. That near every church a parish school, where one does not yet exist, is to be built and maintained *in perpetuum* within two years of the promulgation of this council, unless the bishop should decide that because of serious difficulties a delay may be granted.

II. A priest who within this time prevents the building or maintenance

6 Cassidy, *op. cit.*, p. 416.

of a school through his serious neglect, or after repeated warnings by the bishop does not discharge his responsibility, deserves to be removed from the church.

III. The mission or parish which neglects to aid the priest in erecting or maintaining the school, that on account of this supine negligence, the school cannot exist, is to be reprimanded by the bishop and induced by more effective and prudent means to bring forth the necessary support.

IV. That all Catholic parents are bound to send their children to the parish school, unless it is evident that a sufficient training in religion is given either in their own homes, or in other Catholic schools; or when because of a sufficient reason, approved by the bishop, with all due precautions and safeguards, it is licit to send them to other schools. What constitutes a Catholic school is left to the decision of the bishop."[7]

*   *   *

The decrees of Third Baltimore on the parochial school were never translated from their "glacial Latin text" but their thrust was carried in the long pastoral emanating from the council.[8] In this joint letter Protestantism is no longer identified as the immediate foe. A new enemy had emerged. "In the great coming combat between truth and error, between Faith and Agnosticism, an important part of the fray must be borne by the laity, and woe to them if they are not well prepared." The moral and religious well-being of the people should be promoted to achieve a true civilization. "Take away religion from a people, and immorality would soon follow." Without naming him or his book, Darwin and the *Origin of Species,* published now for twenty-five years, are pointed to: "Civilization without religion would be a civilization of 'the struggle for existence, and the survival of the fittest,' in which cunning and strength would become the substitutes for principle, virtue, conscience, and duty."

The context of 1884 helps to understand this episcopal concern which was still very much shared by the Protestant clergy. Though

[7] *Acta et decreta concilii plenarii tertii* (Baltimore: John Murphy & Co., 1886); Title VI; Latin text of the decrees is found on p. 104. The translation is the author's.

[8] *Ibid.* The English text of the pastoral letter may be read in *Acta et decreta,* pp. lxxviii–lxxix, lxxxii–lxxxvi.

most American scientists had accepted the evolutionary hypothesis, Darwinism had made little progress in other circles. In fact, the last twenty years of the century saw a succession of sensational heresy trials in the Protestant universities and seminaries over evolution, the new higher criticism of the Scriptures, and the scientific method in general. Authoritarianism and protectionism were by no means a Catholic monopoly, and the Roman Catholic bishops of 1884 as a group were no more benighted or enlightened vis-à-vis the challenge of science than any corresponding group in the Protestant world.

In any event, the bishops' solution was the school: education must foster religion in order to safeguard civilization. A key assumption behind this position is that religious knowledge and religious formation can take place *only* in the school—an assumption which by 1884 was being more and more abandoned by the Protestant churches.[9]

The pastoral confronts the point head on.

To shut religion out of the school, and keep it for home and the Church, is, logically, to train up a generation that will consider religion good for home and the Church, but not for the practical business of real life. But a more false and pernicious notion could not be imagined.[10]

Since the school is the principal tool fitting one for practical life, it "ought to be preëminently under the holy influence of religion." The bishops then warn that the avowed enemies of Christianity in some European countries are banishing religion from the schools, in order gradually to eliminate it from among the people."

In the practical order then the fathers of the council had two objects in view: to multiply schools, and to perfect them. "We must multiply them till every Catholic child in the land shall have within its reach the means of education." Still the quality of Catholic education must be kept in mind. "We repudiate," they stated, "the idea that the Catholic school need be in any respect inferior to any other school whatsoever." There is a wistfulness clinging to these final words of exhortation:

[9] The change in Protestant policy is carefully documented in Francis X. Curran, *The Churches and the Schools* (Chicago: Loyola University Press, 1954).

[10] The sections of the pastoral dealing with education may be found in Neil G. McCluskey, ed., *Catholic Education in America* (New York: Teachers College Bureau of Publications, 1964), pp. 86–93.

And if hitherto, in some places, our people have acted on the principle that it is better to have an imperfect Catholic school than to have none, let them now push their praiseworthy ambition still further, and not relax their efforts till their schools be elevated to the highest educational excellence.[11]

* * *

What happened after the council? What impact did the decrees have? Did the Baltimore legislation speed up the building of Catholic schools? This is the one thing we are certain did not happen. However, it should be kept in mind that the drive to establish separate schools had been well under way since the "Instruction" of 1875. The bishops who had pushed vigorously for schools continued to do so, and those who were unconvinced of the need did little more than they had been doing. It can be conjectured that most bishops, while agreeing with the ideal, threw their hands up at the sheer impossibility of the task. To put pressure on their impoverished flocks to multiply schools and to maintain them on a par with the free public schools called for great faith. That so many bishops and pastors did and that their people responded is evidence of the special loyalty the American church has always had toward the Holy See. Many bishops still hoped for some kind of compromise, and even the "Germanizing" bishops promoted arrangements similar to the Faribault-Stillwater Plan.[12]

A study of the school statistics published each year in the *Catholic Directory* makes it plain that the immediate impact of the leg-

[11] *Ibid.*, p. 93.

[12] Ireland's letter to Cardinal Ledochowski, Prefect of Propaganda, cites some of them: "I would not have Your Eminence, however, believe that I was the first ever to introduce such an arrangement into the United States or that the two villages above named are the only places where it actually prevails; on the contrary, Cardinal McCloskey, Archbishop of New York, instituted it 18 years ago in his diocese in the town of Poughkeepsie where it has been maintained there ever since by his successor, Archbishop Corrigan. It is in operation in 8 localities of the diocese of Archbishop Katzer of Milwaukee who also established it in his former diocese of Green Bay. It obtains in a great number of the schools of Bishop Zardetti in the diocese of St. Cloud; in the diocese of Savannah Bishop Becker has it in operation in all the Catholic schools of his Episcopal city. The fathers of the Society of Jesus have applied the same plan with great success in their parish of Conewago in the diocese of Harrisburg; it also obtains in the diocese of Albany, Erie, Buffalo, Rochester, Peoria, etc. etc." (See Appendix E, *The School Controversy*, 1891–93, p. 225.)

islation was generally imperceptible.[13] Certainly, there was no dramatic increase by the end of the two-year period stipulated in the decree, within which every parish was to put up a school. In 1884 there were 6626 churches and 2464 parochial schools enrolling 490,531 pupils. The corresponding figures for 1886 show 6910 churches with 2697 schools and 537,725 pupils. Some 233 new schools apparently were built and the percentage of churches with schools went from 37 per cent to 39 per cent. However, at the end of the two-year interval, 4213 parishes still had not a school. True, the school population grew by 10 per cent, but these were years of peak immigration, which makes that gain less significant. Total enrollment increased steadily, rising from 490,531 in 1884 to 903,980 in 1900. But again it must be kept in mind that the Catholic population between 1880 and 1900 rose from 6,259,000 to 12,041,000, so that it is doubtful if as high a proportion of Catholic youngsters were in parochial schools in 1900 as in 1884. A more significant figure is the percentage of parishes that actually had schools during this sixteen-year span. The 1884 figure was 37 per cent; it peaked in 1891 at 44 per cent; dropped in 1895 and 1896 to 35 per cent; and at the start of the new century was at 36 per cent. Interestingly enough, the figure for 1968 is 57 per cent.

Again, one might expect dioceses with a large German immigrant population to have a higher percentage of parishes with schools than others. On the contrary, no consistent pattern of superiority emerges from a comparison of Milwaukee, St. Louis, and Cincinnati with Boston, Philadelphia, and New York.[14]

The state of the economy strongly influenced the capability of the Catholic community to build and sustain schools, and the last twenty-five years of the century were marked by the sharpest zigs and zags in the nation's economic history. What has been styled "the longest period of economic contraction in American history" occurred between 1873 and 1878. There was widespread unemployment, particularly among railroad builders, from 1882 to 1883, and until 1885 the economy remained in poor shape. A banking panic in

---

13 See appended table.

14 Some of the statistics of the early *Catholic Directories* are inconsistent and suggest error. Boston, for example, in 1884 has 30 per cent of its parishes with schools and in 1894 goes up to 54 per cent but then drops in 1899 to 30 per cent. Milwaukee reports 26 schools in 1884 and five years later lists 125!

1893 resulted in the worst depression experienced by the American people up to that time.[15]

* * *

The school that "within two years" was to be built near every church was a strictly elementary institution of three or four rooms with at most six grades, which satisfied the needs and ambitions of the overwhelming majority of Americans of that era. But needs heighten and ambitions broaden, so that more and more Americans began to lengthen their formal education. Until the high-school movement swept over the country, secondary education was understood as an "academy" for girls or a "college" for boys. In fact, almost any formal schooling beyond the rudiments took place in what was labeled a "college." Before the Civil War, high schools were few and far between. In 1840 one might count around fifty, about half of which were in Massachusetts. *The* Chicago High School, the first in that city, opened in 1856. Among the farming and working classes children were expected to earn their keep at an early age, and the idea of collecting taxes for free high schools for everybody was resisted as a downright luxury as well as an outrageous invasion of family rights. What hastened the multiplication of these schools was the 1872 decision of the Michigan State Supreme Court, upholding the right of the city of Kalamazoo to levy additional taxes for a high school.

Four years prior to Third Baltimore, in 1880, 3 per cent of the youngsters of high-school age were enrolled in high schools. This figure represents approximately 110,000 pupils in about 800 schools. By 1890, when for the first time the U. S. Bureau of Education gathered complete statistics, the comparable totals were 202,969 pupils in 2526 institutions, a rise to 5 per cent of the potential enrollment.[16] Catholics were slow to join the movement to-

---

[15] "The decline in employment in railroad building from 1882 to 1883 came to 500,000 men of a total national labor force of only 18 million. Steel rails, worth $71 a ton in January, 1880, were selling for half that in December, 1883." (Ray Ginger, *Age of Excess,* New York: The Macmillan Company, 1965), p. 43.

[16] Statistical tables printed in Ellwood P. Cubberley, *Public Education in the United States* (Cambridge: Houghton Mifflin Company, 1947 ed.), p. 627. Three out of four Americans now *finish* high school. In 1967 nearly 2,700,000 students graduated and about 40 per cent started college.

ward the four-year high school. The 581 Catholic academies and eighty-three Catholic colleges of 1884 provided whatever there was in secondary schooling. The colleges especially looked to their preparatory division (always by far the larger) for recruits, and hence resented the high schools as rivals. In 1900 there existed 183 Catholic colleges, all with preparatory departments. The first to drop its high-school department and become a strictly four-year collegiate institution was Holy Cross College, and the year was 1914. These schools, conducted by religious orders and congregations, were financed through school fees and benefactions. As the high-school movement spread, provision for Catholic high schools was more and more wanting. Again money was the problem. A continually higher proportion of Catholic youngsters was to be found in state-supported high schools—a situation hardly foreseen by the conciliar fathers of Baltimore—and a new problem.

*   *   *

At the 1889 convention of the National Education Association in Nashville, James Cardinal Gibbons of Baltimore and Bishop John J. Keane, first rector of the newly opened Catholic University of America, gave parallel addresses entitled, "Should Americans Educate Their Children in Denominational Schools?" A paper by Edwin Mead of Boston, "Has the Parochial School Proper Place in America?" and a fourth, "Public and Parochial Schools" by John Jay of New York, represented a sharply divergent point of view. Nonetheless, the two Catholic speakers judged the conference to be beneficial: a large and influential body of educators had heard a well-argued presentation of the Catholic position, and certain valid questions had been raised relating to the place of the parochial school in the American context.

The next year Archbishop Ireland was invited to address the same national group when it met in his see city of St. Paul. A distinguished and forceful orator, John Ireland made a deep impression upon his auditors with his call for a compromise approach, which would provide religious instruction for Catholic children, while making parish schools a part of the public system. This pattern was already operative in two towns within Ireland's jurisdiction, Stillwater and Faribault. However, his address ignited a controversy among

Catholic leaders that "was without parallel in American Catholic history, in point of extent, intensity, and bitterness of feeling."[17]

What did Ireland say that so infuriated some of his brother bishops and began a sharp escalation of the strife between progressives and conservatives which would finally evoke strong papal intervention twice during the decade?

He began his address to an overwhelmingly Protestant audience by stating:

I am a friend and an advocate of the state school. In the circumstances of the present time I uphold the parish school. I sincerely wish that the need for it did not exist. I would have all schools for the children of the people to be state schools.[18]

He dismissed as contemptuous the accusation that Catholics were bent on destroying the state school. He painstakingly set forth the grounds of Catholic opposition to the state schools and what steps could be taken to remove this opposition. The right of the state school to exist he considered a matter beyond the stage of discussion. In fact, he urged its necessity. Though parents have the primary right and function in education, "as things are, tens of thousands of children will not be instructed if parents solely remain in charge of the duty. . . . The state must come forward as an agent of instruction; else ignorance will prevail." Moreover, to achieve universal education the schools must be *free*.

Free schools! Blest indeed is the nation whose vales and hillsides they adorn and blest the generations upon whose souls are poured their treasures! No tax is more legitimate than that which is levied in order to dispel mental darkness, and build up within the nation's bosom intelligent manhood and womanhood. . . .

The Republic of the United States has solemnly affirmed its resolve that within its borders no clouds of ignorance shall settle upon the minds of the children of its people. In furnishing the means to accomplish this result its generosity knows no limit. The free school of America! Withered be the hand raised in sign of its destruction![19]

"Can he be suspected of enmity to the state school," the prelate

[17] Allen Sinclair Will, *Life of James Cardinal Gibbons, Archbishop of Baltimore*, II (New York: E. P. Dutton & Co., 1922), 238.

[18] Complete text can be found in *Catholic Education in America*, pp. 128–40.

[19] *Ibid.*, pp. 129–30.

continued, "because he would fain widen the expanse of its wings until all the children of the people find shelter beneath their cover?"

I turn to the denominational or parish school. It exists. I again express my regret that there is a necessity for its existence. In behalf of the state school I call upon my fellow-Americans to aid in the removal of this necessity.[20]

But the state school itself is laboring under a serious defect. As presently organized this school tends to eliminate religion from the minds and hearts of the youth of the country. The state school is nonreligious. In the absence of positive religion, the impressionable mind of the child comes to regard religion as irrelevant to his life because it is completely outside his school life. The father's long work day and the mother's unceasing round of household chores prevent parents from imparting religious instruction. An hour of Sunday instruction doesn't attract the child. Then is enunciated his pivotal thesis:

Accidentally, it may be, and unintentionally, but, in fact, most certainly, the state school crowds out the church. The teaching of religion is not a function of the state; but the state should, for the sake of its people, and for its own sake, permit and facilitate the teaching of religion by the church. This the state does not do; rather, it hinders and prevents the work of the church. The children of the masses are learning no religion.[21]

He offers the traditional rebuttal to counter the argument that the state school's function is simply to teach morals: "From the principles of religion morals derive power and vitality. Separated from a belief in God and in the existence of the soul beyond the present life, morals are vague and weak commands which passion is not slow to scorn."[22] Nor is he willing to leave the schools to

[20] *Ibid.*, p. 131. Ireland's opponents repeatedly cited these words as proof that he was an enemy of the parochial school. This was "dirty pool." The Archbishop of St. Paul had been surpassed by few in building schools. As he wrote to Cardinal Ledochowski, Prefect of the Propaganda, "My opponents say that I deplored the existence of the parochial school. It is untrue. I deplored the necessity of the Catholics being obliged after paying in tax for the support of state schools to maintain again by voluntary contributions schools of their own, and asked the state for means to maintain schools Catholic as well as Protestant. . . . (Appendix E, *The School Controversy*, 1891–93, p. 251.)

[21] *Ibid.*, p. 133.

[22] *Ibid.*, p. 134.

the secularists and unbelievers. He concedes their rights and has no desire to impose Christianity upon them. In turn, however, let them not impose the religion of secularism upon him and the American school. Nor is a common-denominator type of Christianity the answer. There is large dissatisfaction with the public school because it excludes religion, which will remain until the cause is removed. Ten million American Catholics cannot in conscience patronize the schools paid for by their taxes. This injustice is the more serious because "the ten millions are largely the poorer classes of the population, and . . . they are sincerely and loyally desiring to obtain the benefits of the state school, if only the obstacles be removed."[23]

The archbishop then briefly sketched the compromise plan followed in Faribault and Stillwater, and began his peroration. He protested against the charge that Catholics were the enemies of the nation's schools.

Not one stone of the wondrous edifice which Americans have reared in their devotion to education would Catholics remove or permit to be removed. They would fain add to its splendor and majesty by putting side by side religious and secular instruction, neither of them interfering with the other, each of them borrowing from the other aid and dignity.[24]

He concluded with the proposal that in urging the Christian state school, Catholics were proving themselves the truest friends of the school and the state.

In a later letter to his good friend Gibbons defending his position on the public schools, Ireland repeated his contention that no absolute necessity for the parish school existed. They did not exist in Ireland and England, and they only came into existence in Belgium and France after "infidel governments had made the state school infidel."

The necessity for parish schools is hypothetical—the necessity being not a direct result of the Church's mission, but a provision in certain cases for the protection of the faith. The Church is not established to teach writing and ciphering, but to teach morals and faith, and she teaches writ-

23 *Ibid.*, p. 137.
24 *Ibid.*, pp. 139–40.

ing and ciphering only when otherwise morals and faith could not be taught.[25]

In 1890 there was widespread sympathy and support for this position among the American Catholic leadership. Despite the decrees of Third Baltimore many bishops hoped for some sort of compromise. Nor was this attitude dictated only by economics, granted that lack of money was a critical factor. "The burden upon our Catholics"—and Ireland's words could have been spoken by most of the hierarchy—"to maintain parish schools up to the required standard for all the children of the church is almost unbearable." The true solution would be "to make the state school satisfactory to Catholic consciences, and to use it."

Leaders like Ireland and Gibbons were keenly aware of the value of these schools in assimilating immigrant children and children of immigrants. They fully appreciated the need for compromise. In ideal there should be parish schools but their immigrant workers and farmers simply could not support them. What concerned Ireland, firm believer that he was in the American political philosophy, was that these immigrant children needed the public school, as part of the process of becoming citizens of the great New World republic. Ireland's school stand drew to him the sharpest arrows of the opposition. Moreover, he had aroused bitter feelings among the defenders of *Deutschtum* because of his opposition to the German foreign-language schools and national parishes. During the fight in 1889 over the Bennett law, which would have required all schools in Wisconsin to conduct certain classes in English, he gave no support to the bishops of the Milwaukee province, who regarded the law as trespassing on church and family right. Earlier, along with Keane, he used his considerable influence to have the Abbelen[26] petition rejected. This was a measure to have the national parishes established with full parochial rights. Ireland also used his weight in the defeat of the Lucerne *Memorials* which would have the pope appoint German bishops for America to care for German-speaking immigrants.[27]

[25] Complete text in *Catholic Education in America*, pp. 141–50. This citation, p. 146.

[26] Peter M. Abbelen (1843–1917), vicar general of the Milwaukee archdiocese.

[27] In 1890 and also in 1891 the German emigration societies, meeting in Lucerne, deplored what they considered great losses to the Church among the

The "American" bishops feared the results of parochial schools that tended to preserve European customs and foreign languages at the expense of American ways and the English language. They were also aware of the affection most Americans felt toward the public school and the resentment non-Catholics felt toward what seemed to be an official Catholic attitude of hostility, criticism, and boycott. In an 1890 letter to Leo XIII, Cardinal Gibbons explained to the pope that the divisions between Catholics and their fellow citizens "are caused above all by the opposition against the system of national education which is attributed to us, and which, more than any other thing, creates and maintains in the minds of the American people the conviction that the Catholic Church is opposed by principle to the institutions of the country and that a sincere Catholic cannot be a loyal citizen of the United States."[28]

For his part, Ireland deplored the harsh criticism of the public schools by some bishops. In fact, in their dioceses the parish schools have done "more harm than good." He scoffed at the notion that the public schools were "hotbeds of vice" or that they taught unbelief or Protestantism. "Our public schools are better than those of France and Italy," he wrote, "and in those countries we hear no continuous anathemas."

Not every advocate of the secular nature of the school was an agnostic or unbeliever though Catholic defenders of parochial education often lumped them together. A towering figure in the educational world was William Torrey Harris, superintendent of schools in St. Louis between 1868 and 1881, and U. S. Commissioner of Education from 1889 to 1906. He and like-minded thinkers were making acceptable the idea that, in the nature of things, the school was secular and incompetent to enter the area of religious education. No hostility toward religion or religious values was behind this philosophy, nor was there question of challenging the importance of religion in life. It rather concerned the most apt occasion for efficient instruction in religion and with safeguarding the rights of conscience in a pluralistic society. This last point, in turn, was an

---

immigrants. Under the presidency of Count Peter Cahensley (hence "Cahensleyism" as a name for the movement), they urged the Holy See to provide the equivalent of "national" bishops.

[28] Letter quoted in John Tracy Ellis, *The Life of James Cardinal Gibbons,* I (Milwaukee: The Bruce Publishing Company, 1952), 664.

axiom deriving from the constitutional separation of church and state.

Harris' great friend, Bishop John Lancaster Spalding of Peoria, shared much of this thinking. "I am willing to assume and to accept as a fact," Bishop Spalding said, "that our theological differences make it impossible to introduce the teaching of any religious creed into the public school. . . ."[29]

Cardinal Gibbons also tried to convince Rome that the absence of religious education in American public schools was not due to opposition of the Continental variety. "The public spirit in this country," he said, "is fundamentally religious and there is everywhere a great respect for liberty of conscience well understood and in the legitimate sense of the word." However, the religious question had been set aside in the schools, he went on, in order not to offend the sentiments of the children and their parents, and the care of providing the religious education of the children was left to the church and the Protestant sects.[30]

Evidently these representations did make an impression, if not permanently, at least for a few years. Pressed for a decision on the propriety of cooperating with the public-school system along the lines of the Faribault-Stillwater arrangement, in May, 1892, Rome returned a sphinxlike answer:

The sound decrees of the Baltimore Council as to parochial schools remaining fully in force, the agreement made by the Most Rev. Dr. John Ireland with regard to the Faribault and Stillwater schools, all the circumstances being taken into consideration can be allowed.[31]

Instead of settling the issue, both sides at once interpreted the document in their own favor and claimed victory. Archbishop Corrigan announced in New York that the Faribault system had been condemned and that only the special exception was tolerated. To newspapermen Ireland said that his experiment had been completely vindicated and that he thought it could be adopted in any community where similar circumstances prevailed.

[29] "The Scope of Public School Education," an address in the collection *Means and Ends in Education* (Chicago: A. C. McClurg, 1895). Reprinted in *Catholic Education in America.*

[30] Ellis, *op. cit.*

[31] The document is to be found in *Catholic Education in America*, pp. 151–60.

Everything revolved around the meaning of the Latin phrase *"tolerari potest."* Did the words mean toleration, permission, or approval? The "Church-schools-at-any-price" group could be excused for their perplexity. How in the name of logic could the decrees of Title VI of Third Baltimore remain "fully in force" if Rome gave approbation to a compromise approach? For months the highly partisan press filled the sky with journalistic flak. The attacks took on an ugly note. Even high-ranking prelates blasted one another in print. Alarmed at this disedifying array, in November Pope Leo XIII sent a personal legate, Archbishop Francesco Satolli, to the yearly meeting of the archbishops with a set of fourteen propositions to clarify once and for all the school question. He was also instructed to try to ease the German-Irish antagonism, which was in large part the source of the clash over the schools.

To the consternation and anger of the conservatives Satolli's proposals seemed to allow greater cooperation with the state schools, all the while purporting to be upholding the legislation of Baltimore. The sixth proposition repeated the perennial truth that the church holds for herself the right of teaching the truths of faith and the law of morals in order to bring up youth in the habits of a Christian life, but then adds, "Hence, absolutely and universally speaking there is no repugnance in their learning the first elements and the higher branches of arts and the natural sciences in public schools, controlled by the State. . . ."[32] This was scarcely the tone of the "Instruction" of 1875, and what followed in the eighth proposition was not calculated to add to the repose of James McMaster, who had been buried in 1886.

The separate Catholic schools in America were a necessity, said the document, because the public schools of 1892 were generally "a proximate danger to faith and morals" for three reasons.

1. They totally excluded religious teaching.
2. They used teachers selected indiscriminately from every sect.
3. They educated boys and girls together.

But the proposition made haste to add—and this is where the conservatives felt they had been betrayed—that when these specific dangers to faith and morals disappear, "then it is lawful for Catholic parents to send their children to these schools, to acquire the elements of letters and arts, provided the parents themselves do not

[32] *Ibid.*

neglect their most serious duty, and the pastors of souls put every effort to instruct the children and train them in all that pertains to Catholic worship and life." In other words, if pastors and parents did their job in giving religious education and formation, the state school could care for the profane side of things.

Bishop McCloskey of Louisville wrote Corrigan that the Satolli propositions would be "the death blow, to a certain extent, of our Catholic schools." Even McCloskey's timid wrath smacks of a curial mentality. There is nothing harder to imagine than a "death blow, to a certain extent," unless it is "being pregnant—to a certain extent."

McQuaid was even more aroused. He likewise wrote the New York archbishop:

We are all in a nice pickle, thanks to Leo XIII and his delegate. Just as our arduous work of the last forty years was beginning to bear ample fruit, they arbitrarily upset the whole. If an enemy had done this! It is only a question of time, when present Roman legislation having wrought incalculable mischief, that we, school children of the hierarchy, will again receive a lesson in our catechism from another Italian sent out to enlighten us.[33]

His letter to the pope, however, in which he took issue with nine of the propositions, was couched in more discreet language. Whether one agreed with him or not, McQuaid was a dedicated veteran of some forty-five years in the priesthood, twenty-five of them as bishop, and he had a deep concern for the welfare of his people. His letter eloquently expressed the fears of many American bishops, and, as a matter of record, his thought on the school question within a matter of years replaced the conciliatory approach of the progressives. He wrote:

What we have most to dread is not the direct teaching of the state schools, it is the indirect teaching which is the most insidious and the most dangerous. It is the moral atmosphere, the tone of thought permeating these schools that give cause for alarm. It is the indifferentism with regard to all religious beliefs we most of all fear. This is the dominant heresy that, imbibed in youth, can scarcely ever be eradicated.[34]

Simply look around our large towns and cities, he went on, to see how indifferentism has decimated the Protestant churches and be

[33] F. J. Zwierlein, *The Life and Letters of Bishop McQuaid*, III (Rochester, N.Y.: Art Print Shop, 1927), 191–93.

[34] Letter reprinted in *Catholic Education in America*, pp. 162–63.

educating an elite.[20] There are all-boy schools and all-girl schools. There are big urban day schools and sprawling country boarding schools. There are diocesan, parochial, and private schools. There are coeducational schools and, for those who interpret the encyclical of Pius XI more literally, there are "co-instructional" schools. There are approximately fifty junior high schools.[21]

The 1962 twelfth-grade enrollment in 43 per cent of the secondary schools was less than thirty-eight students.[22] However, there has been a continuous movement toward the consolidation of small schools, paralleling a similar drive in the public-school districts.[23] One large new school is built to replace several schools too old and too small to be operated efficiently without a prohibitive per-pupil cost. The effect can be seen among the Catholic secondary schools by comparing enrollment figures and school totals, even over the past three years. In 1964–65 there were 2465 schools enrolling 1,095,000 pupils but in 1967–68 some 2275 high schools had an enrollment of 1,089,000. Whereas the total high-school population declined by only six thousand, there were 190 fewer schools.[24]

What is the educational objective of the Catholic high school? In 1947, in a survey sponsored by the National Catholic Educational Association, 1581 Catholic high schools were identified by their administrators according to these categories:

Comprehensive	64.4%
Academic	31.6%
Commercial	3.8%
Vocational	0.2%

[20] One Jesuit prep school (and a good one) modestly states that it is dedicated to educating the cream of the country, to which one wag always straight-facedly replies: "Yes; rich and thick!"

[21] The term "junior high school" is used in several senses. At the close of 1965 the NCEA announced that there were 82 Catholic schools in this category. After closer scrutiny of parish and diocesan reports, it was found that only 49 of the total were separately organized units including grades seven through nine.

[22] Neuwien, *op. cit.*, p. 55.

[23] *NEWS* release, NCEA, Sept. 11, 1967. The number of public-school districts was dropped by one-third in five years, from 33,000 in 1962–63 to 22,000 in 1967–68.

[24] *Official Catholic Directory*, 1968. An NC News Service report for the week of June 23, 1968, provides the information that some 313 Catholic schools have been closed completely and more than 300 others have been merged with

Fifteen years later, that is, in 1962, the Catholic high schools were again asked to identify themselves, and this time 16 per cent stated that they were academic plus vocational and 84 per cent identified themselves as *purely* academic! Perhaps the most significant development that is coming with regard to Catholic high-school education is its move in an elitist direction. Some 68 per cent of America's Catholic high schools now require admissions tests and 80 per cent charge tuition.[25] Very quietly the principle seems to be operating that since there is not room for everybody in the Catholic high schools, we take the better-prepared youngsters whose families can afford to pay the tuition and fees. This has undeniably been the trend.

It cannot be repeated too often that, with 22,000 public-school districts and 18,000 parishes in 156 Catholic dioceses, generalizations about public or Catholic education are—to put it mildly—risky. Yet with all this stated, the academic record of the contemporary Catholic high school is generally a record in which Catholic educators can take reasonable pride as they look backwards, and encouragement as they look ahead to new challenges. By all the standard indices, the Catholic high schools share with the public high schools full credit for the qualitative improvement in recent years in American education. Even Mr. Conant concedes that the high-school situation is "better than it was ten years ago."[26] Any temptation to complacency, however, should be quickly dissipated by the reflection that, even if in general, contemporary schools are an improvement over the past, the tasks they are called upon to perform today are awesomely heavier.

There have always been "good" Catholic high schools and "good" public high schools, and one should hasten to define the "good" school as one in which persons of all I.Q. levels are achieving according to their ability. What is important here is that during the past ten years there has been a constantly increasing number of "good" Catholic and public high schools. The teachers are better

other schools since 1966. The report also says that over sixty thousand students were turned away from elementary and secondary schools because of dropped grades and stricter policies on class size.

[25] Neuwien, *op. cit.,* p. 38.

[26] James B. Conant, *The Comprehensive High School* (New York: McGraw-Hill Book Co., 1967), p. 2. No warm friend of nonpublic schools (except on the Harvard level), Mr. Conant's observations were based exclusively on the public high schools.

trained and demand more of the pupils. Science, mathematics, and modern languages are especially well taught. Study programs are more likely to be patterned to fit the student. Counseling and guidance services are widely available. That students are coming to college better prepared is the consensus of college admissions officers.

Yet there is an easy temptation to measure academic success solely in terms of how many Catholic-high-school seniors were awarded plums like National Merit Scholarships, Westinghouse Science awards, and scholarships to the prestige colleges. In some years Catholic high schools have gained more of these glittering honors than their proportion of the total school population would warrant, but in other years they have done less well. On reflection, one begins to suspect that such criteria are only valid when one weighs the awards against the ability of the group. A school should take no credit for graduating tall men if the entrance requirements from the outset screen out anyone under six feet in height. It is possible that some of our Catholic college prep schools and convent schools are taking undue credit unto themselves when the initial screening of entering freshmen pretty well guarantees a high level of ability and consequent achievement. Teachers would have to work hard to hurt them. They could be locked up in a dark basement for four years, and they would still do very well when they went on to college.

Nor do certain claims of superior reading ability or mathematical prowess hold up under close scrutiny. It may well be true that the ninth graders in the Catholic schools of a certain diocese read two years above the national level. However, any temptation to smugness should be averted by simply reflecting that the national reading level is determined by the reading ability of *every* ninth grader in the United States. This includes hundreds of thousands of pupils of marginal and submarginal ability for whom few dioceses have yet made any provision for Catholic schooling, to say nothing of hundreds of thousands of poverty youngsters of Puerto Rican or Indian or Mexican or Southern Negro homes. In the nature of things, then, the public schools must assume the principal care for this group whose substandard reading results will definitely effect the national average. As a matter of fact, few Catholic schools have even made a start on testing the results of their own school effort. Until they do, it seems more prudent to consider them no better nor worse from an academic point of view than the public schools of the nation.

After having surveyed the extant research literature on the scholastic quality of Catholic schools, one is forced into quick agreement with Michael O'Neill's statement that there are "very few studies, most of which are technically weak, limited in application, or now out of date."[27] To no one's surprise the evidence is conflicting, and no clear pattern emerges. Three extensive post-World War II studies indicate superior achievement of parochial-school pupils in comparison with comparable public-school groups.[28] However, several other studies, admittedly more local in nature, come out negative in regard to parochial-school children.[29] The safe conclusion is that much more careful study is needed before an honest comparison of the academic results of public or Catholic schooling can be made.

Leaving aside what invariably turn out to be odious comparisons, it is far more to the point that Catholic educators and school leaders attempt to evaluate the effectiveness of their own schools. In recent years social scientists in numbers have been attracted to Catholic education as a field of study. To say nothing of the novelty, the sheer size of the phenomenon was bound to command the serious attention of scholars and researchers.

Thanks to generous grants from the Carnegie Foundation, both the Catholic Study Office of the University of Notre Dame and the National Opinion Research Council, an affiliate of the University of Chicago, undertook independent studies in the effectiveness of Catholic education. In the fall of 1966, when the completed studies were presented to the public, they touched off much discussion. To char-

[27] "How Good Are Catholic Schools?" *NCEA Bulletin*, February, 1968, p. 16.

[28] Roger T. Lennon, "A Comparison of the Educational Achievement of Public and Parochial Elementary Pupils," *Catholic Educational Review*, XLVI (December, 1948), 647–52; studies in 1959 and 1960: Robert H. Bauernfeind and Warren S. Blumenfeld, "A Comparison of Achievement Scores of Public-School and Catholic-School Pupils," *Educational and Psychological Measurement*, XXIII (1963), 331–36.

[29] Robert E. Hill, "An Investigation of the Educational Development of Selected Iowa Secondary School Pupils from Varied Elementary School Environments," *Yearbook of the National Council on Measurements Used in Education*, XIV (1957), 28–36; David Iwamoto, "Don't Sneer at Public Education," *NEA Journal*, XLVII (February, 1957), 118–19; Seymour Warkov and Andrew M. Greeley, "Parochial School Origins and Educational Achievement," *American Sociological Review*, XXXI (June, 1966), 406–14.

acterize both studies as pioneer is at once to indicate their value as well as their limitation.

The Notre Dame study identified itself as a "pilot" study. It is more descriptive than evaluative, more popular than scholarly, and provided the first comprehensive statistical picture of Catholic elementary and secondary education in the U.S.A. The Notre Dame researchers compiled and tabulated statistics from 92 per cent of the elementary and 84 per cent of the secondary schools of the country. Additionally, visits and depth studies were made of the schools in eleven selected dioceses. Though in some respects the data of 1962 are already outmoded, the study gave answers to many questions and with its companion study provided, in the words of one writer, "a long-overdue look into all those schools which seem to be found on every second corner in cities such as New York, Chicago, and Boston, but have somehow managed to remain as mysterious as Hindu temples to the millions of Americans who pass them every day."[30] The study likewise helped to spot areas of weakness and to identify first-priority needs.

The proportion of seniors continuing their formal education is a much-used criterion of the scholastic seriousness of a high school. Do graduates of Catholic high schools go on to college? The Carnegie-Notre Dame Study found that there were 156,000 graduates in June of 1962 from the 2075 schools in the survey—68,000 boys and 87,000 girls.[31] Of this total 54 per cent went into some type of post-secondary schooling—64 per cent of the boys but only 46 per cent of the girls. One-half of the boys (51 per cent of 64 per cent) picked a Catholic college; one-half of the girls (52 per cent of 46 per cent) likewise picked a Catholic college. The study further shows that students from high schools with well-developed guidance programs were the graduates who in larger numbers went to a Catholic college.

Like their confreres in other schools, Catholic high school seniors are keen on going to college. When asked if the opportunity for college was of extreme importance to them, 71 per cent of the boys and 54 per cent of the girls were in strong agreement. When they

---

[30] John Cogley, "Catholics and Their Schools," *Saturday Review*, October 15, 1966, p. 72.

[31] Neuwien, *op. cit.*, p. 62.

were asked to give an overall ranking of the purposes of a Catholic school, the sample group ranked the five choices in this order:[32]

1. Religious
2. Intellectual
3. Vocational
4. Citizenship
5. Social

If this projection holds up on a national scale, it would seem to indicate that, in general, Catholic high schools create some awareness of what most Catholic educators would agree is the proper hierarchy of purpose in education.

One disturbing attitude disclosed by the Notre Dame study emerges from the response to this statement: "I prefer teachers who teach rather than find out things for myself." Over 50 per cent of the Catholic high school seniors agreed to some extent or strongly with this statement (strongly agree: 22.6 per cent; agree somewhat: 29.07 per cent).[33] This attitude on the part of so many youngsters after twelve years of Catholic education and on the threshold of college is embarrassing, to say the least. It unfortunately lends a handle to the criticism that Catholic schools encourage an intellectually enervating habit of docility which prevents the eager pursuit of truth.

On the other hand, much of the criticism of the academic quality of Catholic education is unfounded. In the wake of wide criticism, a 1963 study undertaken at the National Opinion Research Center by Andrew Greeley began with these hypotheses: Because of the alleged anti-intellectualism and anti-scientism of Catholicism,

1. Catholics will be less likely to go to college.
2. Catholics from the working class will be less likely to go to college than Protestants from the working class.
3. Catholic family ties will interfere with college education.
4. Catholics will be less likely to go to graduate school.
5. Among those Catholics going to graduate school, there will be a smaller proportion going into the academic fields than for the other religious groups.
6. Catholics will not be inclined to go into the physical sciences.

[32] *Ibid.*, pp. 229–30.
[33] Neuwien, *op. cit.*, p. 315.

7. Those Catholics who go into academic pursuits will show a tendency to drift away from the church.[34]

At the conclusion of the study, no confirmation was found for any one of these widely held hypotheses. The study concluded that

it offers no evidence for the alleged intellectual inferiority of Catholics or of Catholic schools at the present time. Those within the church who feel that such inferiority does in fact still exist are now in a position where they must bring up new evidence or at least retreat in silence. . . . As far as scholarship goes, the evidence in this volume suggests that Catholics are much like other Americans. Whatever anti-intellectualism still exists is probably more American in origin than specifically Catholic.[35]

Moreover, according to the same source, the number of Catholics completing college and continuing on to graduate study is at least in their proportion to the total population. This can be considered all the more remarkable because their parents did not. In the adult population Protestants are twice as likely as Catholics to have had a college education. To borrow one last time from this NORC study:

Catholics are more likely to go to graduate school than Protestants; and of those going to graduate school, a higher proportion of Catholics are going into the "arts and sciences" than of the other religious groups. Nor are Catholic colleges inferior in either of these respects. . . . The Knapp studies, as well as earlier ones which are quoted in much of the current literature, are anywhere from one to four decades old; they reflect a situation which once existed but does not any longer.[36]

Catholic high school graduates are interested in the scholarly life to an extent never before realizable in the history of the American church. This development may well be simply a part of a larger phenomenon in the contemporary U.S.A. and may need no further explanation than the same factors of affluence and expectancy which have vastly increased America's collegiate, post-collegiate, and professional ranks. Nevertheless, much, if not most, of the credit must go to the Catholic schools that have generated this new enthusiasm.

[34] *Religion and Career* (New York: Sheed and Ward, Inc., 1963), pp. 15–16.
[35] *Ibid.*, pp. 18–19.
[36] *Ibid.*, p. 88. The Knapp studies found the index of productivity of scientists and scholars from Catholic colleges quite low. R. H. Knapp and J. J. Greenbaum, *The Younger American Scholar* (Chicago: University of Chicago Press, 1953).

Judged from the academic point of view, the modern Catholic school is generally doing a better job than it has been getting credit for. Academically it is pointed in the right direction, perhaps one conspicuous reason being the growth in the area of counseling and guidance.

*   *   *

What is the counseling and guidance picture in the Catholic high school? Quite spotty but slowly improving. Moreover, in all fairness a prefatory remark also has to be inserted here. Almost by definition a priest or religious is assumed to have the kind of people-oriented personality that is the most vital prerequisite in a counselor. By vocation he (or she) gives of himself (herself) because of a formal public commitment to continue Christ's mission to people. The net effect is that many schools under direction of priests or religious have among their personnel a corps of experienced and dedicated—if not always professionally trained—counselors. On the other hand, this argument is at times pushed too far and in some schools is a flimsy subterfuge for not establishing a professional counseling and guidance program.

The best and most recent study indicates that some 95 per cent of large schools, 84 per cent of medium schools, and only 61 per cent of small schools had organized guidance programs. By type, it was found that 81 per cent of diocesan schools, 74 per cent of religious community schools, 73 per cent of inter-parish schools, and 54 per cent of parish schools had organized programs. By student population, 90 per cent of coeducational schools, 75 per cent of boys' schools, 62 per cent of girls' schools, and 35 per cent of co-institutional schools reported organized guidance programs.

The study says that a total of 2589 counselors in 1231 Catholic secondary schools answered individual questionnaires. By size, 46 per cent were in small schools, 30 per cent in medium schools, and 22 per cent in large schools. By school type, 41 per cent were in religious community schools, 23 per cent in diocesan schools, 18 per cent in parish schools, and 9 per cent in inter-parish schools. Some 34 per cent worked in coeducational schools, 33 per cent in girls' schools, 23 per cent in boys' schools, and 8 per cent in co-institutional schools.

The distribution by canonical status and age is interesting.

Among the 2589 counselors, 45 per cent were sisters, 26 per cent priests, 16 per cent lay persons, and 11 per cent brothers. The average age was forty-one years, with lay counselors averaging thirty-five, brothers thirty-six, priests thirty-seven, and sisters forty-six years.

That the battle has not been completely won becomes clear from these statistics:

Respondents were asked to indicate percentage of time spent in various duties. The 1,443 "full-time" counselors held 1,816 additional responsibilities; most full-time counselors had two jobs in addition to counseling and guidance responsibilities. The most frequent additional job was classroom teacher, followed by pastor or assistant pastor, chaplain, and assistant principal. The 1,146 part-time counselors held 1,926 additional jobs. Again the most frequent "other" responsibility was classroom teacher, followed by principal, assistant principal, chaplain, pastor, and assistant pastor.

Among the 2,589 counselors who participated in this study, professional training varied considerably. Forty-three held the doctorate, 1,736 the master's degree (796 of these had additional course work), and 738 had at least the bachelor's degree. Seventy-two were still working on their degrees.

An astounding 810 counselors, or 31%, had *no* graduate courses in guidance; 504, or 20%, were presently taking graduate courses; 881, or 34%, had completed their training within the past 5 years; 214, or 8%, had completed their training 6–10 years ago; 7% completed their training 6–10 years ago; and the remaining 7% completed their training over 10 years ago.[37]

*   *   *

We turn then to the religious dimension of the Catholic school. Has it been a "Christian" success? Has it made a significant difference? In other words, looking at the American experience with its separate system, does eight or twelve or sixteen years of schooling in a Catholic school make a *better* Catholic? Are the products of a full Catholic education truly different in their attitudes toward the broad social, political, and moral issues of modern society? Are they more knowledgeable about things Catholic?

[37] Robert E. Doyle and Joseph C. Duffy, "The Counselor in Catholic Secondary Education: A National Survey," *National Catholic Guidance Journal,* Monograph Issue, XI (Spring, 1967).

Often a loaded question makes a real answer impossible. To ask if religion has been effective in the separate Catholic school is tantamount to asking what effect Christianity has had on civilization. The American faith in the efficacy of the school is astounding, and Catholics too regularly share in the mystical expectancy that the school can do anything and everything. Is juvenile delinquency on the rise in the cities? Then the schools are failing. Is there less respect for law and order? Then the schools are to blame. Is there moral laxity in dress and dating? Then the schools are not doing their duty. Yet with all this stated, some kind of an answer has to be forthcoming on the religious effectiveness of the Catholic school.

The answer is either intuitive or scientific. Some enthusiastic scientists long ago proved that the weight of the bumblebee's body related to its wing span made it impossible for the bumblebee to fly. Just how successful any attempt by social scientists to measure religious understanding and commitment can ever be remains a topic of controversy. Obviously any instrument devised to enter and to explore the murky and mysterious world of the human psyche cannot operate like the chemist's scales or the physicist's rays. Despite its impressive jargon, sociology remains a science only by an extended meaning of the term. The exact physical sciences themselves are incapable of weighing and charting the non-animal side of the human composite. Brute animals of the higher species confound prediction by breaking out of their assigned reactional categories. Even human voting patterns defy forecast.

Ask a priest or sister who has taught in a Catholic high school for ten years if religion is effective. Almost never is there a negative response. Without being able to *prove* the fact, they will tell you unhesitatingly that the religion course (and the total school atmosphere) makes enough difference in the lives of students to make worthwhile the time and effort expended. In some strange way the Catholic faith becomes for most of those students part of a way of life. Perhaps they could have acquired this result in another way. (Other ways must, in fact, be found to achieve this effect!)

In another chapter we are discussing the effectiveness of the religious instruction program sponsored by the Confraternity of Christian Doctrine. It will suffice to mention briefly here that those teachers who have been involved in both programs—the regular Catholic-high-school program with its present defects and the Confraternity instruction program with its defects—unqualifiedly opt for the program in the Catholic high school. They also add that the Catholic high school alone can provide the kind of natural worshiping community in embryo out of which can come leadership for the adult religious community. Sorrowfully, the legalisms and myopia of many of the pastors and bishops impede growth in this direction because they are jealous of the rights and privileges of the canonical parish and the supreme control of the local ordinary so that many schools are not allowed to function as Christian communities.

Probably the distinctive contribution of the Notre Dame Study is the instrument devised to evaluate the school's effectiveness in religious education. The several *Inventories of Catholic School Outcomes* were prepared by a task force of social scientists and theologians to determine "what the students in Catholic schools know about their religion; what their attitudes are to certain questions either directly or indirectly religious in nature; and what their opinions are about their religious and general education in the Catholic schools."[38] Each item was susceptible of five answers, each representing a different level of understanding. The respondent's answer indicated respectively an "advanced," "moderate," "conventional," "moralistic," and "nominalistic" grasp of the Christian truth involved. The Notre Dame Study reports that slightly more than half of the 14,519 students in the sample picked the two more sophisticated alternatives which, it concludes, speaks "reasonably well" for Catholic education. Relative to academic achievement, the Notre Dame Study concluded: ". . . the mental ability measures show the students as superior on the scale of national norms, and more important the measures of achievement showed a comparable superior achievement." Some critics have challenged this conclusion on two counts: (1) the representativeness of the sample was not clearly established; (2) control factors were not clear relative to the comparison with public-school students of similar ability.[39]

The companion study by the National Opinion Research Center attempted more than the Notre Dame Study. A primary objective of the former was to weigh the relative impact of the different levels of education on religious behavior and social attitudes. Personal interviews were held with 2753 American Catholics within the

[38] Neuwien, *op. cit.,* p. 145.
[39] O'Neill, *op. cit.,* p. 15.

twenty-three to fifty-seven age bracket from an already existing probability sample. An additional 1000 respondents were contacted by questionnaire, and a random selection of 1000 readers of the lay-edited, Catholic weekly *Commonweal* was polled by mail to effect a comparison between an ordinary Catholic and his "liberal" counter-part. The all-Catholic sample was then divided into three categories: (1) those who had had an all-Catholic education; (2) those with a mix of public and Catholic education; (3) those with no Catholic schooling at all. To gauge the effectiveness of the Catholic school between 1910 and 1960 was the prime objective of the study. Efforts were made to control the variable factors, such as ethnic back-ground, type and level of the parents' education, and the availability of schools.

The sampling method of this study presents some difficulties. The 2000 respondents are assumed to typify a much larger population. In microcosm this sample of Catholics educated over a fifty-year span ending in 1960 is supposed to represent every meaningful stratum of the much larger group. It is surprising (and disappoint-ing), therefore, to find out that the graduates of Catholic schools during the interval studied who have since entered either the priest-hood or the religious state were omitted. It is not naïve to think that, since most priests and religious are products of Catholic schools, their religious knowledge and behavior is relevant to any conclusions about the whole of Catholic education. (The Carnegie-Notre Dame Study also made this omission.) The distribution of the sample is overbalanced toward the heavily Catholic northeastern United States. A further difficulty is the absence from the sample of respondents who refused to be interviewed. Some 23 per cent of the existing sample (already self-identified as Catholics) did not cooperate. As has been observed: "Those who become disaffected with Catholic education—and perhaps the church generally—are un-derrepresented, possibly critically so."[40]

In the study's pivotal chapter, "Religious Consequences of Cath-olic Education," the authors take up singly what they call the various

---

[40] Robert Hassenger, "Essay Review: American Catholics and Their Schools," *The School Review,* LXXV (Winter, 1967), 448. See also Merton P. Strom-men, feature review of *The Education of Catholic Americans* and *Catholic Schools in Action,* in *Religious Education,* LXII (January–February, 1967), 60–62.

component parts of the Christian life. They ask six questions and at the end of the chapter offer their answers.[41]

The first question asks if Catholics who attended Catholic schools are more likely to engage in "approved formal religious behavior." In other words, do they attend Mass, receive Communion, and go to confession more regularly. They do, but even those who did not attend a Catholic school score relatively well by these measures.

Does the man or woman who has an all-Catholic education more promptly acknowledge the teaching authority of the church and more readily accept church guidance on controversial issues? Greeley and Rossi say that in such matters of disagreement as sex, race, and education, Catholic-school Catholics are more likely to accept the church's authority.

The third question covers doctrinal and ethical orthodoxy. Here the Catholic-schooled Catholic is somewhat more orthodox, "especially in matters such as sexual morality and papal primacy, which have been of considerable symbolic importance in recent Catholic history." The study reports moderate differences in attitude toward family size and mixed marriage.

The greater accuracy of religious knowledge is the fourth item, to which the reply is that those schooled in Catholic schools are much better informed.

The extent of participation in the organizational activities of the church comes next. Though the "K-through-12"-trained Catholics do participate more in church activities, they do not do so to the extent one might expect. The study suggests that family behavior here might be a more important influence than schooling.

The last question is the most important—and the most difficult to put and to evaluate: "Are they more dedicated in their practice of the virtue of charity?" With candor the authors own that "with our admittedly limited tools, we could not discover any relationship between Catholic school attendance and disposition to help others."

The difference, though not great, was considered by Greeley and Rossi to be statistically significant. Those who attended a Catholic school scored consistently higher than those who did not, especially if the family background was strong religiously. The overall conclusion is that there is "a moderate but significant association between Catholic education and adult religious behavior." The Notre

[41] Andrew M. Greeley and Peter H. Rossi, *The Education of Catholic Americans* (Chicago: Aldine Publishing Company, 1966), p. 72.

Dame Study likewise found that the family played the most crucial role. In themselves the schools may have only a slight influence, which can be greatly heightened if the party comes from a religious family and enters into a religious marriage with a partner who shares a similar background. As the NORC study phrases it: "Parental religiousness . . . effects the impact of Catholic education through the mediation of the spouse's religiousness."

A number of commentators on the study seem in agreement that Catholic formal education up until 1960, at least, emphasized the organizational and external side of religion and that its modest success was mostly among those already possessing religious backgrounds.[42] On the other hand, perhaps too much was expected of these studies. Neatly packaged answers are not always available. There are so many imponderables, especially in what concerns the formation of attitudes and ideals, that much of the patient, scholarly work of the social scientist seems pointless and almost irrelevant. To return to an earlier example, what makes a patriotic American? Is it *x* number of times saluting a flag, marching to the national anthem, praying at Grant's tomb, visiting the nation's Capitol, reading the Bill of Rights, making a field trip to Valley Forge or Gettysburg?

One can measure the effectiveness of education as it consists of grasping data or in the possession of skills in almost any academic area. We can fairly accurately determine, for example, how well the fifth-grade parochial-school children of the Archdiocese of St. Louis read or spell or count in comparison with the public-school children of the St. Louis public-school district. A social scientist can then study the relevant factors that might modify any conclusion, like selectivity of pupil intake, economic-ethnic background, professional preparation of the staff, etc., and come up with a reasonably definitive answer. But the conviction of the Catholic school's effectiveness in the area of values and attitudes has to be grounded on something else than the tools of the sociologist or social scientist.

The most serious problem that studies of this nature face is trying to separate religious knowledge and religious behavior. A man can *know* the right thing to do and yet fail to do it. A man can *learn* the correct attitude toward segregated housing but refuse to sell to a

---

[42] Mary Perkins Ryan, feature review of *The Education of Catholic Americans* and *Catholic Schools in Action*, in *Religious Education*, LXII (January–February, 1967), 63.

Negro. A man can be *informed* of the right pattern of communal worship but then perform his religious duties perfunctorily and even without faith. Not since Plato have men seriously argued that knowledge and virtue were one and the same. The NORC study tells us that "if the principal goal of Catholic schools is to provide religious education, the first question we must ask is whether they have succeeded in doing so. Are the Catholics who went to Catholic schools 'better' Catholics than those who did not . . . ?"[43] But just what is a *better* Catholic? It is to be expected that products of parochial schools are *better* Catholics, at least in the sense of being more knowledgeable about Catholic faith and moral teachings. If not, these institutions would be complete failures. It can only be hoped that products of such schools are *better* Catholics as far as commitment and dedication go. But if they are not, are the schools a failure? Not at all. One might just as well argue that the American public school is not a success (or that we really can't say one way or another) because so many of its products do not live fully up to the lofty moral and spiritual values which were held up to them. The whole question is much more complicated.

Perhaps one effect of these studies of Catholic education, albeit unwittingly, is to show beyond any doubt that the Catholic sponsorship of a school on any level does not guarantee its success as either an academic institution or as an incubator of dedicated and devout Catholics. A Catholic school is a good *school* when it is adequately staffed by a professionally trained faculty, is led by an imaginative administration, is properly financed, has clear goals, and is accountable to a concerned school board. A Catholic school is a good *Catholic* school when, with all these components, there is an atmosphere reflecting the special goals and functions of the Christian community.

* * *

Nor are Catholics alone in their efforts to come to grips with the deep issues involved in Christian education. The Lutheran churches of the Missouri Synod have done a study of the effectiveness of their elementary and secondary schools as agencies of Christian education, including the possibility of a larger program of Christian edu-

[43] Greeley and Rossi, *op. cit.*, pp. 9–10.

cation in which the establishment of a parochial school may be an option. The author of the study points out:

> After all, the real issue for all is that of Christian education, not parochial schools. That is, parochial schools are one form, or mechanism, which the church has developed to carry its function of Christian education. The danger is that although of value, one form may begin to absorb so much energy and effort that other forms are neglected, new forms are not adequately explored, and the broad field of Christian education becomes synonymous with one highly specific manifestation in the generalized field.[44]

The Lutheran study attempted to look at Lutheran youth as persons and as members of families, and decided that it had found none of the expected differences traceable to parochial versus public education. The study immediately cautioned, however, that "to discover no differences is an important discovery in itself but is not by definition an indictment of parochial education. All must realize that evaluation must proceed against a backdrop of the objectives an organization has established for itself."[45]

Moreover, no significant differences produced by parochial education were discovered with respect to attitudes toward various social and political issues. The most significant aspect of the discovery of "no differences" in social and political attitudes certainly is "that despite what may be taught here or there, overall that which deviates from mainstream thought in society is not effectively communicated." The study's next words must be recorded:

> We strongly suspect that in the case of many of the variables covered, the strong currents of opinion and interpretation flowing throughout our society would make it extremely difficult for the parochial school to get across effectively a divergent view even if it desired and attempted to do so.[46]

The study did find important differences in the areas of biblical knowledge and doctrinal understanding that gave a definite edge to parochial schools in advancing the level of knowledge and under-

---

[44] Ronald L. Johnstone, *The Effectiveness of Lutheran Elementary and Secondary Schools as Agencies of Christian Education* (St. Louis: Concordia Seminary, 1966), p. 141.

[45] *Ibid.*

[46] *Ibid.*

standing on the part of the Lutheran youth. Yet, even here qualifications were called for.

First, the level of knowledge, understanding, and doctrinal orthodoxy is lower than we suspect most would have hoped. Second, with control for family background, differences in the area of Lutheran doctrine, traced initially to parochial education, almost invariably disappear except again among youth from "marginal" Lutheran families.[47]

Since the Lutheran experience (to mention only one vitally interested group) so strikingly parallels that of the Catholic Church, we, too, must face the implications of their data on the effectiveness of parochial schooling. The study poses the specific question: How should one react to the potential suggestion that parochial schools are now demonstrably ineffective and ought to be phased out as soon as possible and that no new ones ought to be founded in the future? The study answers firmly: "In all probability, as with all simple solutions to complex issues, such a conclusion and decision is overly precipitous." One immediate reason is that parochial-school education has been judged effective, "often highly effective," among youth from marginal Lutheran families. The reason is elaborated upon:

That is, where exposure to Christian education from other sources is minimal, a youth exposed to the parochial school experience finds his level of Biblical knowledge and Lutheran doctrinal understanding, as well as his frequency of participation in the congregational life, measureably raised and improved. The parochial school is an effective agency with these youth.[48]

On the other hand, the study also points out that "youth who have a solid Lutheran background and are from families at least moderately involved in the life and work of the local congregation are hardly ever measurably changed by increasing exposure to parochial education." Lutheran and Catholic educators are then left with the agonizing choice of which youth are best given the experience of the parochial school. It is obvious that the "ideal" Christian families are the moral and financial backers of parochial education, and that the schools presently exist with their children as the chief beneficiaries.

[47] *Ibid.,* p. 142.
[48] *Ibid.,* p. 143.

CHAPTER FIVE

The Support:
Child Benefit vs. Establishment

Every parent and taxpayer in the United States is aware that the nation's school bill is rising every year. This is not simply a matter of inflation nor of a larger population. A good part of the increased cost of educating a child today is explained by new and improved services that the contemporary school is expected to provide its clientele. Today we have not only kindergarten schools but pre-kindergarten and nursery schools. For the elementary-school children there are specialists in remedial work of all kinds, specialists in testing and counseling, specialists in diet and health and recreation, and so forth. For the high-school population there is, in addition to a staff for the services enumerated, a staff for widely diversified athletic and physical education programs, home economics and domestic science, vocational training and industrial arts. For a long time shamefully inadequate, salaries of the clerical, maintenance, supervisory, and teaching staff have now become the most formidable item in the yearly budget. Teaching machines, language labs, and closed TV are as commonplace as are "shop" wings and completely equipped kitchens. These items along with fleets of buses do not come cheaply.

The bill for operating the public elementary and secondary schools during the 1967–68 school year was an estimated $26 billion with an additional $4 billion spent for capital outlay.[1] Operating costs have more than doubled since 1959–60 when the figure was $12.3 billion. Twenty years ago, in 1949–50, the operational cost was $4.7 billion. During the past year, the annual expenditure per pupil was approximately $623, up nearly 10 per cent over 1966–67. The 1966–67 range swung between New York's $912 and Mississippi's $335. A teacher's average salary that year was $6820 but in 1967–

[1] U. S. Department of Health, Education, and Welfare, Office of Education, Report, August 24, 1968.

68 it rose to $7320, a gain of 7 per cent. However, we have seen relatively nothing yet. The total American investment in schools is predicted to increase by nearly 50 per cent over the next decade, according to U. S. Office of Education predictions. Expenditures are estimated to exceed $70 billion by the 1976–77 school year, compared with 1966–67's $48.5 billion.

City and state governments all over the country are operating at a deficit. This year Illinois's puddle of red ink widened to $170,-500,000. The grim fiscal situation in North Dakota is reported to be worse than during the Depression. The farmers' income there is at a low ebb but the teachers are militant in their demand for better salaries and improved classroom conditions. With the passage of the Elementary and Secondary Education Act of 1965 (ESEA), a dramatic shift has occurred in the funding of the public schools. Whereas in 1963–64 the local contribution was 56 per cent, the state's 40 per cent, and the federal government's 4 per cent, in 1967–68 the respective contributions were 52, 40, and 8 per cent.[2] In other words federal aid has doubled over that four-year period. The American people are, albeit with some reluctance, accepting the reality that education is a national problem that can be properly dealt with only on national terms.

The president of Columbia University Teachers College, John H. Fischer, has argued that our national purpose requires us to raise the quality of school programs everywhere and to equalize opportunity for all children.[3] He points out how the Selective Service Mental Test establishes the scandalous inequality across the land. In 1964, the rate of failure in the state of Mississippi was 686 out of 1000; in the states of Minnesota and Washington it was 75 out of 1000. Seventy-five years ago, a sound argument could be made for strictly local control of education but the same argument hardly holds today. The galloping rate of social change has left many communities so far behind that the schools they attempt to run can only be anachronistic and unenlightened. Nor need federal help bring a stifling of local initiative nor elimination of reasonable local control. Fischer and others argue, moreover, that local school leadership should seek help from wider sources than those immediately avail-

[2] U. S. Department of Health, Education, and Welfare, "The Statistics Speak," reprinted from *American Education*, April, 1968.

[3] "Meeting Our Educational Needs," guest editorial, *Parents' Magazine*, September, 1966, p. 52.

able to it—and this, of course, means from the federal government.

Meanwhile, the price tag on Catholic schooling has been rising, in large measure due to salary costs. It is not a question merely of the fast-rising proportion of lay men and women on the faculties but almost as much of the heavier expense of training and supporting religious and priest teachers. Moreover, the Catholic schools are expected to maintain at least the same level of excellence as the public schools—and excellence is costly. So arises the serious question of public support without which the future of parochial schools, at least as we know them today, is very uncertain.

For twenty years a constitutional dilemma has agitated the question of federal aid for church-related education. The Constitution imposes a dual mandate. On the one hand, the state must recognize the parochial schools as part of the educational system for purposes of compulsory attendance laws, but on the other hand it is unable to support them in ways that would violate the First Amendment's injunction against an "establishment of religion."

There really never has been a *Catholic* position on the question of public support for parochial schools. Opinion among Catholics has always ranged widely over the spectrum as it does on every other controversial issue. There is a wide consensus among Catholics that children in the parochial schools are entitled to a more equitable distribution of items that fall under the "child benefit" principle. There are leaders and groups firm in their insistence that Catholic-school children are entitled to everything received by public-school children. There are advocates of tuition plans and tax credit plans. There are also Catholic officeholders, politicians, and just plain citizens, who argue against any form of tax support for parochial schools as vehemently as the most doctrinaire supporter of exclusively public education.

Ten years ago, the general public regarded whatever Cardinal Spellman (or the local bishop) had to say about federal aid as the official Catholic position. Now things are different. A critical new ingredient is the role rapidly being assumed by the Catholic laity across the country. As we have seen in the preceding chapter, what used to be viewed as, and to a large extent was, a clerical operation and responsibility has become something much broader. Hundreds of thousands of Catholic parents in scores of communities are organizing themselves in order to make their case to the public in tones that are clear, strong, and—lay. Much of the impetus toward formal organization is coming from Citizens for Educational Freedom (CEF), a group of parents and other individuals, to quote its own self-description, "dedicated to the cause of securing freedom and equality in education."[4] A platform principle of CEF is its belief "in the constitutional right of parents to direct and control the education of their children without penalty, that is, without suffering the loss of education tax funds if they choose a church-related or other independent school." CEF describes itself as committed to the principle that "every American child is entitled to a fair share of education taxes, and that such participation in tax funds may not be conditioned on attendance at a state-controlled school or on the surrender of freedom of religion in education." Though professedly nonsectarian, its constituency is largely parents and supporters of Catholic schools.

With over a thousand chapters located in every state, CEF has become a force to be reckoned with. Already this organization has been instrumental in effecting action both on the national and state levels for the benefit of nonpublic-school children. Citizens for Educational Freedom played a large role in the enactment of Fair Bus Laws in Michigan (1964), Ohio (1965), Pennsylvania (1965), and Wisconsin (1967). The Wisconsin law has special significance because an earlier busing law had been struck down by the state supreme court as a contravention of the Wisconsin constitution. To allow the legislature to pass a new bill the citizens of the state had to vote in referendum to modify their constitution so that public busing could legally be extended to children in nonpublic schools. The Citizens for Educational Freedom went to the people of Wisconsin, convinced them of the fairness of its position, and won its case.

Some critics find Citizens for Educational Freedom hard to take and resent its political successes. By some curious logic these people contend that CEF tactics are somehow subverting the democratic process and undermining the Republic. Conversely, the pressure which they bring to bear on officials and legislators is, in their eyes, patriotic virtue. When CEF works to elect candidates for public offices favorable to busing for nonpublic-school pupils, this is sinister. When an organization like Protestants and Other Americans United (POAU) (at its founding, "Protestant and Other Americans

---

[4] Citizens for Educational Freedom, Wisconsin State Federation, S. 81 W. 12511 Hi View Drive, Hales Corners, Wis. 53130.

United for the Separation of Church and State") works to defeat such candidates, it is defending America!

No influential group has been more in the thick of the battle to deny tax benefits to youngsters in parochial schools than the American Jewish Congress. Its 1966 "Resolution on Religious Freedom" typifies the argument of the hard-core opposition. After expressing concern over the "recent grave erosion of the principle of separation of church and state," the Congress deplores the steadily increasing amount of aid provided to religious institutions by current federal and state laws.

These include aid given directly to religious groups under the Anti-Poverty Act of 1964 as well as the inclusion of nonpublic schools in the programs of the Elementary and Secondary Education Act of 1965, which "embodied a compromise of the principle of separation as it has always been understood and applied." Moreover, even though there has been "some pretense that the benefits are to flow to the child and the teacher rather than to the institution, the reality has been institutional aid—strengthening of the religious institution itself."

The resolution continues:

These developments pose a grave threat to the public schools of America. The public schools will have to compete for funds with religious groups, themselves competing with each other. They will be deprived of the services of the teachers who are sent into the nonpublic schools. There will be increased involvement of representatives of religious school systems in the day-to-day operation of the public schools. Finally, the public financing of religious schools will aggravate the problem of racial segregation in public schools and may ultimately reduce the public school system to the role of educators of the poor.[5]

The emotions, assumptions, and premises underlying this statement excite conflicting reactions. One can overlook the poverty of the reasoning and even the slanted reading of American history. What saddens and disturbs is the total lack of social concern.

Debate is a healthy thing. To air social grievances is a good thing if it can be done in a civilized fashion. It is dangerous and unhealthy when an important segment of society feels itself the victim of social injustice and simmers in an aggrieved silence. It would be sad

[5] American Jewish Congress, Resolution on *Religious Freedom* adopted at its Biennial Convention, April 27–May 1, 1966.

indeed to find one day on American shores that painful Continental phenomenon—the making and unmaking of governments over the issue of support for religious schools. Calling forth as it does such deep-seated loyalties and ancient animosities, the issue is almost as highly volatile as the question of racial integration. If for no other reason then, the dialogue should continue but always in calm and restrained terms. Unfortunately, the school question has not usually been approached with the responsibility it warrants.

The historical complexities and subtleties with which the issue has been bedeviled intermittently since the 1840's are often ignored. At times even the terms of the debate seem stale nineteenth century. Slogans and clichés are incanted ritually. One faction aims broadsides at the other, or rather, at positions that either were never held or that have long since been abandoned or substantially modified. One side triumphantly establishes a case which the other side never hears. The argument goes on loudly and with impeccable logic but from premises that are miles apart—and the two sides stay miles apart. Citizens for Educational Freedom are deceiving themselves if they think the issue will be settled by a simple appeal to constitutional rights guaranteeing freedom of religion. Nor will POAU, the American Jewish Congress, or the Horace Mann League—all inveterate opponents of public benefits to nonpublic schools—wave the problem away by quoting what they think Madison and Jefferson meant by the "wall of separation" between church and state.

"The wall" has not only served as a descriptive symbol dividing the spheres of authority but often simply shuts off dialogue between groups of Americans that usually are quite ready to listen to one another on the subject of civil rights. The word "separation" is not in the Constitution. It is Jefferson's word and so is the wall, and when the two are taken together as the "wall of separation," we have, at best, a loose description of the historic American pattern of church-state relations.[6] The phrase appears in a U. S. Supreme Court decision for the first time in 1879, and then to stress the fact that a Mormon's religious belief does not exempt him from the act of Congress outlawing polygamy.[7] Those who claim that the wall is breached when children in parochial schools climb into a public-school bus or when they share in a special remedial-reading program,

[6] The expression first appears in a letter written by President Jefferson to the Danbury (Conn.) Baptist Association, January 1, 1802.

[7] *Reynolds* v. *U.S.*, 25 Law Ed. U.S., p. 249.

point specifically to the First Amendment of the U. S. Constitution. They argue that providing tax support in any form for the educational work of a church-related or church-sponsored school violates the "no establishment" clause of the amendment, and taking money from nonmembers to finance the work of a church infringes on the "religious liberty" clause of the same amendment. The "wall," however, is a relatively recent phenomenon.

As one writer has pointed out: "The idea of an absolute separation of church and state was carefully ignored during a century and a half of Protestant political and cultural hegemony in the United States, when little dissent was audible over the use of public funds for the support of Protestant institutions of welfare and education. Absolutist thinking on the separation question comes to us with no reliable historical credentials whatsoever."[8] He is so right.

The serious mischief preventing rational discussion is that legislators and journalists simply fall back on the metaphor as a substitute for historical analysis and informed discussion. Provided it is not overworked, however, there is still much to be said for the metaphor of the wall separating church and state. More precisely the concept is "independence" or "autonomy" rather than "separation."[9]

Absolutism applied to church-state relations leads to trouble and contradiction. In his dissent in the 1947 *Everson* New Jersey bus case, Justice Wiley B. Rutledge wrote what under scrutiny becomes historical fantasy, when he argued that the objective of the First Amendment was "to create a complete and permanent separation of the sphere of religious activity and civil authority by comprehensively forbidding every form of public aid or support of religion."

[8] William Ball, "Church and State: the Absolutist Crusade," *Saturday Review*, January 21, 1967, p. 58.

[9] It was in this sense that Jefferson's famous metaphor was used by Innocent XI a century before the United States became a nation. The French church was struggling to maintain its independence in face of the encroachments of regal power, so the pope wrote to Louis XIV of France: "Everyone sees what destruction and ruin, not solely in France but in the rest of the Christian world, would follow for the Catholic Church, what confusion of sacred and profane things, if the wall between the spiritual and the secular power were to be breached, with the influence of such an example spreading daily ever wider. In addition, unless so absurd and so certain an error is corrected a grave risk and danger to souls in this kingdom will result." *Innocentii Pp. XI Epistolae ad Principes*, I, 225 (Romae: Typ. Vaticana, 1890).

For one thing, Mr. Rutledge can't have it both ways. If separation must be *complete, permanent,* and *comprehensive,* then, to quote one of America's most scholarly historians of education, "we can seriously call into question the practice of state control of secular education in the parochial schools, which already has been judged to constitute 'an establishment of religion.' Since the state is prohibited from making any law about 'an establishment of religion' with reference to financial and other subsidies, it follows that under the same prohibition, as stressed by Mr. Justice Rutledge, the state cannot make any law which regulates the parochial school, which is obviously a part of a religious establishment."[10]

If a parochial school is simply an extension of the church, then, for example, the state can no more require attendance in the church classroom than in the church itself, and it is monstrous to permit a church school to become a place where society's compulsory school law may be fulfilled. The question is simple but the answer ignites controversy: Can the state distinguish (this is different from "separate") the secular from the religious in education? Then those states with mandatory certification for teacher employment in all schools, public and parochial alike, are poaching on an ecclesiastical preserve.[11]

On the other hand, this is precisely the direction in which the child-benefit doctrine has developed. Ever since the Oregon school case in 1925, as Justice Byron R. White has indicated, "a substantial body of case law has confirmed the power of the states to insist that attendance at private schools, if it is to satisfy state compulsory-attendance laws, be at institutions which provide minimum hours of instruction, employ teachers of specified training, and prescribed

[10] William W. Brickman, "For and Against Public Aid to Religious Schools," *School and Society,* May 20, 1961, p. 248.

[11] Certification is required for nursery-school teachers in four states, for kindergarten teachers in six, for elementary-school teachers in nine, and for high-school teachers in seven. More commonly, however, the states exercise an indirect control over the nonpublic schools by granting accreditation only to schools employing teachers who hold state-issued teaching certificates. This holds true in four states for nursery schools, in ten states for kindergarten schools, in nineteen states for elementary schools, and in twenty-two for high schools. State control through accreditation is the current trend. (These figures are for 1957, the latest year surveyed. They were made available through the courtesy of the NEA research division.)

subjects of instruction."[12] Because of the state's interest in school standards, the courts have ruled that instruction at home does not comply with compulsory-education statutes. Mr. White argues that these cases were "a sensible corollary of *Pierce* v. *Society of Sisters.*" Moreover, he states: "If the state must satisfy its interest in secular education through the instrument of private schools, it has a proper interest in the manner in which those schools perform their secular educational function."[13]

* * *

The constitutional argument is easily stated: Can church-related schools share in any general provision for government aid to all schools without violating the First Amendment to the Constitution? Or is such support forbidden because it would favor church groups with educational commitments over other groups, church and non-church, without them? Does the United States Congress have the authority to make funds available for religiously-related nonprofit schools in its legislation for the common good? Or does the prohibition in the First Amendment to the Constitution, "Congress shall make no law respecting an establishment of religion," extend to legislation which would incidentally promote the interests of church-sponsored educational enterprises?

May the federal government, as part of a comprehensive program to promote educational excellence in the nation, provide secular educational benefits to the public in private nonprofit schools, church-related as well as nondenominational? This is the broad constitutional question. It is not a question of whether religion or a church is helped or hurt by the fact that such benefits are provided in these schools as well as in the regular public schools. It is a question of whether the help or hurt that results is the kind of benefit or detriment forbidden by the First Amendment.

Arthur E. Sutherland of the Harvard Law School has pointed out that there are only three sources of information on this subject: (1) the mind of the Founding Fathers who prepared the First Amendment; (2) the decisions of the U. S. Supreme Court which interpret

[12] The United States *Law Week,* June 10, 1968, 36 *LW* 4540.
[13] *Ibid.,* 36 *LW* 4541.

the amendment; (3) the actions of the different Congresses and Presidents in carrying out the amendment.[14]

Regarding the first course, the difficulty of accurate inquiry is formidable. The senators and congressmen who authored the amendment, and the legislators from the dozen states that ratified it, were indeed numerous. They represented sharply contrasting points of view in their political and religious philosophies.

With regard to the deliberations of the Constitutional Convention itself, one legal scholar has shrewdly observed: "It is possible that an ambiguous expression was intentionally chosen by the conference committee. Such want of candor is not unknown—even in ecclesiastical legislation."[15] In any event, the pertinent point is whether it is in the best interests of the nation that the Congress in 1969 should have its powers delimited by "an uncertain guess at the frame of mind of men" who lived 178 years ago. To know the thought of our forefathers on a given point of political philosophy is important for the historian, but more immediate factors often have to guide decisions in the social order.

A study of the decisions of the U. S. Supreme Court in cases involving church-state relations is the second source of light on the meaning of the "establishment" clause. Even greater ambiguity is to be found here than in a study of the full intentions of the Founding Fathers. There are few direct judgments regarding "establishment," and most of the incidental opinions or *obiter dicta* that have at times been expressed on this point can be juxtaposed to cancel one another out. As Mr. Sutherland has underlined: "While all lawyers properly pay respect to such dicta, still, statements of this sort, not directly relevant to the decision of the court, do not carry the weight, as precedent, of an actual adjudication."

From the third source, presidential and congressional action, comes a great variety of precedents in what concerns public support of church-related undertakings that are in the public service.[16] Even

[14] Hearings before the Senate Subcommittee on Education of the Committee on Labor and Public Welfare on the Elementary and Secondary Education Act of 1965, 89th Cong., 1st Sess., pp. 163–64 (1965).

[15] Wilber G. Katz, "The Case for Religious Liberty," in *Religion in America,* John Cogley, ed. (New York: Meridian Books, 1958), p. 101.

[16] The most complete treatment of this subject is to be found in Richard J. Gabel, *Public Funds for Church and Private Schools* (Washington: Catholic University Press, 1937).

a cursory study of how the First Amendment has been interpreted in practice by men sworn to uphold the Constitution removes any ambiguity about the meaning of the "no establishment" clause in the document. From the beginning of our national history the federal and state governments have used public funds to support religion and religiously-sponsored enterprises on a nondiscriminatory basis under certain conditions.

Examples could be multiplied: orphanages, hospitals, boarding schools for Indian children, the national leprosarium, institutes for the special preparation of teachers, colleges for the Negroes, etc. The sectarian or private nature of the group sponsoring the activity was considered no obstacle because the service rendered was held to be a public benefit. Direct and indirect support was given to religiously-sponsored institutions through land grants, extension of credit, sharing in state lotteries, and even direct payments out of both the state school fund and common tax funds.

However, government subsidy is no longer given on the scale of former years. Today it is generally limited, at least the direct and substantial aids, to protective and eleemosynary institutions, most notably orphanages and hospitals. Public support here seems to present less the aspect of aid to a sectarian operation, and society is quicker to grasp the common-welfare aspect of the work. Nonetheless, the principle of public service remains valid, and the same theory would still justify direct support of parochial and church-related schools—as is done in so many other countries around the world.

The evidence is unquestionable that on both national and state levels countless forms of cooperation between government and religion have been meshed into our political system. The interpretation of absolute separation would require the dismantling of all those arrangements, some of which go back to the cradle days of the American Republic. Even the proclamation of Thanksgiving Day each November by the President, for example, is an "aid" to religion, for it violates the alleged neutrality between believers and non-believers. Publishing the Thanksgiving Day proclamation requires money—and this obviously runs afoul of the supposed prohibition on the use of any tax, large or small, to support religious activities and instructions, whatever they may be labeled. Until the Everson case there had never been any serious acceptance of the claim that these practices violated the constitutional separation of church and state or were the equivalent of an establishment of religion.

Separation of church and state has validity only as a means to an end. In other words, the principle of separation is instrumental and subordinate to the end—religious liberty. The concept of religious freedom will, accordingly, determine how much separation of church and state there should be. As Professor Wilber Katz has remarked: "Separation ordinarily promotes religious freedom; it is defensible so long as it does, and only so long."[17] The same authority warns those who would make separation an end in itself that the basic American principle of church-state relations is not separation but religious liberty. And Milton Himmelfarb makes the point that it is not true that separation of church and state guarantees freedom of religion, and he instances the most secular society in what used to be Christendom—the Soviet Union—where absolute separation has been decreed and where there has long been flagrant persecution of religion. Even in America, he says, "separationism is potentially tyrannical; separationism needlessly repels some from the democratic consensus; it is harsh to those who prefer nonpublic schools for conscience's sake and it stands in the way of a more important good (and a more important safeguard of Jewish security), the best possible education for all."[18]

Many people fail completely to understand how Catholics can argue that their own religious liberty is involved here. They concede that Catholic parents and pastors have the right to establish and operate separate schools but they cannot see the basis of any additional right to have these schools financed in whole or in part from common tax funds. If any religious liberty is at stake, they feel, it is that of non-Catholics. Their sentiment is embodied in this statement of Justice Rutledge in his Everson dissent, that "like St. Paul's freedom, religious liberty with a great price must be bought. And for those who exercise it most fully, by insisting on religious education for their children mixed with secular, by the terms of our Constitution the price is greater than for others."

But the issue of religious liberty is not so easily waved away, least of all by a price tag. In fact, this argument in the American context boomerangs. The last thing our Founding Fathers intended to do

---

[17] Katz, "The Case for Religious Liberty," p. 115.

[18] Milton Himmelfarb, "Church and State: How High a Wall?" *Commentary*, July, 1966, pp. 27–28.

was to put a price on the religious liberty protected by the First Amendment that would put it beyond the reach of the less affluent. But this is precisely what has happened, and this is precisely what pinpoints the Catholic grievance.

The states have passed compulsory school attendance laws, and to assist parents to comply with this legislation, have established a system of free public schools, but without any provision in them for religious training. To achieve the common good of accessible free education, the states tax all citizens alike to form a common pool for the support of education. As a result the states are able to provide for their school-age children the substantial benefit of free education and certain auxiliary benefits related to schooling. But more and more for Catholic families of moderate or small means, this can only take place within the type of school the state itself chooses. The higher school taxes rise, the greater the squeeze on the Catholic parent and the less real freedom of choice he has in choosing a school for his child.

Many Catholic parents judge that in all conscience they must send their children to a Catholic school because they believe that secular education during the child's formative years is best integrated with religious training. Or they simply may prefer this kind of schooling. The Catholic parent looks to the public school not reproachfully but regretfully. As a policy statement issued only a few years ago by a joint commission of the ruling group of America's most powerful public-school national organizations has solemnly told him: "As public institutions, the public schools of this nation must be non-denominational. They can have no part in securing acceptance of any one of the numerous systems of belief regarding a supernatural power and the relation of mankind thereto."[19] In the next chapter we shall take the point up more fully.

Opponents of the Catholic case still press their contention that to take tax dollars from non-Catholic pockets to support Catholic schools would be an intolerable violation of religious liberty—their own. This argument is raised sincerely by many people. The temptation is to make the quick retort that this is an absurd piece of fiscal logic, for public taxes must always go for policies adopted for the common good. Dollars from a Methodist teetotaler might be paying

[19] National Education Association and American Association of School Administrators, Educational Policies Commission, *Moral and Spiritual Values in the Public Schools* (Washington, D.C.: The Commission, 1951).

for an embassy cocktail party in Paris, Jewish dollars might be paying the salary of a Lutheran prison chaplain in Atlanta, atheist dollars might be paying a Senate page's tuition at Georgetown Prep, a pacifist's dollars might be paying for the latest Polaris missile, etc. After all, where does an argument like this end? The principle here, however, is that legislation is not void if it achieves a public purpose, even though in the process a private end is incidentally aided. Education and its auxiliary services are public benefits to the individual citizen. "There is no requirement that the church should be a liability to those of its citizens who are at the same time citizens of the state, and entitled to privileges and benefits as such."[20]

The courts have made it clear that the government must leave parents free to send their children to schools of their choice. Mr. Justice Felix Frankfurter has admitted that "parents who are dissatisfied with the public schools thus carry a double burden," which, he says, raises the problem of "consistence." American judicial opinion has not yet fully faced the corollary to parental freedom to educate according to religious convictions. In the same opinion the Justice raised these questions:

What of the claims for equality of treatment of those parents who, because of religious scruples, cannot send their children to public schools? What of the claim that if the right to send children to privately maintained schools is partly an exercise of religious conviction, to render effective this right it should be accompanied by equality of treatment by the state in supplying free textbooks, free lunch, and free transportation to children who go to private schools?[21]

*   *   *

Back of the intransigence of some people to accept even the court-approved general welfare benefits for parochial-school children like bus rides and textbooks is the worry that "child benefit" has no limitations other than what the Catholic community feels it can successfully push for. It is not so much today's buses and textbooks

[20] *Chance* v. *Mississippi State Textbook Board,* 200 So. 706 (1941). This was a suit of free nonreligious textbooks to parochial-school children, which was rejected by the state supreme court. In 1930 the U. S. Supreme Court had unanimously upheld a suit based on a similar law in Louisiana, declaring that "the school children and the State alone are the beneficiaries."

[21] *West Virginia State Board of Education* v. *Barnette,* 319 U.S. 624 (1943).

but tomorrow's salaries, buildings, and eventually a fully subsidized-parochial-school system that rouses some non-Catholic opposition. What guarantee is there, they ask, that Catholics will limit their demands on the public purse to the so-called "child welfare benefits"?

On Catholic assumptions this is a loaded question, and the only answer is the frank question: Why should there be any guarantee? Catholics do not look upon the claim to share in general welfare benefits—including education itself—as a raid on the public treasury but as an issue to be argued in the civic forum because they feel it concerns civil rights.

No, the school question will not be solved by simply applying the old formulas or shouting the old battle cries that held through the nineteenth and into the twentieth century. For one thing, the pattern of American education has substantially changed. The sheer dimensions of the nonpublic-school system—which is 90 per cent Catholic —make its needs and interests more than the concern of the groups immediately sponsoring it. This is the first argument in favor of public support for all schools.

At the beginning of the 1968–69 school year there were an estimated 5,250,000 pupils in the Catholic private and parochial schools or nearly 11 per cent of the nation's total elementary-school and secondary-school population. But that figure of 11 per cent doesn't tell the complete story. In dozens of towns and suburban communities, the Catholic schools enroll 40, 50, and even in some cases, 60 per cent of the school population. In Detroit and Cincinnati it is 24 per cent and in Philadelphia, 40 per cent. One out of every four pupils in all of Pennsylvania is in a parochial school. The figure for Boston is 30 per cent, for Milwaukee and New Orleans, 33; for Buffalo and Pittsburgh, 40. One-half the children of Green Bay, Wisconsin, and of Manchester, New Hampshire, are in Catholic schools. The Catholic-school systems in many of the largest cities of the United States enroll one-quarter or more of the total school population. Every third school child in the cities of New York and Chicago is enrolled in a Catholic private or parochial school. Last year, in Cook and Lake counties, the area comprising the Archdiocese of Chicago, there were 342,403 children in the Catholic elementary and secondary schools.[22]

[22] Statistics furnished by Catholic Superintendents' Offices.

When a concerned President tells the American people that our progress as a nation "can be no swifter than our progress in education," neither he nor the total American community can exclude from their concern progress in the Catholic schools of Chicago, Pittsburgh, and New Orleans.[23] The quality of the education in these cities can be no better than the quality of the Catholic schools in them. It is inconceivable that the youthful talent of the nation can be adequately developed without the inclusion of nonpublic schools in government programs designed for this purpose.

A family seeking to follow simultaneously the dictates of conscience and the compulsory-education law may not now, for all *practical* purposes, share in the state's provision for the common welfare. In the practical order, the state has set up what amounts to a religious test. Children in Catholic schools would qualify for free schooling and all related benefits provided by the state for its junior citizens *except* that their parents have placed them in a Catholic school. If public benefits are so administered that citizens must do violence to their consciences in order to share in them, then the benefits are discriminatory. Perhaps Catholic parents should look at things differently. Their feeling of frustration, however, is not assuaged by telling them that they are "free" to have their own schools, as they watch increasing subsidies for public schools steadily pricing Catholic-school education out of the market.

*   *   *

There are four key cases, decided by the U. S. Supreme Court in recent years, which have guided national and state legislation with reference to the public school's relationship to religious programs and religiously-oriented schools. They are *Everson* (1947), *McCollum* (1948), *Zorach* (1952), and *Allen* (1968). Something should be said here about each one.

In the first case the Court sustained a ruling of the New Jersey State Supreme Court that a transportation law which provided also for parochial-school pupils was not a violation of either the state or the federal constitutions. In 1941 the state legislature had passed the law. A taxpayer, Arch R. Everson, challenged the legal right of the school board of Ewing under this statute to reimburse the parents

[23] John F. Kennedy, Education Message, 87th Cong., 1st Sess., February 20, 1967, *Congressional Record,* CVII, 2429.

of parochial-school children. The Ewing township had authorized payment for the transportation of local pupils to "the Trenton and Pennington high schools and Catholic high schools by way of public carrier." Though the decision was welcomed by supporters of non-public education, there were serious misgivings about the extreme separatist interpretation of the First Amendment upon which it was based.

In its 5 to 4 decision upholding the constitutionality of school bus transportation for parochial-school students, however, the Court compared such facilities to fire and police protection offered to all schools without discrimination. The Court recognized that the New Jersey law did no more than implement the compulsory-education law by providing "a general program to help parents get their children, regardless of their religion, safely and expeditiously to and from accredited schools." In this case for the first time, the Court employed the child-benefit theory to interpret the First Amendment though in several earlier cases involving education, it had followed the theory. The Court said that a valid constitutional line could be drawn between acts which directly aid religion and are, therefore, unconstitutional, and acts which are constitutional because they achieve a larger social purpose even though they incidentally may aid religion. Though the absolute separatists miss no opportunity to quote those sweeping passages of *Everson* which sustain their high and impregnable wall, they mute or ignore the central point of the decision: the State Supreme Court of New Jersey *did* approve publicly-supported bus transportation for parochial-school children on the basis of the child-benefit theory. The court decision said:

> Other language of the First Amendment commands that New Jersey cannot hamper its citizens in the free exercise of their own religion. Consequently, it cannot exclude individual Catholics, Lutherans, Mohammedans, Baptists, Jews, Methodists, Non-believers, Presbyterians or the members of any other faith, because of their faith, or lack of it, from receiving the benefits of public welfare legislation.

The next year, the *McCollum* decision dealt with a "shared time" program. In 1945 Mrs. Vashti McCollum had sued in an Illinois court to test the legality of a voluntary religious instruction program in the Champaign public schools. As an officer in a secular humanist organization she wanted no part of the program for her ten-year-old son Terry. The religious instruction program, then in its sixth successful year of operation, was a joint undertaking of some fifty churches and synagogues in the area. Pupils were admitted to the thirty-minute-weekly classes held inside the public-school buildings only on the written request of the parents. No public funds were involved, all expenses being borne by the sponsoring churches. Though the Illinois State Supreme Court upheld the constitutionality of the practice, the U. S. Supreme Court, by an 8 to 1 decision, deemed it a violation of the First Amendment. By cooperating, even on a nondiscriminatory base, with the churches in giving religious instruction, Illinois, said the Court, had breached the high wall separating church and state.

In attempting to lay down precise norms for legislation that would be constitutional, the Court gave a definition of "establishment" which many thought established secularism as our national philosophy. It definitely was in conflict with a venerable legal tradition and the instincts of most American people on the proper relations between government and religion. In any event, four years later the Court did what appeared to be an about-face, and Justice Stanley F. Reed's lone dissent in *McCollum* became the majority opinion in *Zorach*.

The 1952 decision did not so much as mention the "wall of separation" though it did formally profess adherence to *McCollum*. In *Zorach* the court sustained the action of the New York City School Board in providing a program for religious instruction that differed in one important particular from the Champaign program: the instruction was not given within the public-school buildings. The pupils were simply permitted to leave their classrooms on a voluntary basis to attend religious instruction elsewhere. The religion-in-public-education aspects of both *McCollum* and *Zorach* will come in for further discussion in the following chapter.

The latest decision was in June of 1968, when the High Court by a 6 to 3 majority upheld the constitutionality of a New York textbook law.[24] In 1965 that state had passed a bill that required public-school districts to lend fifteen dollars' worth of textbooks each year to every pupil in grades seven through twelve in nonpublic schools. The decision stated that the New York program was a benefit to the

---

[24] At the same time the court ruled in the *Flesch* decision that federal taxpayers are permitted to litigate the constitutionality of federal spending programs that involve church-state issues.

student in the church school and not to the school itself and thus did not violate the First Amendment prohibition of public support of religion.

All four decisions under discussion agreed that the religious prohibitions of the Constitution were absolute. But backtracking from the *Everson-McCollum* position, in *Zorach* the Court isolated the precise area of separation, saying: "The Constitution does not say that in every and all respects there shall be a separation of Church and State. Rather it studiously defines the manner, the specific ways, in which there shall be no union or dependency one on the other. That is the common sense of the matter."

How *absolute* is constitutional separation to be? The Court ruled:

And so far as interference with the "free exercise of religion" and an "establishment" of religion are concerned, the separation must be complete and unequivocal. The First Amendment within the scope of its coverage permits no exception; the prohibition is absolute.

Justice William O. Douglas, who wrote the 6 to 3 majority opinion, carefully explained that the separation of the state from religion must not result in a relationship that is "hostile, suspicious, and . . . unfriendly." The decision affirmed that "when the state encourages religious instruction . . . it follows the best of our traditions." The state may "encourage" religion, though it cannot aid it; the government should "sponsor an attitude" that lets each religious group flourish. There was no hint at the desirability of union between church and state. On the contrary, the Court insisted there was not the slightest doubt that the First Amendment "reflects the philosophy that church and state should be separated."

Now of course there is a school of thought that immediately equates any kind of cooperation with some form of *establishment*. For these people any collaboration between church-sponsored schools and state becomes a union of church and state or an establishment of a state church. Seemingly there is no depth of absurdity to which they won't plunge. It was only a few years back that the executive director of the Northern California–Nevada Council of Churches filed a complaint with the Board of Education of San Francisco, charging that the employment of publicly-paid truant officers to enforce attendance of children in parochial schools was "a complete violation of the separation of church and state," and three years ago a New York City Board of Education lawyer ruled that if a Jewish high-school lad wore a *kippah* on his head during class hours, he would be breaching the wall of separation between church and state.[25]

*   *   *

What then does "separation of church and state" mean, and what are its historical antecedents? There are two passages in the federal Constitution that are the main sources of the American doctrine of separation between church and state.

The first sentence of the First Amendment, part of the Bill of Rights, reads:

Congress shall make no law respecting an establishment of religion, or prohibiting the free exercise thereof.

The Fourteenth Amendment, added after the Civil War, which has come to be interpreted by the courts as incorporating the guarantees of the First Amendment and extending them to the states, reads in part:

No State shall make or enforce any law which shall abridge the privileges or immunities of citizens of the United States; nor shall any State deprive any person of life, liberty, or property, without due process of law; nor deny to any person within its jurisdiction the equal protection of the laws.

Except for another brief passage in Article 6, Section 3, forbidding any religious test as a qualification for public office, the Constitution is silent about religion or any relations between state and church. Why?

Commentators on the history of the Constitution are generally agreed that there was no mention of religion because the federal government was to have no control over the subject, just as the document made no mention of education or intrastate commerce for the same reason. In addition, the religious beliefs and practices of the people, as well as the extent of the control exercised over religious affairs by the states, were so diverse that it would have been impossible to attempt any uniform system of relationships between religion and the government. It is important to keep in mind that when the Constitutional Convention convened in Philadelphia in 1787, New York, New Jersey, Virginia, North Carolina, and Georgia had only recently discarded their established state

25 Himmelfarb, *op. cit.*, p. 25.

church; that by law the Congregational Church in Massachusetts, Connecticut, and New Hampshire was still the established church, as was the Church of England in South Carolina.

Confirmation for the silence in the Constitution about religion is readily found in the records of the debates in the various state conventions called to ratify it. The new Constitution of the *United States* forbade it to place disabilities upon any citizen because of his religion. The Constitution did not lay the same restraints upon the individual states. According to the common legal interpretation, this development came only in 1868 with the ratification of the Fourteenth Amendment. It is a matter of historical fact that Connecticut did not disestablish the Congregational Church until 1818, Massachusetts not until 1833, and that New Hampshire by its constitution to this very day may legislate for "adequate provision . . . for the support and maintenance of public Protestant teachers of piety, religion, and morality."[26]

Justice Joseph Story, the first great commentator on the Constitution, said that every American colony down to the Revolution, excepting possibly Rhode Island, "did openly by the whole course of its laws and institutions, support and sustain in some form the Christian religion." It would be fantastic to suppose that the day after the colonies united in a federal union, the new states individually or collectively would have adopted a policy of hostility toward, or even indifference to, religion.

It is regrettable that since the 1947 *Everson* decision, the doctrinaire separatists have succeeded in widely publicizing some poor history. They found support in the definition of *establishment* given in that case by the Supreme Court in which it was stated that "establishment" meant at least this:

Neither a state nor the federal government can set up a church. Neither can pass laws which aid one religion, aid all religions, nor prefer one religion over another.

This may have become the current understanding of establishment for many people today—but it was by no means the original understanding. The question is not of opinion but of historical fact. Certainly the overwhelming majority of the citizenry in 1788, the year the states ratified the document, would have been shocked to learn that the new Constitution forbade the federal government

[26] New Hampshire Constitution, Part I, Bill of Rights, Art. 6.

to adopt a benign attitude toward religion. Justice Story has commented: "An attempt to level all religions, and to make it a matter of state policy to hold all in utter indifference would have created a universal disapprobation, if not universal indignation."

Any remaining ambiguity about the intentions of the framers of the Constitution is resolved by even a cursory study of how the document was interpreted in practice. From the first years of our corporate political life as the United States, the federal and state governments have used public tax monies to support certain kinds of religious and philanthropical activities sponsored by church groups. That is the simple fact of the matter.

Though the contemporary school of absolute separatists dates only from 1947, they have had kindred spirits throughout American history. In the name of separation of church and state, an important suit was brought in 1853 to eliminate the chaplaincies in the Congress. The Senate committee appointed to study the charge that this practice allegedly violated the constitutional separation of church and state reported (their report was adopted by the Senate) on the meaning of establishment in the minds of the men who framed the Constitution. The committee stated that the idea

referred, without doubt, to that establishment which existed in the mother country, and its meaning is to be ascertained by ascertaining what the establishment was. It was the connexion with the state of a particular religious society, by its endowment, at the public expense, in exclusion of, or in preference to any other, by giving to its members exclusive political rights, and by compelling the attendance of those who rejected its communion upon its worship, or religious observances.[27]

The Senate committee defended the institution of congressional chaplains, denying that this constituted an establishment of religion, because no church or ecclesiastical association or system of religious faith thereby had introduced in its favor "all or any one of these obnoxious particulars—endowment at the public expense, peculiar privileges to its members, or disadvantages or penalties upon those who should reject its doctrines or belong to other communions."

Nor is this to argue that exactly the same policies, practices, and procedures must prevail today. Perhaps some, many, or all of them should be abolished as no longer serving the common good.

[27] Reports of Committees of the Senate, 32d Congress, 2d Session (1852–53), Senate Report No. 376, January 19, 1853.

Then we are deciding *new* policies, practices, and procedures on new social grounds. Maybe the government should no longer pay for chaplains in the Congress. Perhaps a case can be made out for having the sponsoring churches pay for chaplains in the armed forces so that these men may be free to speak out on the morality of a given war. Moreover, in a later chapter of this book a case will be made out for acceptance of a new secularity in American education. The point here, however, is that it does not advance the argument to fabricate history. Despite possible interpretations of the First Amendment that would have completely separated the American state and the churches, in practice there was cooperation and collaboration. The First Amendment was not devised by the Founding Fathers to prevent church and state from working together. They and those who succeeded them actually did work together. Any other interpretation is bad history whether penned by a Supreme Court Justice or a propagandist from the POAU or the American Jewish Congress.

*   *   *

The absolutist school of separation never seems to have reflected on the startling implications of its position. Take these examples. When the Continental Congress proclaimed in the Northwest Ordinance of 1787: "Schools and the means of education shall forever be encouraged," the absolute separatists would have tried to modify the passage to read: "Schools, except for parochial schools and other nonpublic types of schools, and the means of education, except those means which might directly or indirectly benefit pupils in nonpublic schools, shall forever be encouraged."

When President Johnson sent the Elementary and Secondary Education Act (ESEA) of 1965 to the Congress, he stated: "I propose that we declare a national goal of full educational opportunity. Every child must be encouraged to get as much education as he has the ability to take. We want this not only for his sake—but for the nation's sake." And he added: "We must demand that our schools increase not only the quantity but the quality of America's education. For we recognize that nuclear age problems cannot be solved with horse-and-buggy learning." Had the absolute separatists had their way, they would have edited Mr. Johnson's words somewhat as follows:

I propose that we declare a national goal of full educational opportunity for all children who attend the public school. Every child must be encouraged to get as much education as he has the ability to take within our public schools. We want this not only for the sake of the public-school youngster—but for the nation's sake. We must demand that our public schools increase not only the quantity but the quality of America's education. For we recognize that nuclear-age problems cannot be solved with horse-and-buggy learning in our public schools.

Here again in its most graphic form is the dilemma: if the state recognizes the nonpublic school as an appropriate institution for the fulfillment of the compulsory-education laws by a significant part of the school population then the state must be concerned with its well-being.

Fortunately, neither the President in presenting the administration's bill nor the Congress in overwhelmingly enacting and in 1967 extending it, followed the absolute separatist philosophy.[28] The title itself enunciated the comprehensiveness of the act: "a bill to strengthen and improve educational quality and educational opportunities in the nation's elementary and secondary schools." The President's message spelled out the four major tasks to be met by the law:

1. To bring better education to millions of disadvantaged youth who need it most;
2. To put the best educational equipment and ideas and innovations within reach of all students;
3. To advance the technology of teaching and the training of teachers;
4. To provide incentives for those who wish to learn at every stage along the road to learning.

It was attested by the constitutional authorities consulted that the power of Congress to pass this kind of legislation "rests on its constitutional authority to appropriate funds to provide for the general welfare of the United States." All parties responsible for this piece of legislation were aware that many earlier bills had been scuttled in part over the church-state issue. However, the administration and the Congress had an immediate responsibility to resolve a grave social situation.

President Johnson, fresh from his overwhelming mandate in the

---

[28] Voting on HR 2362, Senate: Yeas, 73; Nays, 18; Not voting, 9. House of Representatives: Yeas, 263; Nays, 153; Not voting, 17.

election of 1964, reminded the Congress that five million children in the five to seventeen age bracket were in families whose annual earning was less than two thousand dollars, that one-third of the 3,700,000 children enrolled in the fifteen largest school systems of the country required special educational help, that about 60 per cent of the sophomores in inner-city high schools would probably drop out before graduation from high school, that some 69 per cent of the public elementary schools and 56 per cent of nonpublic elementary schools had no library. This final item meant that in 1965 there were 9,850,000 public-school youngsters and 1,740,000 nonpublic-school children without school library service.

Given the explosion of knowledge and the consequent need of a continual updating and widening of curriculums, the need for new textbooks was patent. "The obsolete textbook," as the President's message said, "can suffocate the learning process." Yet books are more and more costly and are putting additional strains on the purse of moderate-income and low-income families.

The ESEA of 1965 made provision for supplementary educational centers and services which would be open to *all* school children—from parochial as well as public schools. The exciting experiments—hitherto subsidized by the National Science Foundation, by the Office of Education, and by some private foundations—were now to be made more widely available. Not only the "new" math but the new techniques in teaching science and foreign languages were to be open to all through joint programs combining the public and private sectors of American education. Likewise the act envisaged cooperation between public and nonpublic schools in things like remedial reading programs, and special provisions for the physically handicapped, for the mentally retarded, and for the specially gifted. More than any single piece of legislation from Washington, D.C., already has the Elementary and Secondary Education Act of 1965 contributed to bridge-building. The presidential message said:

Within each community, public and private nonprofit schools and agencies will cooperate to devise the plan and administer the program for these supplementary centers. Their services should be adapted to meet the pressing needs of each locality.

The senators and congressmen who wrestled long and diligently with the church-state problems involved here can hardly be categorized as lackeys or tools of an ecclesiastical pressure group. They carefully worked out patterns that have proved an advance in American education, despite the reluctance of important individuals and groups whose doctrinaire devotion to a monopolistic public-school system blinds them to the broader issues and needs of American education.

Some of the most authoritative constitutional scholars in the land were assiduously consulted in the preparation of the bill to ensure that what the President called "the number one business of the American people—the education of our youth" would not founder on the rock of the church-state question.[29] In view of the impending and forthcoming court tests of the principles upon which participation of parochial-school children were included in ESEA, it is worthwhile pausing here to study some of the points these men made. Their thought was gathered in an extensive memorandum prepared by the general counsel for the Department of Health, Education, and Welfare, which was supplied to the senators and representatives.[30]

The basic premises set forth in the memorandum are:

1. The Supreme Court has ruled that the First Amendment to the Constitution forbids the use of public funds to "support religious institutions" or "finance religious groups."
2. Legislation that renders support to church schools is unconstitutional in some circumstances and constitutional in others.
3. Laws designed to further the education and welfare of youth may not be unconstitutional if they afford only incidental benefits to church schools.
4. The line between direct support and incidental benefits is not always easy to determine.

From 1947 until today the series of U. S. Supreme Court decisions have established certain negative norms which have been followed with more or less consistency. Across-the-board grants to church schools may not be made. The Court reasons that lacking specific designation such broad grants would inevitably facilitate the performance of the school's religious function. The same reasoning is followed in what concerns across-the-board loans at less than the going interest rate.

[29] Among them, Professor Arthur E. Sutherland, Professor Wilber G. Katz, and Professor Mark De Wolfe Howe, Hearings before the Senate Subcommittee on Education, p. 158.

[30] *Ibid.*, pp. 159–72.

The memorandum goes on to say that tuition payments for all church-school pupils are invalid "since they accomplish by indirection what grants do directly." Actually, however, the Court has never decided a case involving tuition; but in the 1908 *Quick Bear* v. *Leupp* case, it did approve something analogous.[31] The decision upheld the use of public trust funds for the education of Indians in sectarian schools at their request. Yet there are at least two more general practices that are consistent with this interpretation. For generations public funds have been used to pay the tuition of Senate and House pages attending church schools, and on the college level hundreds of thousands of veterans of World War II and the Korean war have been given public monies to finance their education. Granted that neither of these situations has undergone Supreme Court scrutiny, it is highly doubtful that the Court would rule them unconstitutional. Why not? The unusual working hours of the page boys require special arrangements for their schooling, so that often it is simply more practical for them to attend a private institution. This is a fringe benefit that doesn't seem to ruffle the feathers of absolute separatists any more than, say, the use of an official government limousine to take an assistant secretary of state to Mass. With reference to the G.I. Bill of Rights, inconsistent though it may be, there is a public acceptance that college-level institutions are different from church-related elementary and secondary schools.[32]

The memorandum stresses the distinction between governmental programs that "aid institutions as such [including sectarian institutions] or aid them on behalf of all their students and, on the other hand, programs that aid a small number of selected students whose choice of institution alone results in benefit to a sectarian school." In the first case, the aid to sectarian institutions is "an automatic consequence of Government action; in the latter, it is a matter of chance so far as Government is concerned." Under terms of the original G.I. bill, the individual chose the college he wished to attend, but the government made the tuition payment directly to the

---

[31] 210 U.S. 50 (1908).

[32] The general counsel's guiding memorandum added another reason: ". . . a program of educational grants to returning war veterans for their readjustment into civilian life perhaps could not have constitutionally excluded from its benefits applicants who wished to attend sectarian institutions. This would probably be regarded as a classification so unrelated to the expressed public purpose as to offend due process requirements."

institution. The memorandum goes on: "If the Government had selected the institution, however, it would obviously have presented a very different situation, and the mode of selection would have been more relevant than the identity of the payee of the Government check."

Moreover, special programs to subsidize qualified students to develop their full potentialities or to encourage study "in subjects where there is a shortage of adequately trained persons to serve national needs, does not seem to raise a serious question." Whatever financial support would accrue to a particular religious institution would depend upon the student's choice and would seem, therefore, both "indirect and incidental." From the point of view of the government, "it would depend upon chance, not governmental decision. There would seem to be no constitutional significance to the fact that, like other problems of probability, some statistical prediction might be possible of how much aid particular religious institutions might receive."

Four criteria are spelled out for determining the constitutionality of general-benefit legislation:

1. How closely is the benefit related to the religious aspects of the institution aided?
2. Of what economic significance is the benefit?
3. To what extent is the selection of the institutions receiving benefits determined by government?
4. What alternative means are available to accomplish the legislative objective without resulting in the religious benefits ordinarily proscribed? Could these benefits be avoided or minimized without defeating the legislative purpose or without running afoul of other constitutional objections?

Just what is the permissible area of legislation which, in rendering incidental benefits to pupils, does not subsidize their church school? The favorable decision of the Supreme Court in the *Everson* case with its 5 to 4 split illustrates how one justice's benefit is another justice's subsidy.[33] In upholding busing, a form of assist-

---

[33] The appropriation of funds to reimburse parents directly and the fact that only Catholic parents were involved were the factors that prompted Justice Jackson to enter his separate dissenting opinion in *McCollum;* he said that if the resolution of the school board in *Everson* had been "for the protection of the safety, health, or morals of youngsters it would not merely have been constitutional to grant it. It would have been unconstitutional to refuse it to any child merely because he was a Catholic."

ance in no way related to a church's religious function, the majority opinion said that the New Jersey statute "approaches the verge" of impermissible acts under the First Amendment. The memorandum we have been following goes on to say that "other collateral benefits like provision of milk and lunches appear equally constitutional since the benefit is plainly to the health of the child and not to the school itself."

Moreover, loans for specific purposes not closely related to religious instruction or ceremony were included in Title III of the National Defense Education Act of 1958, so that church schools (including secondary and elementary schools) could borrow funds for equipment to improve the teaching of science, mathematics, and languages. This precedent was cited in the preparation of the Elementary and Secondary Education Act of 1965. Programs of this nature "advance specific national purposes, and their relationship to the religious function of a church school is remote." Let us look at some of the specific programs and their antecedents.

The federal school-lunch programs originated during the Depression years prior to World War II. In 1935 the Congress passed legislation to provide milk and hot lunches in cooperation with the states. The purpose of the program, renewed and expanded by subsequent Congresses, is set forth in the 1946 Act: "It is the declared policy of Congress . . . to safeguard the health and well-being of the nation's children. . . ." In addition to the ordinary protection through police, fire, and sanitation service, the community provides its school children with other welfare benefits without discriminating between public and parochial schools. School property is protected by zoning regulations because the community judges that school children might be harmed by the proximity of factory smoke, heavy trucking, or tavern traffic. The city will close off its streets during part of the day to form recreation areas for school children. That is, public property is temporarily put at the disposal of a sectarian institution to supplement its recreational facilities. Again the principle justifying these programs is simply that the health and safety of the nation's children is a public concern, regardless of the school they happen to be attending. Moreover, it has long been accepted that the most convenient spot to gather children for medical and dental examinations is the school, and the most efficient way to administer such a program is through the school's administrative machinery. It taxes belief to realize that some states continue to exclude parochial-school youngsters from these welfare benefits on the grounds of separation of church and state. But they continue to do so.

The time may be at hand when the federal government, if not the state's, will have to step in and establish special clinics, hospitals, and cafeterias in the schools of the inner city, where these children may be examined and treated for such things as dietary insufficiency or the effects of strontium 90, as it does now during a polio outbreak. The state of its children's health is hardly a matter of indifference to the government. No one, moreover, has yet explained how a town or city can curb polio, eradicate tooth decay, or eliminate tuberculosis by confining its public health measures to children in the public-school system.

*   *   *

A more controversial and less accepted application of the child-benefit principle is the supplying of textbooks to all school children indiscriminately. Nine states—Indiana, Iowa, Kansas, Louisiana, Mississippi, New Mexico, New York, Rhode Island, and West Virginia—presently provide textbooks to nonpublic-school children, though the statutes of Kansas, Indiana, and West Virginia contain a needs test. On the other hand, a South Dakota case and an opinion by Florida's attorney general ruled out a law permitting issuance of textbooks to pupils in the nonpublic schools of these two states. For twenty years Oregon had also provided books for all its school children but in 1961 the state's highest court decided that the textbook statute was in violation of the Oregon constitution.

By statute the California State Board of Education has authority to provide for "the sale at not-less-than-cost price of state textbooks to private schools, individuals, or dealers under such rules and regulations as may be adopted by the board of education." Private schools in Kansas communities have the same privileges of purchase of state school textbooks as have public schools in the same communities. Yet a Kentucky law prohibits the sale of state textbooks to private or sectarian schools.

The first free-textbook law was passed in 1929 by Louisiana. The statute was challenged but upheld as constitutional by the Louisiana Supreme Court. Two suits were decided together. In the *Borden* case the Louisiana court declared that children in parochial schools have a right to share in textbook programs, for the schools "obtain nothing from them, nor are they relieved of a single obligation, because of them. The school children and the state alone are the beneficiaries." The *Cochran* case, upheld by the state supreme court in the same action, was the one appealed to the U. S. Supreme Court. On behalf of the Court, Chief Justice Charles Evans Hughes gave the Court's unanimous opinion that the Louisiana law was constitutional.

The decision underscored the point that since the taxing power of the state is exerted for a public purpose, "the legislation does not segregate private schools, or their pupils, as its beneficiaries or attempt to interfere with any matters of exclusively private concern." The Court's 9 to 0 decision confirmed the principle that legislation is not void if it achieves a public purpose, even though in the process a private end is incidentally aided. The state's "interest is education, broadly; its method, comprehensive. Individual interests are aided only as the common interest is safeguarded."

Mississippi enacted legislation in 1941 providing for the free loan of textbooks to the pupils in all qualified elementary schools in the state. Suit was brought to prevent the state textbook board from extending this piece of legislation to pupils in private and parochial schools. The Supreme Court of Mississippi upheld the constitutionality of the measure in an opinion which spoke eloquently of what would be involved in a denial of the state's welfare benefits to all its children. "There is no requirement," said the court, "that the church should be a liability to those of its citizens who are at the same time citizens of the state, and entitled to privileges and benefits as such." The decision stated further:

If the pupil may fulfil its duty to the state by attending a parochial school it is difficult to see why the state may not fulfil its duty to the pupil by encouraging it "by all suitable means." *The state is under duty to ignore the child's creed, but not its need.* It cannot control what one child may think, but it can and must do all it can to teach the child how to think. The state which allows the pupil to subscribe to any religious creed should not, because of his exercise of this right, proscribe him from benefits common to all.[34]

The tribunal finally scored the narrow construction contended for by the complainants, which would compel the pupil to surrender the

[34] *Chance* v. *Mississippi State Textbook Board,* 200 So. 706 (1941). (Emphasis added.)

use of his books "when and because he elected to transfer from a public school to a qualified parochial school." This, the court said, would constitute "a denial of equal privileges on sectarian grounds."

The unanimous decision in 1930 by the U. S. Supreme Court in the *Cochran* case was settled on the child-benefit principle but was not contested on the issue of the First Amendment, that is, the "establishment of religion" problem. However, this issue, too, should henceforth be laid to rest after the U. S. Supreme Court ruling of June, 1968, which by a 6 to 3 decision upheld the New York textbook law. Speaking for the majority, Justice Byron R. White said:

We are unable to hold . . . that this statute results in unconstitutional involvement of the state with religious instruction or that [the law], for this or the other reasons urged, is a law respecting the establishment of religion within the meaning of the First Amendment.[35]

Earlier, two judges of the Appellate Division of the Supreme Court of New York in upholding the constitutionality of the New York textbook law, had drawn a meaningful analogy with the availability of books from a public library to parochial-school students. Even the most fanatical separationist has stopped short of proposing that access to public libraries be denied these children. Yet public libraries contain myriad books, paid for out of *public* monies, that could be used to promote religion!

* * *

Justice White made reference to the 1947 *Everson* ruling which insisted that the Constitution "does not prevent a state from extending the benefits of state laws to all citizens without regard for their religious affiliation." The norm laid down in the earlier decision was the purpose and the primary effect of the enactment. "If either is the advancement or inhibition of religion then the enactment exceeds the scope of legislative power as circumscribed by the Constitution. . . ." The purpose of the New York law, however, was to further the educational opportunities available to the young. The court challenge of its adversaries has "shown us nothing about

[35] *Board of Education* v. *Allen*, June 10, 1968. A similar textbook aid law, under litigation since its passage in 1963, was upheld by the Rhode Island State Supreme Court on October 27, 1968. The Rhode Island decision cited the *Allen* case.

the necessary effects of the statute that is contrary to its stated purpose," said Justice White.

The premise upon which the New York law was based got strong support in these words of the decision: "This court has long recognized that religious schools pursue two goals, religious instruction, and secular education." After citing the 1930 *Cochran* dictum, "the state's interest is education, broadly; its method, comprehensive; individual interests are aided only as the common interest is safeguarded," the justice pointed out:

Underlying these cases, and underlying also the legislative judgments that have preceded the court decision, has been a recognition that private education has played and is playing a significant and valuable role in raising national levels of knowledge, competence, and experience.

Americans care about the quality of the secular education available to their children. They have considered high quality education to be an indispensable ingredient for achieving the kind of nation, and the kind of citizenry, they have desired to create.

Considering this attitude, the continued willingness to rely on private school systems, including parochial systems, strongly suggests that a wide segment of informed opinion, legislative and otherwise, has found that those schools do an acceptable job of providing secular education to their students.

This judgment is further evidence that parochial schools are performing, in addition to their sectarian function, the task of secular education.

Opponents of the textbook law based their case on the contention: "There is no such thing as secular education in a sectarian elementary or secondary school. The whole curriculum is permeated by religion." It is true that some Catholic writers on education have long talked about how religion permeates the Catholic school, sometimes to the extent that a legitimate wonder arises whether they are not discussing a church service. Sometimes Chesterton's remark that there is a "Catholic" way even of teaching mathematics is used to buttress the permeation philosophy. Whatever the great G.K. had in mind, his remark is meaningful only when understood as reflecting the influence of Catholicism on *any* phase of a man's life. As St. Paul long ago reminded people, whether they are eating or drinking or traveling or thinking, they should be doing it for God—so that "in all things God may be honored." In this sense there is a Catholic way of eating strawberries and a Catholic way of teaching mathematics and a Catholic way of practicing politics.

If there are no legitimate God-given values in human activity outside of revealed religion, then we reach ultimate absurdities. The
profane or secular order must be outside the sanctuary and temple.
If there is no valid education of the secular order given in the
Catholic school, then "millions of parents and their children have
deceived themselves by imagining that, through sending their children to New York's religiously-affiliated schools, they were fitting
them to compete for their future livelihood and to take their places
as citizens"—as the defendants' brief argued. Moreover, "if there is
no secular education in such schools, then New York's Compulsory
Education Law, as related to these schools, is completely baseless
and New York's public policy . . . is unfounded." Finally, if there
is "no such thing as secular education" in Catholic schools, the
state should suppress them. The Court did not agree, and so upheld
the law.

In his vigorous dissent Justice Douglas insisted that there is no
reliable standard for distinguishing secular from religious textbooks.
The New York Legislature felt that science was a nonsectarian subject. "Does this mean," Mr. Douglas asked, "that any general science textbook intended for use in grades 7–12 may be provided by
the state to parochial school students?" To make his point the
justice cited a passage from a textbook which teaches embryology
in the following manner:

> To you an animal usually means a mammal, such as a cat, dog, squirrel,
> or guinea pig. The new animal or embryo develops inside the body of the
> mother until birth. The fertilized egg becomes an embryo or developing
> animal. Many cell divisions take place. In time some cells become muscle
> cells, others nerve cells or blood cells, and organs such as eyes, stomach,
> and intestines are formed.
> The body of a human being grows in the same way, but it is much
> more remarkable than that of any animal, for the embryo has a human
> soul infused into the body by God. Human parents are partners with God
> in creation. They have very great powers and great responsibilities, for
> through their cooperation with God souls are born for heaven.[36]

Justice Douglas hastens to point out that, although the author is
a priest, the text in question contains no imprimatur and no nihil
obstat nor is it marked in any manner as a "denomination edition"

[36] John M. Scott, *Adventures in Science* (Chicago: Loyola University Press,
1963), pp. 618–19.

but is simply the general edition of the book. He concludes then that *Adventures in Science* is put out as "nonsectarian."

Mr. Douglas' dismay here is a perfect illustration of the myopia of the secularists. It doesn't seem to come through to him that the premises and assumptions from which he argues are just as "sectarian" as is the example he cites. Apparently *Adventures in Science* would not be offensive and could pass as "nonsectarian" if it taught human embryology from an atheist's point of view, omitting any reference to "God," "creation," and "heaven," or if it taught pure Darwinian evolution, or if it were silent about any ultimate explanation of man's existence. But then this makes hash out of the educational process.[37] Here we have a good example of what happens when the doctrine of separation is pushed to its logical extreme: education becomes impossible.

* * *

Then there is the school bus—which has almost become the symbol of church-state tension in education. The consolidation of schools and concern for the safety of the school child today have ringed many a school with shiny yellow buses. In 1929–30 approximately 1,900,000 public-school youngsters, or 7.4 per cent of the total public-school enrollment, rode the buses, for which the tax tab was $54,800,000 or $28.81 per pupil.[38] In 1957–58 a total of 10,900,000 pupils, or 36.5 per cent of the enrollees, were transported to school and the taxpayers' bill was $416,500,000—again not counting the purchase of new buses or other capital expenses. In 1968–69 the total number of pupils carried by America's 230,000 school buses was over 17,000,000 at a cost of $720,000,000, which averages out to more than $42 per child. Busing accounts for an average of better than five pennies of each dollar in an average school budget but the item can be much greater in the budget of a suburban or rural school district.

Every legislative season bills are introduced across the land to authorize or to make mandatory bus transportation for nonpublic-school pupils. Nebraska voted it down, New York expanded it, and

[37] It is important, however, even for junior-high-school youngsters to realize that there are conflicting explanations of the origin of man and the universe. On the other hand, there is no need to pretend that they are all of equal validity.

[38] *Standard Educational Almanac,* 1968, pp. 117–18, 181; and *American Education,* October, 1968.

Pennsylvania decided it was constitutional—all in the same year of 1967. Apropos of the New York event, the *New York Times* fretted editorially over the way things were going. The archpatron of all that is good and liberal aggrievedly had pointed out earlier how "the original New York State constitutional ban was weakened in 1938 by the adoption of an amendment permitting the use of public funds for transporting students to and from religious schools."[39] The *Times* failed to mention that the vote among the delegates to that constitutional convention was 134 to 9—another case, perhaps, of democracy being too precious to entrust to the people and their representatives.

What is the present picture? Inconsistent and kaleidoscopic, to say the least! Twenty-one states by constitutional or special statutory authority, i.e., by an act of the legislature, allow free transportation in varying degrees of generosity: California, Colorado, Connecticut, Illinois, Indiana, Kansas, Kentucky, Louisiana, Maine, Maryland, Massachusetts, Michigan, New Hampshire, New Jersey, New Mexico, New York, Ohio, Oregon, Pennsylvania, Rhode Island, and Wisconsin. Though not provided for by law, some transportation is provided in six other states through interpretations of general pupil transportation statutes. In sum, parochial-school youngsters in over half the states with the bulk of the nation's population are riding in school buses at public expense.

In those states where transportation is authorized for parochial-school pupils but public-school funds may be expended only for public-school purposes, transportation is provided only along regular routes to and from public schools, or is financed through funds that have not been raised or levied for public-school education. Indiana, where, it is estimated, only one out of every three parochial-school youngsters eligible for transportation gets it, falls into the first category, whereas Kentucky and New Mexico exemplify the second. The Maryland authorization is limited to certain counties. In Montana nonpublic-school children may ride the public-school buses, provided parents or school pay a proportionate share of the cost. Since 1967, New York nonpublic-school and public-school children receive exactly the same transportation service. In most cities reduced fares at least are made available to all school children on bus and trolley lines, whether these facilities are owned by the munici-

[39] October 15, 1966, p. 28.

pality or by a private corporation, with the city putting up the difference in fare.[40]

On the issue of tax-supported transportation for parochial-school pupils the state courts have been divided. Maryland (1938 and 1942), Kentucky (1944), New Jersey (1944), California (1946), Massachusetts (1955), Maine (1959), Connecticut (1960), and Pennsylvania (1967) have approved such measures. On the other hand the supreme courts in Wisconsin (1923 and 1962), South Dakota (1931), Delaware (1934 and 1966), New York (1938), Oklahoma (1942), Washington (1943 and 1949), Iowa (1947), New Mexico (1951), Missouri (1953), and Alaska (1961) have handed down negative decisions but for varying reasons.

The Iowa and Pennsylvania decisions were not based on the constitutional issue but rather on the lack of statutory authority to transport other than public-school students. Following the court's decision, New York citizens amended the state constitution to provide bus rides for all pupils. Pennsylvania likewise passed enabling legislation, which was upheld by its state supreme court in 1967. The Alaska, Washington, Oklahoma, and Wisconsin decisions were based on constitutional prohibitions on the use of public monies for sectarian institutions, societies, establishments, or schools of instruction. The people of Wisconsin voted to change the constitution so as to have a "fair bus law" which would cover nonpublic-school youngsters. Twice the Washington state legislature had passed bills to allow parochial-school children limited bus transportation, and twice the state supreme court declared the measure unconstitutional according to the literal reading of certain passages in the state constitution.

For anyone who has considered the pile of court cases since 1947 dealing with the question of publicly-supported bus transportation for nonpublic-school children, the inconsistencies, contradictions, and prejudices which are interlarded with the decisions rendered are bewildering to say the least.

An incisive decision handed down in 1945 by the Kentucky Supreme Court cut through the rhetoric and falderal of the absolute separationists in words that deserve pondering. An earlier decision had pointed out that there was no enabling legislation to provide for this service to parochial-school youngsters through payment

[40] In some states, like Illinois, the legislature helps the cities by picking up part of the tab.

from the public-school fund. Thereupon the state legislature passed a statute, so that general county funds could be used to provide transportation for nonpublic-school children, and when this action was challenged, the Kentucky High Court said:

In this advanced and enlightened age, with all of the progress that has been made in the field of humane and social legislation, and with the hazards and dangers of the highway increased a thousandfold from what they formerly were, and with our compulsory school attendance laws applying to all children and being rigidly enforced, as they are, it cannot be said with any reason or consistency that tax legislation to provide our school children with safe transportation is not tax legislation for a public purpose.[41]

Safety was one of the primary reasons for convening the first national conference on school bus standards in 1939. Safety was the major reason for the enactment of the "school bus stop law" in most states. Currently, safety is the main reason for the movement for adequate standards and for training programs for school bus drivers.

It is true, as in Missouri and Washington, that explicit provisions of the state constitution bar the use of money from the public-school fund or the general fund for anything but public-school purposes. When court tests are made, the judges are bound to follow the literal wording of the document. However, the citizens of New York and Wisconsin and other states modified their state constitutions in order to extend this benefit or protection to all its school children.

On the reasoning of *Everson-McCollum-Zorach,* several state cases involving the use of public funds to pay tuition grants at church-sponsored schools below the collegiate level have been decided in the negative. Many but not all of these cases were complicated by efforts in some Southern states to circumvent the U. S. Supreme Court rulings on segregation and integration of public schools. In Virginia, *Almond* v. *Day* held that state payments to sectarian elementary and secondary schools for the education of war orphans violated the First Amendment because such payments utilized public funds to support religious institutions in opposition to the principles in *Everson.* Moreover, such legislation "affords sectarian groups an invaluable aid in that it helps to provide pupils for their religious classes through use of the state's compulsory pub-

---

[41] *Nichols* v. *Henry,* 191 SW 2d 930 (1945).

lic school machinery. . . ." It also compelled "taxpayers to contribute money for the propagation of religious opinions which they may not believe."

The Vermont Supreme Court decision in *Swart* v. *South Burlington* was directed to another kind of situation. A school district without its own high school paid tuition for its youngsters to attend the nearest Catholic high school. The court interpreted *Everson, McCollum,* and *Zorach* as raising this query, to which the court replied affirmatively: "Does the payment of tuition to a religious denominational school by a public entity finance religious instruction, to work a fusion of secular and sectarian education?" In the later light of the *Allen* case, perhaps now the court would recognize a valid distinction between secular and sectarian.

On the other hand, other state cases have upheld tuition payments to other kinds of sectarian institutions in special circumstances. Thus grants for the support of dependent, wayward, neglected, and physically handicapped children in church-sponsored homes and institutions have been upheld on the reasoning that such payment was reimbursement and not use of appropriated funds that are governed by the state constitution. Again the point should be made that tuition grants directly to the pupil do not contravene the federal constitution and, given the appropriate enabling legislation, it would seem now that any individual state can do for the general-category student what it now does for the special-category student.

Those who refuse to acknowledge the child-welfare principle as operative here dismiss the weight of the *Everson* decision, claiming that it settles only the federal question; i.e., the New Jersey bus law does not violate the establishment of religion clause of the First Amendment of the U. S. Constitution. They point only to the wording of the individual state constitutions, most of which contain explicit bars to the use of public funds for any but public-school purposes. This remains an anomalous situation: a state constitution in contradiction to the federal Constitution.

One may be excused some visible impatience after hearing that some proposed bus law in Missouri or Indiana would violate the First Amendment of the federal Constitution or breach the "wall of separation" between church and state. The federal question *is* settled, and it is hard to understand how anyone can raise the issue with sincerity. This is all the more true since the U. S. Supreme

Court in 1961 again reaffirmed its 1947 position in the *Everson* case by declining to review an appeal from a decision of the Connecticut Supreme Court favorable to busing parochial-school children. Maybe there are valid arguments from expediency or public policy which opponents of tax-supported buses for parochial-school children might call upon. Separation of church and state is no longer one of them.

In his concurring opinion in the 1948 *McCollum* case, Justice Jackson made an observation about *Everson,* however, which, like an unexploded time bomb, is still ticking away. He said that if the resolution of the school board in the *Everson* case had been "for the protection of the safety, health or morals of youngsters it would not merely have been constitutional to grant it. It would have been unconstitutional to refuse it to any child merely because he was a Catholic." That is the central question, which has yet to be squarely faced by the courts. It is not whether the extension of such "auxiliary services" to pupils in nonpublic schools is permitted by our fundamental laws, but whether our fundamental laws do not *require* such extension under the "equal protection of the laws," guaranteed by the federal Constitution. Someday the principle must be tested. Legislative provisions which attempt to outlaw any and every form of indirect assistance to church-sponsored schools are most probably unconstitutional because they conflict with the First Amendment guarantee of religious freedom. In American society religion touches much of everyday life, both in the home and in the school. Ours is a society, to quote from the Willcox brief,

in which customs, practices, morals, and ceremonies have been importantly influenced by religion. Fundamental as are the principles contained in the First Amendment, it is clear that they cannot always be absolute. The problem is to draw a line between what is permitted and what is prohibited in accordance with applicable constitutional principles. Since this must be done in the society in which we actually live—a society in which aspects of religion are inextricably entwined with knowledge and culture —history and experience may be sounder guides to locating Jefferson's "wall of separation between church and state" than abstract logic.[42]

One can readily agree with Mark De Wolfe Howe's wish that Justice Hugo L. Black, who wrote the briefs, "had spoken with

[42] Alanson W. Willcox, Memorandum on the Impact of the First Amendment to the Constitution upon Federal Aid to Education, Hearings before the Senate Subcommittee on Education, p. 119.

greater caution in the *Everson* and *McCollum* cases." The eminent
member of the Harvard Law School faculty stated the critical point
when he wrote that Mr. Black's "resounding absolutes with respect
to the religious disabilities of American government" represent a
"simplistic analysis" and that they "may still serve to delay and possibly to prevent the adoption of a national educational program of
the dimensions which the times require."[43]

*   *   *

Much of the opposition to the claims for children in nonpublic
schools derives from two concerns. Some Protestants and other non-
Catholics fear that granting even a few incidental benefits to Catholic schools will serve to strengthen what they consider to be the
growing power of the Catholic Church in American society. Much
of this fear is—in Catholic eyes—unreasonable, inherited prejudice.
In any event, it exists and must be taken into account.

An even larger group of Americans bases its opposition on the
fear that whatever favors the growth of private education serves to
weaken public education—that any government step facilitating the
expansion of parochial schools redounds to the harm of public
schools. If Catholic schools were to get basic support, these people
are convinced, a profusion of other church schools will spring up in
a chain reaction that could ultimately destroy our traditional public-
school system. Those who share this opinion profess to see a nightmare, in which dozens of church-sponsored or sectarian-sponsored
schools with state subsidy will fragmentize American education.

How could a town of five thousand inhabitants support a dozen
sectarian schools, each competing for community support and patronage? In place of a single strong public school for all children,
the town would end up dividing its children and its money among a
dozen mediocre schools. In the parochialism, bickering, and rivalry
that would ensue, what would happen to civic unity and harmony?
Moreover, the argument continues, consider the consequences of
helping some of the splinter denominations to get into education.
Oddly enough, those who propose this difficulty never seem to consider the manner in which the identical situation is handled in any
one of a score of other countries that legally subsidize independent

---

[43] *The Garden and the Wilderness* (Chicago: University of Chicago Press,
1965), p. 174.

religious schools, and whose citizens count themselves lovers of freedom and democracy as much as do Americans.

Separate school systems, subsidized in whole or in part by the government, under the auspices of the major church groups are actually operating with success in many countries—England, Ireland, Scotland, Belgium, Holland, Canada, and others. After all, there are reasonable requirements and standards that the state can lay down to avoid exactly the kind of educational chaos and dissipation of school resources these objectors fear. Only sponsoring groups that can guarantee stability and continuity may qualify for a school charter and assistance. Some countries, like Great Britain, supply only a portion of the funds needed to establish and operate the school. The sponsoring group must still undertake much of the support. The government office of education prescribes the general curriculum, licenses teachers, and supervises examinations for promotion for these schools, just as for others.

What is the current status of church-sponsored education in the United States? Though statistics are not complete, in 1967–68, out of some 250 Protestant groups, 9 have schools in some kind of an organizational way.[44] There are about 3500 elementary schools which enroll approximately 500,000 pupils. On the secondary level, there are almost 70,000 students in 360 schools. The two largest Protestant groups, Methodist and Baptist, comprising the bulk of Protestant church membership have no tradition of church schools. There are Baptist-sponsored schools, however, in the South and the Southwest. Hebrew schools number 234 on the elementary and 105 on the secondary level with respective enrollments of 55,300 and 13,600.

The parents of children in parochial schools have always been free as citizens and voters to work for legal measures that would alleviate the double burden of school taxation they presently bear. They have the right to expect that the federal and state governments will assist them in every way legally possible to finance the education of their children in schools of parental choice. These parents insist that their children have every right to share in all of the state's general welfare benefits, and in any special legislation designed to develop academic and scientific leadership for the nation.

A series of provisions in Title I, II, and III in the ESEA of 1965

[44] Board of Parish Education, The Lutheran Church–Missouri Synod, St. Louis, Missouri, December 12–20, 1967.

have brought additional benefits to nonpublic-school children in terms of audio-visual and other advanced educational equipment, programs for special categories of pupils, remedial programs in speech and reading, etc. The political and professional alignment that agreed to this bill comprised such strange bedfellows as the National Education Association, the National Catholic Welfare Conference, and the National Council of Churches. Shaky as was the alignment, it surprisingly survives. The original understanding so painfully worked out among these organizations left some ambiguities that have soured the concord and may jeopardize further cooperation.

On the principle that it is a lot easier to have one teacher move than to have twenty-five pupils move between schools, in some cities public-school teachers of remedial reading or basic English have gone directly into Jewish and Catholic schools to perform their specialized chores. Watchdogs on the wall, however, have barked out the alarm and suits have already been entered in the courts to right this egregious wrong. So the sinister shadow of establishment falls across the office of some exhausted and harassed principal who now may have to laboriously rework schedules and class loads to preserve the ambiguous letter of the law.

The ESEA of 1965 was born of expediency without real agreement upon means and ends. A decade of impasse over federal aid legislation undoubtedly motivated the cooperating parties in 1965 but this past summer when the act was extended for an additional two years, the NEA and the U. S. Catholic Conference found themselves again on opposite sides of the fence. The NEA strongly backed an amendment to the bill for renewing the ESEA introduced by Representative Albert H. Quie of Minnesota, which would have consolidated all federal education funds into block grants to be turned over to the states. Had the amendment been passed, no federal funds would have reached parochial schools in some thirty-five states whose constitutions forbid either direct or indirect state aid to any institution under sectarian control. Under the present administration of the ESEA, the funds are channeled into the hands of local public-school authorities and not state agencies.

On the other hand, the NEA strongly supported the Supreme Court decision in the New York textbook case. "We agree with the U. S. Supreme Court that the textbook loaning program—the basis for NEA support of Title II of the Elementary and Secondary School Act of 1965—benefits students and not parochial schools and therefore does not constitute state support of religion," said the organization's spokesman this past fall.[45]

The Supreme Court has not yet passed on the ESEA law but if it does, and finds the measures for assisting parochial-school children unconstitutional, the scene may heat up. As one concerned observer has pointed out: "Catholics might become school aid opponents in an effort to persuade Congress either to find new grounds for a church-state compromise or to revise the Constitution. If Catholics as a bloc began to oppose, their position as a balance of power and their influence over 20 to 25 per cent of congressional seats could cause defeat for future school aid bills for some time to come."[46] Such concern is not yet called for and there is hardly a remote possibility that it will be. The "school question" is not a genuine constitutional issue: it is a social one. Since 1947 there have been a dozen cases decided by the Supreme Court of the United States involving religion and education and each decision has ostensibly piled another layer atop the wall separating church and state. Despite these judicial acts more public tax-support goes to the children in parochial schools than before 1947. What is the explanation? American society has decided that there are ways of helping children in nonpublic schools within the letter and spirit of the Constitution—and has gone ahead and done it, "wall" or no "wall." To state all this is for some people to argue for a union of church and state.

It is a temptation simply to categorize modern-day defenders of the absolutist position of complete exclusion of parochial-school children from common benefits as antisocial, antiprogressive, antiliberal, and antiquarian. They actually seem to have forgotten that life is essentially a dynamic process. Man's life is mirrored in his institutions which are governed by a social metabolism: they adapt and reconstitute or decline and die. China and Britain had their ancient walls. France dug a wall known as the Maginot Line. Berlin today has an ugly wall of division. We neither need nor want walls like these. The only kind of American "wall" that makes sense is the stout affirmation that the church will stay out of the state's business and the state out of religious affairs. The issue then is, at heart,

[45] John M. Lumley, assistant executive secretary for legislation and federal relations, quoted in *School and Society,* October 12, 1968.

[46] James W. Guthrie, "A Political Case History: Passage of the ESEA, *Phi Delta Kappan,* February, 1968.

a social one which the American people are continuing to resolve in their own good sense, in their own practical way, and in their own good time.

In 1925 the *Pierce* decision affirmed that Catholic and other private schools meeting reasonable state standards had the right to exist. It took another twenty-two years before the High Court got around to including formally Catholic-school youngsters and others in private schools in a state's welfare benefits, notably free bus transportation. Now, after another twenty-one-year interval, the Court has ruled that a state may provide free secular textbooks as a valid part of its concern for the quality of nonpublic-school education. Undoubtedly, it will require more time for the U. S. Supreme Court to finish the guidelines within which the state's concern for all of its school children may be spelled out.

CHAPTER SIX

Double Dilemma:
The Church, Public Education, and Values

The attitude of the American Catholic community toward the state-supported public school has fluctuated widely over the nearly two centuries of our national existence. Nor should this surprise. Since the public school mirrors society, it reflects a changing countenance. It has meant something different for each generation of Americans. However, what has divided and confused Catholic approaches to public education has been the absence of a rounded philosophy of education. Had there been a coherent and consistent theory of the school—that is, an understanding of its relation to profane learning, technical and professional skills, religious formation, and civic education—the Catholic community might have entered fully into the public-school movement, if not from the beginning, at least before the close of the nineteenth century, lent it strength and inspiration, and worked to achieve its own distinctive educational aims in other ways.

Indeed, though there has always been an abundance of episcopal and papal statements on education written in the most eloquent of terms, the arguments for Catholic schooling are invariably aimed at the ultimate goal of education, i.e., preparation for eternal life itself, with accompanying insistence on the need for moral and religious training. While the eschatological and the theological may illuminate a philosophy of education, they can never substitute for it. Yet given the hostile climate in which the American Catholic Church grew to maturity, it is understandable how things happened the way they did, and it is easy to sympathize with the uneasiness Catholic Church leadership has nearly always felt vis-à-vis the state-supported public school.

The nineteenth century, no more than the twentieth, was not the ideal time for absorbing a set of values in the quiet fashion of the "traditional" Catholic home. Even then the industrial and social revolutions were shattering the order of the past. The unencumbered piety of the European village or country parish was not transplantable. For the young it was fast disappearing behind the smoke and bustle of the raw new cities and towns. Catholic leadership came to hope that the parish school would play surrogate for the agencies that during the age of devotion has kept men loyal and obedient sons of the church. For the first time in history, the school was asked to become what it had never been: the primary guardian and tutor of the faith.

The parochial school was established, accordingly, in response to the church's pastoral concern. If a single theme characterizes the collective pronouncements of the American hierarchy on education over the past one hundred years, it has been the insistence that education was primarily moral training and religious formation to be achieved through the separate confessional school. So true is this that the questions must be asked: was the school expected to replace the priest and the parish in fulfilling Christ's commission to teach or, even more fundamental, was the school expected to assume the natural obligation of parents to prepare their young for admission into the Christian community?

Social and religious factors have conditioned the Catholic attitude toward the public school. Chief among them was reaction to Protestant anti-Catholicism and the defense mechanisms to which this gave rise. Inseparable from and only second to Protestant-Catholic tension was Catholic perplexity in face of the drive for mass education, which, with its mystical vision of the public school as the unique font of America's greatness, seemed to smack so strongly of Protestantism itself. When Justice Robert H. Jackson of the U. S. Supreme Court wrote in his dissent in the New Jersey bus case that "our public school, if not a product of Protestantism, at least is more consistent with it than with the Catholic culture and scheme of values," he was only voicing a sober truth.

A third factor was the conservative reaction here and abroad to a Europe rocked to its Christian foundations by successive waves of revolution, particularly the French Revolution, from the end of the eighteenth century onwards. And equally to be weighed in an analysis of the social forces which shaped Catholic attitudes toward education was the inability of traditional Europe and official Rome to comprehend the distinctive genius of the American experience.

Those episcopal leaders who early saw how, freed from the social and political encumbrances of its tired past, the church could take on renewed life and wax strong in the New World setting, were engulfed by reactionary forces. The traditions of Catholic Europe ran counter to much of what the young country was beginning to stand for—opportunity for all (including state-supported education), the end of class privilege (including a favored position for the church), a trust in the new science to ameliorate man's lot on earth (including encouragement for independent thought and initiative). Where the nineteenth-century liberals exalted individual liberty, the Roman establishment stressed papal authority, and where the progressives glorified reason and humanism, traditionalists emphasized obedience and devotionalism. Church control over civilization was loosening. It was, in Gabriel Vahanian's later words, "the end of what might be called the ecclesiastical era of Western culture." Perhaps what church leadership in Latin Europe found hardest to accept was the political philosophy so boldly expressed by one of America's greatest churchmen, John Ireland, when he stated: ". . . I say that government of the people, by the people, and for the people is, more than any other, the polity under which the Catholic Church, the church of the people, breathes air most congenial to her mind and heart."[1] After a brief ascendancy, he and like-minded bishops fell out of favor with Rome and their influence came to be neutralized. They fell under the shadow of "Americanism," a phantom heresy which has never truly existed nor, for that matter, been completely laid to rest in the minds of nervous officials of the Vatican curia.

* * *

Even during the pre-World War II period, when it began to be more and more argued that by its nature the school must remain completely out of the sphere of religion and be true to its secular nature, this new secularity was erected upon some loose interpretation of "natural" law and the theism of the Judaeo-Christian tradition. In other words, despite creedal differences, a loose consensus prevailed among the American people that moral and spiritual values were rooted in some kind of transcendent value system. There was universal acceptance that American democracy drew its strength from the conviction that divinity was a reality, that the guarantee

[1] John Ireland, *The Church and the Modern Society,* I (New York, 1903), 1.

of the rights of man defined in America's first political documents was the Almighty God.

In the historic working out of Horace Mann's compromise, the unavoidable became the inevitable. In the effort to remain "neutral," the educational process in the schools officially turned "secular," for the compromise approach bore the seeds of its own dissolution. The area of agreed-upon tenets contracted inexorably, leaving almost nobody happy with the state of things. The only group which seemed to profit was that which held a minimum of positive doctrine or none at all. Though the substance of religious-based ethical formation had disappeared, uneasy parents for a while longer could take some assurance that this side of education was still receiving some attention. After all, Bible-reading, general prayer formulas, observance of certain religious seasons and days continued.

Alas, "neutralism" had no future in the secular age. The final factor in converting the public school, in principle, from neutral to secular was the ascendance of the modern philosophies of secularism—ethical culturalism, instrumentalism, pragmatism, social psychologism, and scientific humanism. In common these philosophies took a new set of assumptions as their point of departure in rejecting the concept of the supernatural and limiting the real order to the exclusively natural. The strictly secular outlook, which sees man as the beginning and the end of his own life and which looks upon human existence as a problem to be solved by man unaided as he confronts nature and ignorance, is a new faith based on assumptions unverifiable by scientific investigation. Man's supernatural origin and destiny and his relation to a transcendent deity, the starting point and primary assumption in traditional Christian education, went by the boards. The compromise approach of the 1840's had at last come to bankruptcy. The public schools no longer were nonsectarian Protestant; they were no longer Christian; they were no longer religiously oriented. From the judicial point of view they were "neutral" but from the social point of view "secular."

A series of post-World War II decisions by the U. S. Supreme Court has imposed a theoretical neutrality upon the public school. The Court has interpreted the no-establishment and religious freedom clauses of the First Amendment to the federal Constitution as imposing upon the public school a posture of neutrality between those who believe in the God of the Judaeo-Christian tradition—or, for that matter, any notion of a transcendent personal or impersonal deity—and those who do not. Yet such neutrality could only be theoretical. Of necessity, every school must rest upon a set of value-assumptions.

Our public schools take as their starting point and basis the value-assumptions of secular democracy. The moral and spiritual values they inculcate lead to civic or political virtue exclusively. The public school officially has only one objective in the ethical order: to train up the "good" citizen. More significant in the total social order is the fact that responsibility for educating the child has effectively passed from the family to the state.

The social conflicts and resulting pressures which in effect have secularized the American public school are themselves reflected in the same series of decisions regarding religion and public education, while the decisions themselves have accelerated the secularization process.

The first major post-World War II decision was in the *Everson* v. *Board of Education* case over the use of public monies to transport children to parochial schools.[2] In upholding the bus law as a legitimate exercise of New Jersey's social concern for all school children and not a contravention of the First Amendment, the Court laid down certain *obiter dicta*. The establishment-of-religion clause means that neither a state nor the federal government "can pass laws which aid one religion, aid all religions, or prefer one religion against another." Still more sweeping was the interdiction in *Everson* on use of public funds and cooperation between the state and religious groups: "No tax, in any amount, large or small, can be levied to support any religious activities or institutions, whatever they may be called, or whatever form they may adopt to teach or practice religion." On the surface, one could take these words as demolishing a 150-year-old tradition, the more so after considering the Court's next statement: "Neither a state nor the Federal Government, can openly or secretly, participate in the affairs of any religious organizations or groups, and vice versa."

Perhaps the fault lies in the language but, taken at face value, this dictum is simply impossible to implement. It would seem to demand that American citizens, who may likewise be members of a religious group, sort their lives in such a fashion that no part of their civic affiliation touches their religious affiliation. Carried out to its logical conclusion, this dictum would require the unraveling

---

[2] *Everson* v. *Board of Education*, 330 U.S. 1 (1947).

of hundreds of cooperative undertakings between philanthropic societies with church relationship and the federal and state governments. It would have demanded an end to chaplaincies in the armed forces and public institutions; to invocations by ministers or priests at official dedications and functions; to programs for Indians, orphans, lepers, unmarried mothers, the incurably cancerous and the blind; to draft deferment for clergy and clerical students; to exemption of church property from certain direct taxes, etc.

In 1948 came the *McCollum* decision, which outlawed the released-time program, a cooperative venture that had been providing religious instruction on public-school premises.[3] Basing its decision on the grounds set forth in the *Everson* case, namely, that neither a state nor the federal government can pass laws which "aid one religion, aid all religions, or prefer one religion over another," the High Court ruled that the practice in the school district of Champaign, Illinois, breached the wall separating church and state. The *McCollum* decision tolled the death knell for released-time programs in thirty-seven states and set off a furious national reaction. The U. S. Attorney General publicly deplored the decision and the *Journal* of the American Bar Association lambasted it in an editorial. During the four years of its life, the *McCollum* decision was not used as the basis for any important ruling in American law.

With the 1952 *Zorach* v. *Clauson* ruling, the Supreme Court appeared to return to what many observers judge its "traditional" position.[4] In sustaining the legality of a New York program for religious instruction, the Court pointed to what it said was a substantive difference between this program and that in Illinois: in the New York program instruction took place off public-school property. Justice William O. Douglas wrote the 6 to 3 majority opinion and took pains to explain that the separation of the state from religion must not result in a relationship that is "hostile, suspicious and . . . unfriendly." The decision affirmed that "when the state encouraged religious instruction . . . it follows the best of our traditions." The state may encourage religion, though it cannot aid it; the government should "sponsor an attitude" that lets each religious group flourish.

There were of course some caustic observers who suggested that *Zorach* had forgotten with unseemly haste what *Everson* had said

[3] *McCollum* v. *Board of Education,* 333 U.S. 203 (1948).
[4] 343 U.S. 306 (1952).

so serenely four years earlier: "Neither a state nor the Federal Government can, openly or secretly, participate in the affairs of any religious organizations or groups, and *vice versa.*"

Ten years later the pendulum seemed to swing back to the other side, when the Court reviewed the *Engel* case.[5] The question was the legality of the optional recitation of a brief prayer composed by the New York State Board of Regents for classroom use. This was a step toward an establishment of religion, the Court ruled, and, by consequence, a violation of the First Amendment despite the fact that New York State courts on three levels had upheld the practice.

During the 1962–63 session the Court also ruled on three other cases which touched on religious practices in the public schools. The *Schempp* and *Murray* cases, from Pennsylvania and Maryland respectively, were ruled on in a single set of opinions.[6] The Florida *Chamberlin* case was remanded to the Florida Supreme Court to be reconsidered in the light of opinions covering the *Schempp* and the *Murray* cases.[7] The mandatory reading of Bible passages without comment was the common issue. The Maryland and Florida cases also involved the opening of the school day with a nonsectarian prayer. The Court declared all three practices unconstitutional.

These decisions of the nation's highest law tribunal have, in each instance, been followed by praise and blame. What many critics have failed to see is that the U. S. Supreme Court has simply been caught up on the horns of a dilemma. The state-sponsored public school cannot *itself* provide what millions of American families consider an essential dimension of education. It is an impossibility in the practical order because by definition the school is "common" and must then yield to all reasonable compromises worked out by the community. Yet, the people of America continue to charge the school with a large responsibility for character formation but have no consensus as to what constitutes the ethical side of education and the best means of accomplishing it. What makes this mandate impossible to fulfill is the inherent contradiction in the idea that a single *common* school (and officially neutral) can totally satisfy the educational demands of a religiously fragmented society.

Americans would generally agree that the public school is a civic

[5] *Engel* v. *Vitale,* 370 U.S. 421 (1962).

[6] *Abington School District* v. *Schempp,* 374 U.S. 203, 225 (1963); *Murray* v. *Curlett* (June 17, 1963), Part V.

[7] *Chamberlin* v. *Dade County,* 143 So. 2d21 (1962).

and not a religious institution, and that, in the nature of things, it cannot and should not become a community of worship. But with this stated, there remains a deep concern among many people that the official neutrality, so often stated in beautiful rhetoric by the U. S. Supreme Court, does not leave the public school neutral at all but establishes conditions which: (1) allow cooperation with the school exclusively to areligious, nonreligious, and antireligious groups in society; (2) establishes a full-blown "religious" value-system; (3) infringes thereby the religious liberty of most Americans. Let us pursue these points.

* * *

Donald Appewal writes perceptively of the two powerful trends in our contemporary society which are "on a collision course *via* court decisions" to produce a confrontation. They are, he says "the consistent, persistent, and deliberate withdrawal of civil government from influence by, grounding in, or cooperation with anything called religion; and the steady, persistent broadening of the definition of the term 'religion.' "[8] But when these two forces collide, the molders of public-school policy including the courts will more and more have to choose (1) between cutting educational policy free from all value-commitments and sanctions, or (2) taking sides and aligning policy with some of the competing value-systems rather than others. However, adoption of either alternative, according to Appewal, is to court "educational and social disaster." Serious pursuit of the first is to emasculate the educational process; serious adoption of the second alternative puts us back in the messy labyrinth of "establishment."

As we have seen elsewhere, the attempt by the state to remain neutral made educational and social sense so long as there was some loose consensus built around Protestant theism. Values—religious, moral, and spiritual—were in the public school. But as the nineteenth century became the twentieth, and as the early twentieth becomes the late twentieth century, a bewildering array of conflicting value systems has made consensus an impossibility. Whereas once even the courts could refer to the United States as a "Christian"

8 "Religion and Public Education: an Emerging Quandary," *The Educational Forum,* March, 1967, p. 324.

nation, today we are officially secular.[9] In the attempt at neutrality state after state has built into its constitution prohibitions against public support of *any* religion in education but in effect the gainers have been the newer "religions" of the secular and purely humanist varieties. It is clear from a look at the language in these documents, such as "sectarian religion," "no Christian sect," "denominational-ism," that the prohibitions were aimed at traditional Christianity, rather than at the new secularisms and humanisms.[10]

All might have been well except that the presently tolerated value-roots are themselves thrust into forbidden soil. Actually the state's withdrawal from *all* religion has not in fact meant that "the state has abandoned all rootage in value systems; it means merely that it has abandoned any allegiance to supernaturalisms, to theism." It is all well and good to talk, as did the educational policies commission of the NEA-AASA, about the need to provide sanctions for behavior, but their national policy-making document on moral and spiritual values listed only sanctions of the natural order. Moreover, it went out of its way to warn that religious sanctions "may not be explicitly invoked in the public-school classroom," adding that "of course they may play a powerful role in the moral and spiritual in-struction of home and church."[11]

As illustrative of what the teacher may properly do in guiding Johnny to see why he should give back the dime returned him mis-takenly by the corner candy store man, the commission suggests these sanctions: sense of justice, respect for law, property rights, feeling of integrity, group approval, teacher's authority, and adult guidance as sanctions or motives. While these are all good and worthy, they are the total basis of the secular-value-systems. The conclusion is inescapable: by excluding sanctions of religious creeds and doctrines, the commission (and the courts) are favoring, i.e.,

[9] With a few distinguished exceptions like John Courtney Murray and Harvey Cox, Christian theologians have been tardy to develop a theology of the secular. Most of us would do well to ponder Christ's own words: "When God sent His Son into the world, it was not to reject the world, but so that the world might find salvation through him" (John 3:17); ". . . I have sent them into the world on my errand" (John 17:18); "I am not asking that you should take them out of the world, but that you should keep them clear of what is evil" (John 17:15).

[10] Samuel W. Brown, *The Secularization of American Education* (New York: Columbia University Press, 1912), p. xi.

[11] National Education Association, *Moral and Spiritual Values in Public Schools,* 1951, p. 16.

establishing, natural religion in the public schools, and hence limiting, i.e., *infringing* upon, the religious freedom of citizens who believe in a theistic or supernatural religion. Why? Because the old definition of religion has been so stretched that today it covers in law any and every value-system.

At an earlier time, philosophers, dictionaries, and courts were agreed that religion had to have something to do with *God* (upper case "G")—a Supreme Being or the transcendent deity. As recently as World War II, in handling conscientious objectors the U. S. Supreme Court upheld the definition of religion included in the Selective Service Act of 1940:

> Religious training and belief in this connection means an individual's belief in a relation to a Supreme Being involving duties superior to those arising from any human relation, but does not include essentially political, sociological, or philosophical views or a merely personal code.

But a generation later, things had changed. In 1961 the High Court reversed a Maryland court decision in upholding the right of a notary public to retain his office, even though he refused to declare belief in the existence of God. The Court cited the *Everson* and *McCollum* decisions in attempting to plot a course of sheer neutrality between theism and atheism—a something that can only be done with mirrors. Rejecting the traditional understanding of religion, the Justices ruled that neither a state nor the federal government "can constitutionally pass laws or impose requirements which aid all religions as against non-believers, and neither can aid those religions based on a belief in the existence of God as against those religions founded on different beliefs."[12]

There is an obvious riposte here which one commentator has seized, arguing that if neutralism in religion means anything at all the Court's proposition can be reversed: "The state cannot pass laws or impose requirement that aid nonbelievers as against religion or which aid religions that are *not* based on a belief in God as against those that are."[13]

[12] *Torcaso* v. *Watkins,* 376 U.S. 488 (1961). To clarify its intention, the Court in a footnote instanced Buddhism, Taoism, ethical culture, and secular humanism "among religions in this country which do not teach what would generally be considered a belief in the existence of God."

[13] Francis Canavan, "Implications of the School Prayer and Bible Reading Decisions: The Welfare State," *Journal of Public Law* (Atlanta, Ga.: Emory University Law School), XIII (1965), 443. (Emphasis added.)

The dilemma of "neutrality" sharpens when transferred to the area of public education because of the Court's premise that it is the state, not the community, that is the educator in the public schools. *L'école, c'est moi!* Since the state is by nature secular, it must be above conflicting and differing religious philosophies and, in fact, neutral between believers and nonbelievers. And there is no argument. However, in the realm of education, can the state as paramount educator follow the same line of neutrality within the schools?

To quote again from the same authority:

What the state cannot do, according to the Court, the school cannot do either, because the school is the state in action. The state has no religion. The school, therefore, not only has no religion, but cannot make a place for religion in its curriculum. It cannot do this even for those who want it, and even when private persons rather than public school teachers are allowed to use public school classrooms for religious instruction on a voluntary basis.[14]

* * *

Perhaps it is time for a hard new look at this premise. Should education in the public school be exclusively an activity of the state? Or is education the kind of human activity with a dimension extending beyond the exclusive competence of the state and, therefore, better achieved by actively enlisting the cooperation of other social agencies whose qualifications in this respect are larger than the state's? Given our present social structure and the necessary adaptation of the structure of public education to accommodate itself to this structure, one may readily grant that the public school by itself is incapable of providing religious education and formation. But this is not to grant the necessity or desirability of refusing the cooperation of agencies in society that possess peculiar competence here.

At this interval one often hears the argument that religious education ought to have its place in the church or home, leaving the public school appropriately busy with the business of secular and profane education. This solution has about it the beauty of simplicity but it is simply impractical. A new factor complicates the picture, that is, the greatly enlarged place which the modern school occupies in the life of the average youngster. Given the conditions of family

[14] *Ibid.*

living in our industrialized and urbanized society, among other new factors—married women now constitute about one-third of the working force—what other major educational influences on the life of the child remain?

It is no exaggeration to say that the contemporary school, especially for the twelve- to eighteen-year age group, consumes the majority of the waking hours. What with school-sponsored activities, athletic events, the social whirl, field trips, etc., the youngsters' interests and friendships are almost circumscribed by the school. Married women constitute about one-third of the working force. Such was not always the case. There was a time when philosophers of education could legitimately talk of dividing the time of the pupil, and earlier their efforts at reaching compromise on the religion-in-education question were based on some such theoretical division. Columbia University's respected historian of education, Lawrence A. Cremin, has observed: "Jefferson was a great believer in schooling, but it never occurred to him that schooling would be the chief educational influence on the young."[15] It is only with John Dewey and his time, the same writer continues, that "public education has become coextensive with the education of the public."

As a matter of fact, it was Dewey himself who insisted that education must be related to the whole of life. When all activity within a school is carefully antisepticized against the influence of religion, the youthful mind just may get the impression that religion is the one area without relevance to *real* life. This is, of course, a secularist dogma. In quietly following it out, the public school puts its weight squarely on the side of secularism.

Moreover, all-out defenders of the "neutral-secular" approach to education seem never to understand that culture rises out of a values system, and that every value system is rooted in religion—at least in the broad sense of the word. To attempt to convey a total culture minus its religious dimension is to substantially alter and thereby to falsify the culture. If the paramount educational agency, here the public school, makes no provision to ensure a supplementary role for outside agencies, is it to be wondered at that only secularist ideals and values come to govern the lives of most graduates of our public schools?

Due to the religious and spiritual diversity in modern American

15 *The Genius of American Education* (New York: Random House, 1966), p. 6.

society, there is a narrowing basis for any general agreement on values and none at all as to their sanction. In times past, Protestant and Catholic alike could talk of a Christian ethic built on the Old World legacy of Greco-Roman natural law and the central religious concepts of the Judaeo-Christian tradition. But such a consensus has long since faded away. It could be argued that an overwhelming consensus favoring such an ethical base remains, but even if true, it can no longer figure in any public-school program of moral and spiritual values.

The U. S. Supreme Court has decided that even the traditional theistic bias in the public schools conflicts with the constitutional rights of nonbelievers. The point cannot simply be dismissed with an impatient shake of the head. A person may disagree with the philosophy behind the Court ruling and still appreciate the attempt to safeguard individual freedom. Conscientious public-school administrators and boards of education have long agonized over the issue. To what extent should the children of Jehovah's Witnesses, Orthodox Jews, Zen Buddhists, ethical culturists, Christian Scientists, Asian Moslems, atheists, and agnostics—all equally American citizens along with Protestants, Jews, and Catholic—be made to conform to a religious tradition that is alien to them? Before unqualifiedly condemning the U. S. Supreme Court, a person would do well to reflect what his own feelings might be, were his child required to follow even minimal, state-required religious observances in a public school in Pakistan, Israel, or Japan.

The defense of individual religious freedom is a priceless principle. If not always in the realm of action, certainly in the area of belief religious freedom must be an absolute. However, given the continuing dilution of the meaning of religion, the question can fairly be asked: Are we broadening it to the point of absurdity or non-meaning in using such a rubbery, emptied-out term in formulating policy for public education? And we have not yet talked about including in the category of religion atheistic Christianity and atheistic Judaism. Those who proclaim that the supreme being of their religion is no longer alive, let alone concerned with man, Thayer S. Warshaw reminds us, "have not thereupon given up their claims to religiosity, have not renounced their pulpits or their chairs in institutions of religious education."[16]

---

[16] "Teaching about Religion in Public School: Eight Questions," *Phi Delta Kappan,* November, 1967, p. 129.

Anyone who still imagines that there is no such thing as a "religion of democracy" and that it cannot soon become the established religion of America's public schools must never have read John Dewey's *A Common Faith* or the voluminous writings of those who follow his philosophy there.[17] The master taught that "democracy contained all the elements for a religious faith that shall not be confined to sect, class, or race. Such a faith has always been implicitly the common faith of mankind." Nor is this religion simply one more to take its place among many. Dewey warned that "the opposition between religious values as I conceive them and religions is not to be bridged. Just because the release of these values is so important, their identification with the creeds and cults of religions must be dissolved." The public school was intended to be the chief instrument for propagandizing the religion of democracy. Has it become so or is it well on the way to becoming so? Without even deciding an answer, it should be evident that the public school will be by default the principal purveyor of the "ism" of democracy unless a new interest is taken in public education by the many millions of American families who would regard such an eventuality as less than a blessing for their country.

Admittedly, for good or for ill, the character of public education in America has moved by stages from nonsectarian Protestant Christian to ever broadening neutral to unabashedly secular. But is this necessarily a retreat from America's spiritual greatness? Has the process of secularization already destroyed the moral fiber of the public school? Not if two things are kept in mind: the first is the distinction between "secularization" and "secularism"; the other is the full acceptance by the American Catholic community (and other groups as well) of its civic and religious responsibility for the public school.

Harvey Cox speaks of secularization as implying "a historical process, almost certainly irreversible, in which society and culture are delivered from tutelage to religious control and closed metaphysical world-views." In contrast he points out that secularism "is the name for an ideology, a new closed world-view which functions very much like a religion."[18] Secularization is rooted in biblical faith and is,

[17] For a complete discussion of this point see the author's *Public Schools and Moral Education*, chaps. 9 and 10.

[18] *The Secular City* (New York: The Macmillan Company, 1965), pp. 20–21.

Cox argues, to some extent an authentic result of the impact of that faith on the history of the West, seeking to free itself from man's superstitious enchantment with nature. It was man's growth in understanding that open-ended history was the locus of God's action and not a blindly repetitive nature which opened up a brand new world of possible changes in the social and political sphere.[19]

*   *   *

It comes as a surprise to many people that in 1884 the same Third Plenary Council of Baltimore, which symbolizes rigorous Catholic allegiance to the parochial school, discussed with sympathy the necessarily secular nature of the public school: "The friends of Catholic education do not condemn the state for not imparting religious instruction in the public schools as they are now organized: because they well know it does not lie within the province of the state to teach religion."[20]

Ten years later John Lancaster Spalding, the scholarly Bishop of Peoria, spoke even more to the point: "I am willing to assume and to accept as a fact that our theological differences make it impossible to introduce the teaching of any religious creed into the public school. I take the system as it is—that is, as a system of secular education. . . ."[21]

Much of America's school problem has arisen because, for good or ill, there are two independent systems, each with its own relationships to society to be continually defined. The public school's failure or success, competence or noncompetence, in coping with the moral side of schooling has evoked nearly as much discussion and emotion as the question of federal aid to church-related schools. Yet neither question can be adequately answered without reference to the other. The preceding chapter has discussed the federal aid issue, but here it may be worthwhile to treat the underlying assumptions, general attitude, and specific problem areas which enter into the relationships between Catholic-school people and those in the public-school system.

*   *   *

[19] *Ibid.*, p. 25.

[20] Cited in Neil G. McCluskey, ed., *Catholic Education in America* (New York: Teachers College Bureau of Publications, 1964), p. 92.

[21] *Means and Ends in Education* (Chicago: A. C. McClurg, 1895), pp. 140–50.

A new and different Catholic attitude has been developing toward the nation's public schools. While there have always been friendly associations and mutual respect between individual leaders of both systems, the general attitude of both camps was more characterized by suspicion, coolness, and often downright hostility. Much of the credit for the improvement is attributable to the School Superintendents' Department of the National Catholic Educational Association. A decade ago, the superintendents formed a committee which for four years studied the whole area of relationships with public education. Though the committee's report was limited largely to the membership of the department, its appearance did initiate broad discussion and has contributed to the change in attitudes.

The key to understanding is acceptance: not a blind and uncritical surrender to the vagaries of every aspect of the public-school enterprise but an acceptance of the fact that the public school is a respected and necessary institution. The periodic polemic with public-school protagonists over the sharing of federal aid by nonpublic schools did harden long-standing antagonisms, but even as early as 1955, the American Catholic bishops said publicly in their annual statement:

The rise and vigorous expansion of the American education system is cited, correctly, as one of the major achievements of Western civilization. During the past hundred years, in particular, general education, sponsored by states and communities, religious groups and private bodies, has come very near to the goal of providing adequate educational opportunities for every American.

It would be blind prejudice which would refuse to acknowledge, in this connection, the tremendous accomplishment of the public educational agencies. Whatever uneasiness may or must be felt on the score of educational theory and philosophy as illustrated in large areas of American teaching, the plain physical fact of the school system is a matter for unanimous congratulation. This, at least in part, is what freedom has achieved.[22]

The occasional harsh and unqualified statement by a bishop on the "godless nature" of the public school is no longer listened to, and the Catholic community no longer needs to be reminded that the public school is here to stay. The choices then are simple. Will Catholics help to isolate the public schools from all religious influ-

[22] "The Place of the Private and Church-related Schools in American Education," *Catholic Mind*, February, 1956, pp. 112–13.

ence, even indirect, and make them breeding grounds of pure secular humanism and our school children more and more religiously illiterate? Or will they join with those, even of different religious faith, who are seeking reasonable and constitutional ways to work with the schools in accomplishing the moral and spiritual objectives of education? The alternatives are either to support and to strengthen a form of public education which of necessity will take place within a less than perfect religious atmosphere, or to continue to promote by indifference the purely secular school, which can then be condemned for its godlessness.

It should not be hard for Catholics to accept the *secular* basis of public education in the same sense that they accept the *secular* basis of the American government. We can respect the secular order for the same reason that the Founding Fathers did: it is from God and, ultimately, for God. Because "we are a religious people whose institutions presuppose a Supreme Being," we can view only with dismay the success of those groups that have given a new meaning to the traditional American consensus, and that are making the common Father less common and less a Father.

For historical reasons Catholic interest and energy have been expended almost exclusively on Catholic parochial and private schools, in some areas to such an extent that the public schools were considered exclusively Protestant domain. Whatever there was in the way of religious influence or activity seemed to be related to the local Protestant churches. The image of the public schools as a Protestant institution once did correspond to reality. In some communities outside the mainstream it may still be true. That this image should be perpetuated as somehow typical everywhere neither corresponds to the reality, nor is it in the best interests of contemporary society.

With Vatican II Catholic isolation from public education had to end. The ecumenical winds unloosed by the council have begun to blow down many ghetto walls and, though old ways and old attitudes do not fade away overnight, for the record the church has told Catholics to open their arms wider to men and institutions of the larger society. Quite understandably, during pioneer years emphasis was on the schools serving the church. In our day the emphasis is on a reversed relationship: the church's vocation to serve the schools—and not merely church-related schools. For a Catholic citizen there can be no more obvious religious concern than the quality of the education of the nation's children.

There is a mutual interest here that should unite those who are convinced of the importance for the common good of the moral and spiritual dimension of schooling. This common interest should forever lay to rest that strange attitude found in some Catholics who regularly become incensed when they hear of a rabbi or minister urging public-school students to obey the moral code. Education has a valid dimension in time with values common to all citizens. The quality or healthy state of national education affects all. Christian concern for the well-being of the temporal order should inspire service. It is a good thing, therefore, to teach or administer in a public school or to serve on a public-school board, and active church membership should be no bar. The public schools are public institutions and can be expected to welcome legitimate interest on the part of individuals or groups. While social concern is no license to proselytize, neither should fear of possible abuse be a warrant for automatic disqualification.

Nor should Catholic interest in public education be interpreted as some kind of mandate to "take over" the public schools. It may have required Vatican II and the American political experience to have reversed the tide, but the church no longer tries to "Catholicize" society; that is, it no longer tries to impose beliefs, practices, or institutional forms that lie beyond the civic consensus. Perhaps all religious groups learned something from the dismal results of Volsteadism, though many individual states continue to impose fundamentalist morality on all through their stringent Sunday "blue laws" governing entertainment and drink. In America we have never had, nor do we want, Catholic political parties, labor unions, or department stores. We decidedly do not want "Catholic" public schools.

Nor is the new Catholic concern for public education a subtle attempt to erode the religious freedom of others. For American Catholics, too, freedom of conscience must mean at least this much: within the accepted bounds of reason, nothing in the atmosphere should directly or indirectly coerce a child into accepting or rejecting a moral or religious position at odds with his family belief. The consensus of reason has to be invoked here because tranquillity in the domestic order is postulated upon a basic agreement on the broad ethical patterns in social behavior. At one time or another, marriage, divorce, birth control, gambling, drinking, narcotics, blood transfusions, vaccination, nudity, flag saluting, and military service have all been defended or attacked as part and parcel of religious freedom. Moreover, it belongs to freedom of conscience for a parent to have his request honored (again within the obvious limits of reason and right order) when he asks that his child be excused without any recrimination from a public-school activity that he judges an infringement upon the family prerogative.

Were there not a single Catholic child in the public schools of the nation, the church as such would still have a valid concern for the public-school population. The church's pastoral love embraces all the nation's school children. This is simply a part of the church's care for the soul of America. As parents and citizens Catholic Americans have an important stake in the public schools, including parents with youngsters in parochial schools. Their membership in the church enhances this stake. There is nothing in Catholic dogma or belief that makes a virtue out of shirking the responsibilities of citizenship. Catholic citizens have as grave an obligation toward the common welfare of the nation as has anyone else, and the concept of the common welfare today certainly includes publicly-supported education. Because many Catholics, when offered the choice, prefer to send their youngsters to parochial rather than to public schools, they are not, therefore, absolved from the civic obligation of moral as well as reasonable material support of the public schools.

Catholic interest then extends to every area of the school world: the training of teachers and administrators; curriculum and textbooks; methods and objectives; cocurricular and extracurricular activities; finance, etc.

To dispel any reluctance in accepting this responsibility, let us look at a parallel instance of the church's role in society. Few question the church's right and duty to be present in, to watch over, to influence, and when necessary, to call for reform in the economic order. Leo XIII and Pius XI are two universally acclaimed residents of the pantheon of labor because of their great encyclical letters on the condition of the working class, *Rerum novarum* and *Quadragesimo Anno*. In part, Pope John's encyclical *Mater et Magistra* is a call to Catholics to work for appropriate reforms in industrial society in order to bring the economic order more in line with the principles of Christian faith.

For historical reasons already discussed at length, the church's maternal interest in what is patently one of the most important social institutions in American society has generally been late in coming on the scene. This new attitude makes for a more sympathetic understanding of the moral and academic problems that regularly plague the public school. School administrators themselves do not generally initiate the policies that bring them under community fire, relative to controversial topics like banning prayer or excluding religious symbolism from Christmas displays, etc. Outside pressure groups and court decisions are most often the source of such policies.

It might also be recalled that state legislation or city ordinances require the public schools to admit and to retain "problem" children, including those dismissed for disciplinary reasons from the neighboring Catholic school. These points should be kept in mind when reading newspaper accounts of the increase in pregnancies or dope addiction among youngsters in certain public schools to avoid any temptation to utter the prayer of the Pharisee.

If the official school leadership of the church appears at times to be isolated from the public-school world, it is because the superintendent can hardly do the job by himself. Often enough he is the only Catholic school official with upwards of ninety public-school superintendents scattered over his diocesan territory. Here is where the pastor and, even more importantly, the lay parochial-school board have a role to play. Even in more compact dioceses the pastor is often the nearest representative of church authority, which at times puts him in a more influential position with local and district public-school officials than the diocesan superintendent.

If religious leaders and educators today are willing to accept the state-supported school system as a valid institution of the secular order, the public-school leadership must be willing to take positive steps to enlist the services and make use of the resources of other agencies that share concern for the education and formation of the child. In effect, this means the quiet burial of the "no communication" philosophy formulated in the *Everson* and *McCollum* cases.

The first step the public schools should take on national, state, and district levels is to acknowledge loudly and clearly that they accept the responsibility pinpointed in this statement of the National Council of Churches:

Religious ideas, beliefs, values, and the contribution of churches are an integral part of our cultural heritage as a people. The public schools have an obligation to help individuals develop an intelligent understanding of the role of religion in the life of the people of this nation. Teaching for religious commitment is the responsibility of the home and the couple of faith (such as the church or synagogue) rather than public schools.[23]

Cooperation requires some familiarity with the local situation, and school officials generally encourage the interest of the taxpaying (and bond-voting) public in what goes on within the public school. Efforts of public-school officials to strengthen an academic program or to promote some sound school activity call for recognition and congratulations. Though many times the charges made about what takes place in the public school are based on rumor, hearsay, or distortion, on occasion some policy or practice might require critical scrutiny and polite protest. Successful schoolmen are hardheaded and they realize that they need community support. Though he will probably have better motives, the administrator can find even here reason enough for welcoming interest.

The key to the classroom is in the hands of the teachers. Policy directives are simply so much paper without a teacher willing and able to implement them. Cooperative projects and experiments in curriculum are foredoomed without an interested teacher, but this interest can be won. In most areas of the country a good start is yet to be made in building lines of communication between the local teacher-training college and the parish or diocese. (This is often true even with reference to Catholic teacher-training institutions.) These institutions are aware of the increased pressures from society to train the teacher to cope in some way with the problem of religion in education. Support at the strategic moment can spell the difference between the successful launching of some religious education project and its floundering.

Catholics can make their own this thought of the National Council of Churches:

Teachers should be trained to deal with the history, practices, and characteristics of the various religious groups with competence and respect for diverse religious convictions. Their greatest influence will be through the life and attitudes they reflect in the classroom. They should be free as persons to express their own convictions in answer to direct questions from pupils when appropriate to the subject matter.[24]

[23] A policy statement adopted by the General Board, June 7, 1963.
[24] *Ibid.*

Almost every special interest group in the country has published a handbook presenting information and embodying its point of view for the use of the classroom teacher. A striking example is the discussion guide on religion in public education put out by the American Jewish Committee's Institute of Human Relations.[25] This beautifully prepared handbook has had wide influence among teachers. Jewish groups have shown the way with their well-prepared brochures and periodicals designed to correct hostile attitudes and to win understanding for the Jewish community. How many of the hoary canards about Catholic belief and practice could be corrected by this means! Another way of achieving this objective is to issue reprints of outstanding articles or studies and have them mailed to public-school teachers and personnel with the compliments of the diocesan school office.

Another fertile field for cooperation can be found in the cocurricular and extracurricular programs. In many cities and peri-urban areas Catholic-school teams join in athletic leagues with public-school teams; where this is not the case, it is usually because they are unwelcome. There are a number of other student activities which cut across the high-school population and can bring students from public, private, and parochial schools together. Recreational facilities can be shared. Assemblies and convocations can be exchanged. Cooperative community projects can be undertaken.

Catholic concern for the welfare of the public school is something that should exist independently of any involvement in what is in a certain sense a competitive school. Moreover, adoption of a more cooperative attitude toward the public schools is not to abdicate the right to be interested in a reorganization of public education that would be more equitable to the rights of Catholic parents and children. Tax-supported education has no consecrated structure but has continually responded to new demands put upon it by the American consensus.

The 1962 decision of the U. S. Supreme Court, which banned from the New York public schools the optional recitation of a short nondenominational prayer adopted by the State Board of Regents, caused strong reactions throughout the country. In the "no official prayer" decision the Court argued that the First Amendment of the Constitution clearly intended "that each separate government in this

[25] Philip Jacobson, *Religion in Public Education,* Institute of Human Relations, 165 E. 56 St., New York, N.Y. 10022.

country shall stay out of the business of writing or sanctioning official prayers." To date the further point has not been reached wherein any and every prayer, e.g., the fourth stanza of "America" or the verses of "God Bless America," has come under a similar ban. The New York State Commissioner of Education, however, has ruled that even the fourth stanza of "America" cannot be recited with prayerful intent in public classrooms. These decisions have patently strengthened the secularist drive to eliminate all religious observances and practices from the public school.[26]

For school children to turn to God in some prayer before school opens, before lunch, or at an all-school assembly is better than no prayer at all. Despite the slight risk of indifferentism (an eventuality that can be forestalled by a proper explanation for the young), even minimal prayer in the public school has its values. Though it may give some appearance of a "least-common-denominator" religion, the recitation of prayers does not differ in principle from the accepted practice of marking important civic occasions by a "nondenominational" prayer.

In stating that "we are a religious people whose institutions presuppose a Supreme Being," the *Zorach* decision of the Court is perhaps the most accurate reflection of the safe and solid basis for common prayer the nation possesses. For there is an almost universal fund of love and respect for God as Father and Giver of Life to whom men are accountable for their actions, and who, in turn, exercises a paternal providence over all human activity. The accidents of history and grace will not forever divide us if we deepen awareness of our common paternity and brotherhood and find opportunities to unite at times in common prayer.

The "no official prayer" decision has widely curtailed such activity in public schools but "homeroom devotional services" still take place in many of them, particularly in the South. Where group prayer can take place on a completely optional basis and in such a manner that no one can be singled out for ostentatiousness because he does or does not participate, the practice should be encouraged.

---

[26] Despite the logic of the decision, the popular furor against it continues. For years Senator Everett M. Dirksen has tried to get a constitutional amendment which would permit prayer in the public school. Cartoonists have had a field day. One classic cartoon shows the entrance to a public school's air-raid shelter and a neat sign on the door saying: "In case of atomic attack, prayers may be said in school."

The ultimate solution may be a cooperative pattern where pupils may arrive late or leave early to attend some special commemorative service in a neighboring church.

There is much to recommend in silent prayer. A few moments of silent meditation would not be a bad substitute for formal vocal prayer and yet would achieve the same purposes. By statute the United Nations General Assembly begins its opening and closing session with "one minute of silence dedicated to prayer or meditation," and thus far not even the Communists have raised a protest. Some directors of the Confraternity of Christian Doctrine have discussed the desirability of preparing "minute meditations" on scriptural quotations or the liturgy which could be distributed in the weekly CCD classes. About the size of an ordinary matchbox with five to a strip, they could provide the material for the week's daily minute meditations.

The baccalaureate has become an integral part of commencement week. The National Association of Secondary School Principals conducted a 1968 survey of 1050 high schools of all sizes and learned that 80 per cent of them include some type of baccalaureate service in commencement activities. Though school graduation is formally and primarily an academic function, it has two distinct aspects which tradition has always linked together: the academic and the religious. The same people take part in both, the same formal attire is worn, and the institution is the official sponsor of both. When because of the sectarian nature or choice of a Protestant atmosphere for the service, Catholics are forbidden to participate, many feel aggrieved. They feel that their youngsters are being left out of the community celebration of an important occasion in their young lives.

To have no baccalaureate is hardly a solution; to eliminate all religious parts of the ceremony makes the occasion hollow. This policy also plays into the hands of secularists and those who would gladly separate all religious influence from the public schools. Division of the graduating class according to confessional affiliation for separate baccalaureate ceremonies destroys the social nature of the celebration. The strength of the bond among members of a class should be recognized. Separation by religious categories is likewise impractical in many places. For example, without a sufficient number of Catholic graduates, a separate ceremony in the parish church would be wanting in the éclat which means much to impressionable youngsters. Yearly rotation of the locale for the service among the principal churches of the community or district is objectionable from many points of view. In off-years, some pastors or bishops would not allow Catholic students to attend a baccalaureate service in a Protestant church.

Because of local personalities, deep-rooted traditions, and particular situations, Catholic policy regarding these ceremonies will no doubt continue to differ from place to place. However, if conditions did lend themselves to it, a plan along these lines might be acceptable in a surprising number of communities. First of all, the baccalaureate would have to be regarded as in the same category as inaugurals, dedications, or the laying of cornerstones—that is, as a civic event with a more than purely secular meaning shared in by citizens whose confessional allegiance is divided. The school board could then invite a multi-faith committee to prepare a baccalaureate ceremony within this framework:

1. The ceremony is to be held in a suitable auditorium if a church or church hall cannot be agreed upon.
2. The auditorium should have no distinctively sectarian ornamentation, e.g., no Bible or cross surrounded by candles, though candles and flowers could be used in other ways.
3. The participating minister or priest or rabbi is not to dress in robe or cassock but in clerical street costume, or academic robe.
4. The address—to be given in annual rotation—should be hortatory and inspirational, moral but not doctrinal, spiritual but without obvious sectarian overtones.
5. The organ and choir music should be selected for its universal classical quality and not be associated exclusively with church services.
6. The invocation or blessing should resemble that made use of for the analogous occasions cited above.
7. Any scriptural passages selected for reading should be appropriate to the event.
8. The prayer or hymn for common recitation or singing should be something generally acceptable like the final stanza of "America" or "The Star-Spangled Banner" or the Lord's Prayer.

*   *   *

Even without the severe legal restrictions laid down by recent Court decisions, the public school *as such* hardly qualifies as the appropriate pedagogical agency to teach distinctive or general religious beliefs through prescribed prayer or reading of the Bible for either understanding or commitment. No longer should the point be a subject of debate in our pluralistic society. We have talked about optional prayer, but what about the reading of the Bible without comment? Outside the metropolitan areas there are communities of a homogeneous religious make-up where a long-standing tradition of Bible-reading has been left undisturbed. In communities, however, where these practices have become subjects of litigation and bitterness, one can wonder if the struggle to maintain them is worthy Christian behavior.

The importance of Bible-reading in the public school should not be exaggerated. Often it is little more than a ritualistic routine or perfunctory salute to the Deity. In no sense is the reading of a psalm or a passage from the Sermon on the Mount a substitute for the study of Christ's life and teachings. Yet, it remains a shame that the Bible cannot be as accessible to youngsters in the public school as the Gideon Society makes it for Mr. Hilton's hotel guests. Would it rock the foundations of the Republic if there were a meditation room somewhere in the junior and senior public high school equipped with copies of the Old and New Testament? The practice of Bible-reading does have its values, perhaps more appreciated in the Protestant churches than in the Catholic Church. By making God's Word available, the school would be helping somewhat to inspire reverence for the things of God. It would help to underline the importance of the role of religion in life.

Someone has pointed out that the average high-school senior has already seen fifteen thousand hours of television in addition to hundreds of hours in movie houses. Add to these the staggering total spent with newspapers, magazines, and comic books and one can begin to appreciate the "formidable display of violence, cruelty, dishonesty, and inhumanity to man" to which he has been exposed. The Bible alone is not the whole antidote but it can be a part of one.

At least we no longer cling to the old shibboleth about whose version of the Bible should take precedence. The King James and the Douay versions have been replaced by fresher translations enriched by the latest in biblical scholarship. Significant differences in textual understanding no longer divide Catholic and non-Catholic scholars. Protestant, Jewish, and Catholic scholars today share the discoveries of the archaeologist and the psychologist, which throw increasing light on the meaning of the scriptures.

As far back as the 1840's, opinion among Catholics was divided on the real worth of Bible-reading in the public schools. In their pastoral letter of 1840, the Catholic bishops expressed the desire "that at an early period, children should be instructed in the Sacred History . . . and be judiciously led by proper selections, under discreet and pious guides, to the right use of this rich treasure."[27] But they immediately went on to say, "We are disposed to doubt seriously whether the introduction of this sacred volume as an ordinary class book into schools is beneficial to religion." Their reasons were that thereby the Bible risks exposure "to that irreverent familiarity, which is calculated to produce more contempt than veneration"; that the sacred book would be placed "side by side with mere human productions, with the fables of mythology and the speculations of a vain philosophy," finally making the Bible "the subject of a vulgar jest" and sinking it "to the level of task-books."

*   *   *

If one accepts the secular character of the contemporary American public school, does it follow that this type of school should be altogether excluded from religious education? If the public school is considered an extension of the political state, the answer is Yes; it would have to be, like the state, neutral. But functioning as an extension of the social community, the public school can and should work together with the community's legitimate undertakings in religious education.

Nor by religious education is intended here the classroom study of religious events in history or religiously inspired literary pieces in an accepted curriculum, which is normally called for in proportion to their relative importance to the larger fields of history and literature. If the schools must keep silent or give a non-interpretative presentation of everything over which there has been some dispute among religions, honest education is not taking place. The Crusades, the breakup of Christian unity, the age of slavery, the Russian Revolution are topics which demand balance and sensitivity in their

[27] *Catholic Education in America*, p. 6.

treatment. If there are no teachers who can assume this kind of responsibility, then perhaps we should shut down the schools.

After the negative ruling on the constitutionality of the Bible-reading practice, the Supreme Court itself did go out of the way to suggest that, despite its own decisions, the teaching *about* religion can be a legitimate area of public-school instruction.

The major professional society of public-school officialdom, the American Association of School Administrators, is on the record as saying:

A curriculum which ignored religion would itself have serious religious implications. It would seem to proclaim that religion has not been as real in men's lives as health or politics or economics. . . . Whatever else the Supreme Court decisions may or may not have done, they have stimulated the public schools to a search for appropriate means to deal effectively with religion as one of the great influences in man's history.[28]

It can be doubted whether there is the personnel, the audience, or the genuine need to promote courses in "Comparative Religions" or "Great Systems of Religious Thought" at the sixth- or ninth-grade level. But at the eleventh- or twelfth-grade level, one or more units in "American Civics" or in "Modern Social Problems" discussing these areas would be much in order. Ignorance (to say nothing of plain distortion) of what one's neighbor believes has in the past led to misunderstanding and mistrust. It is a normal preparation for full membership in our pluralistic society to have learned as part of social studies the background and at least the rudimentary content of the value-systems which govern the lives of Americans. Courses in the Bible and other points of collaboration between the public school and religious groups will be discussed in the final chapter.

The reason that the public school as an extension of the community must at least be a cooperating partner in religious education is that somehow ways must be found to educate our young people to commitment to value-systems. Perhaps the impasse has come about because we have failed to understand that its social side is the deepest aspect of the problem and requires concerted social action. Many responsible leaders in public education are unhappy over the present situation in the public schools. They and other

28 *Religion in the Public Schools* (Washington, D.C.: The Association, 1964), p. 55.

leaders in society are concerned lest the democratic faith in the dignity of man will erode without some formal awareness of Deity and transcendent values on the part of the public school.

It is erroneous to think that the role of religion in public education can be settled by judicial review alone. As one observer has remarked: "It depends most of all on the initiative of responsible leaders in local communities—schools, churches, and synagogues."[29] The ultimate resolution of this problem, like the racial problem, will in great measure be decided by the formation of a public consensus. Niels Nielson is correct in stating that the basic issue "is no longer whether government and religion can remain indifferent to each other, but how they are to be related."[30] Nor should social action be indefinitely postponed through the utopian hope that if government simply keeps looking away, church-state tension will disappear. Government, on every level, can no longer afford to assume an attitude of indifference before the claims of religion.

It is clear, and we are deliberately repeating, that the teaching of religion and the basic formation of the Christian must remain the responsibility of religious groups. Yet this does not preclude the responsibility of the public school for indirectly creating an awareness of the importance of religion, i.e., "the building of desirable convictions about the meaning of life and personal commitments based on them."

Human rights, human dignity, and human life are wobbly resting on a purely secular base—George Washington tried to make the same point in his Farewell Address. In our anguished modern society where there seems to be such little respect for life and order, the solution is not to destroy the positive neutrality of public education because it has been forced outside the pale so far as the inculcation of all but the most fundamental secular and humanist values goes.

If every family or tribe or nation must at length take its stand on basic social values or risk engulfment by totally alien value-systems, so must America. So must the American public school in

[29] Arthur Cohen, ed., *Religion and the Free Society* (New York: Fund for the Republic, 1958).

[30] For an excellent discussion of this point see Dr. Nelson's chapter 2, "Public Policy and the Separation of Church and State," in *God in Education: A New Opportunity for American Schools* (New York: Sheed and Ward, 1966).

collaboration with religious groups. Anabaptist piety in frontier America joined with Enlightenment conviction in making religion "a personal if not a private matter." All well and good—up to a point. And today we have gone beyond that point. In the nature of things, values are never exclusively private or personal. In its anxiety to protect the rights of the individual, the courts seem to have overlooked the social dimension of religion. The social approach to the problem of religion and education must again be stressed if we Americans are to find the creative solutions appropriate to the dynamic pluralistic society in which we live.

CHAPTER SEVEN

Catholic Higher Education: Its Prospects

David Riesman, a shrewd and knowledgeable observer of the contemporary scene, has recently expressed the hope that today's prophets of Catholic higher education

can retain their sanity in the face of so many competing expectations, so many overpowering pressures abroad and at home, so many disappointments in the very face of growing openness and success.[1]

Probably there is an element of foolhardiness in an author's attempting a one-chapter treatment of Catholic higher education, where a complete book or even several would remain inadequate. However, since the major problems besetting Catholic elementary and secondary schools (as well as their causes) are more or less shared by the Catholic universities and colleges—redefinition of purpose, change in government, financing, and adjusting to a new context— the present volume would be lopsided without the present chapter. Moreover, whatever adjustments, modification, and solutions the future holds ideally have to be brought to bear on the entire edifice of Catholic education, not on its separate parts.

An immediate impediment to the sane approach urged by Riesman is that Catholic education will not stay still long enough to be properly analyzed. Sociological studies of 1957 or 1962 have about the same relevance to what is going on today in the Catholic collegiate world as something out of the Chaucerian or Elizabethan world. Though this statement is, of course, an exaggeration, the substantive changes in "style" or "stance" of almost any social institution, over even a four-year period, are dramatically illustrated by the difference, say, that distinguished the Kennedy and the Johnson administrations. We need to remind ourselves that four years is a complete college generation.

[1] Robert Hassenger, ed., *The Shape of Catholic Higher Education* (Chicago: University of Chicago Press, 1967), foreword.

A further complication is the recurring necessity of speaking in general terms of liberal arts colleges and universities, of obsolete liberal arts colleges for men or women and forward-inclined colleges of tomorrow, of the very good and the very mediocre, of the six or seven major Catholic universities and some thirty-two other institutions that style themselves universities by grace of a charter from the state legislature.

Counting everything in any way in sight, one can come up with a grand total of 457 American institutions of higher learning under the loose rubric of "Catholic Higher Education—1968."[2] Of these, 253 have fewer than 300 full-time students. Of this latter number, 189 are for clerics or sisters and 64 for lay students. But 165 institutions have less than 100 full-time students. In this last grouping are 147 colleges run primarily for religious and clergy, with 18 for the laity. Of the 139 institutions founded since 1950, only 3 have more than 300 full-time students. One can be readily excused for wondering why Catholic educators never came up with an academic "pill" to control institutional fertility.

*   *   *

"Building quickly, borrowing freely, expanding rapidly," says Edward Wakin, "educators at Catholic colleges and universities, often seem intoxicated with their success in the postwar education boom." Most of them, he adds, "rushed into the 1960's as if there were no tomorrow in which they would have to take stock and re-examine their enterprises."[3] Tomorrow has dawned with a vengeance and the day of reckoning is already begun.

Despite the fact that an increasing number of Americans are going to college, enrollment in Catholic institutions is dropping. At the same time more and more money is needed to operate these schools. It is not simply a question of rising costs that threaten to price private higher education out of the market. The immediate question is whether or not public policy will continue to support a strong dual system of higher education and if not, except for a few institutions, whether quality education under private auspices is headed

[2] Figures taken from Charles E. Ford and Edgar L. Roy, *The Renewal of Catholic Higher Education* (Washington, D.C.: National Catholic Educational Association, 1968).

[3] "How Catholic Is the Catholic College?" *Saturday Review*, April, 1966, p. 92.

for oblivion. The trend since 1945, when the private institutions enrolled 60 per cent of the college population, has been steadily downward, until today their share is just below 30 per cent. The prediction is that within ten years 85 per cent will be enrolled in public institutions.

Particularly among the 800-plus church-related collegiate institutions, administrators are nervously eyeing the barometer, whose reading tells of financial storms, already beginning to sweep across private-school campuses. In fact, many of these institutions—including the 233 senior colleges and universities related to the Catholic Church—face an uncertain future.

The irony of the situation is that total college enrollment for the 1968–69 academic year was at an all-time high—over 7,000,000—and the U. S. Office of Education predicts that enrollment, beginning this year and continuing through the rest of the decade, will increase by 49 per cent, four times the growth of the total population.

Data from 170 of the four-year Catholic colleges and universities show that for the last two years slightly less than one-half met their predicted freshman enrollment.[4] In some cases the drop in freshman students was one-fourth of the anticipated total, and this while the 1968–69 freshman enrollment was increasing nationally by an estimated 8 to 10 per cent.

Scattered reports from other private institutions verify the conclusion that almost all America's private collegiate institutions are facing a critical period from which some will not emerge and that, as the price of survival, others will have to amalgamate with other institutions, surrender partial or total control, change their purpose, or settle for a less selective clientele. From the point of view of strengthening the totality of American higher education, these prices may not be too high. Yet there remains a note of dismay, particularly at the thought of the threatened passing of many small liberal arts colleges with church connections that in the past have so much enriched American society. They deserve a better fate than to follow the corner grocery store into the belly of the educational supermarket. For them and private schools generally, money—or lack of money—is the root of almost all evils.

All but the most handsomely endowed private colleges must lean

[4] Unpublished study done by the Office for Educational Research, University of Notre Dame. For other statistics see *The Chronicle of Higher Education,* November 11, 1968.

on student tuition and fees as their principal source of revenue. These institutions, lacking a solid endowment, must build their operating budget almost completely upon the predicted income from anticipated enrollment. A drop of 20–30 per cent in numbers can have disastrous effects on the year's operation, forcing drastic austerities that can well-nigh suffocate the life of the institution. In near-panic, the ax is swung. Funds for research or publication or travel to meetings are slashed. Faculty members get heavier teaching loads. Class size is enlarged and seminar-type classes are curtailed. Salary increases and promotions are slowed. Teachers with modest credentials and no experience replace distinguished professionals departing in frustration. Admission standards are lowered and, at length, the very reason for the existence of the private college—personalized quality education—becomes forgotten except in the proud prose of the catalogue.

And as yet we have said nothing about capital expenditures. The Higher Education Facilities Act, which provides federal grants up to one-third of construction costs, still leaves the problem of finding the two-thirds matching funds required by the law. At first sight, a private gift of $500,000 or $1,000,000 for a memorial building looks most appealing. But every additional building, like each new member of a family, increases the operational budget. Since the post-World War II boom, the Catholic colleges and universities have diverted a huge proportion of their unrestricted income into buildings. Heavy interest payments have blotted up current funds, and the academic budget has been starved.

To what extent Catholic collegiate institutions, in general, depend upon tuition revenue can be gathered from the fact that the ten largest endowments among Catholic universities combined just about equal the endowment of Princeton and are less than one-fifth that of Harvard.[5]

On the other hand, Catholic institutions, at least so far, have had an equivalent kind of endowment in the contributed services of the

[5] The most recent endowment statistics are in *American Universities and Colleges* (American Council on Education, 1964). The figures are (in millions): Notre Dame, $38.1; St. Louis, $22.0; Loyola (Chicago), $11.9; St. John's (N.Y.), $11.4; Georgetown, $11.0; Catholic University, $10.4; Marquette, $9.1; Seton Hall, $7.6; Boston College, $7.2; San Francisco, $5.6. No figures are listed for Fordham. Princeton's endowment is $133.6 and Harvard's is $765.5. In the past three years Notre Dame and Georgetown have doubled their endowments, but Harvard's is now almost $1 billion.

staff persons with priestly or religious order vows. These people, many of whom are scholars and teachers of top-level earning power, receive no actual cash recompense for their services except living expenses. Where priests, brothers, and sisters are still the mainstay of the faculty and administration, as is the case with practically all but the twenty-nine major Catholic institutions with enrollments of over 2000 students, this "living" endowment has meant fiscal salvation. Given a college of fewer than 750 students (131 Catholic schools fall into this category) and a faculty of forty that might include thirty nuns or priests, the contributed equivalent salaries can mean as much as $250,000 or the interest at 5 per cent on a real endowment of $5,000,000.

But what of the future? It is a blunt fact that the orders and dioceses no longer have the manpower to staff and administer their institutions as they have in the recent past. Vocations to both the priesthood and religious life are dropping sharply. Since Catholic enrollment in the secular and state collegiate institutions will continue to rise sharply, more and more talented religious and priests will find these campuses the locus of their Christian service. Though over 1300 Newman chaplains are on the roster, fewer than 500 are full-time. There are Newman programs on over 1200 secular and non-Catholic campuses but only 300 centers with chapel and meeting facilities. The need here is great. It is predictable that an increasing pattern will be the Catholic center on the secular campus, staffed by a group of priests and religious. These latter will hold professorial chairs, work in counseling, and do pastoral work—all the while helping to build a Christian community.

*   *   *

If the American college-going population is on the increase—and it certainly is—how explain the declining enrollment among these church-related institutions? There are two good reasons: tuition and competition.

The price of a college education, like that of most commodities involving labor costs, has soared. The U. S. Office of Education reports that in the decade 1955–65, college costs tripled.[6] The rise was from $5 billion to $15.2 billion. In 1955, a student could figure

[6] *Digest of Educational Statistics and Projections of Educational Statistics,* U. S. Office of Education, 1966.

on spending $1815 for his year at college, but ten years later his younger brother had to spend $2442. If they have a brother in college in 1975, he will have to pay out an estimated $2976 for his year of schooling. These are average figures, for all types of colleges. If the brothers have attended or will attend a private college, however, the average costs are and will be higher for each of the three interval years: in 1955, $1875; in 1965, $3102; in 1975, $4294. These figures include tuition and fees, board and room, and ordinary related living and educational expenses. Catholic schools that in 1960 were charging $200 to 400 per year now ask a tuition of $800 to 1200, in many cases a 400 per cent rise. A score of Catholic institutions have moved into the $1500 to 2000 bracket.

Competition for the better and best students is an old story. A number of Catholic institutions shared in what was once a widely held assumption that, in general, private colleges and universities had superior faculties, attracted more of the outstanding students, and offered a more ideal learning environment. Whatever imbalance may have earlier existed here is rapidly being righted, at least so far as quality of faculty goes. The scramble for "name" faculty and the auction for the brilliant young Ph.D.'s whose acquisition promises to add to a school's academic prestige grows costlier year after year.

And of course this largely explains why the customer must pay more and more for an education and why the state legislatures continually add to the tax load. Moreover, competition among schools, not simply to attract but to hold on to glamour personnel, is as keen as if it were a question of professional quarterbacks, Italian movie actresses, or Madison Avenue vice-presidents. No school dares fall too far behind in the race or it weakens its appeal to better students. An outstanding faculty draws outstanding students, who give an institution an outstanding reputation, which attracts financial support to pay an outstanding faculty, which draws outstanding students, etc. Despite the grotesqueness that the competition at times assumes, behind it all is the sober awareness that academic quality results from the encounter of good minds in the proper atmosphere. No institution openly pledges itself to the achievement of mediocrity. Whether it be by the catalogue or the public relations office or the president, Alma Mater is invariably festooned in paraphrases of "quality," "excellence," "distinction," "leadership," and "superiority."

By dint of enormous expenditures, hard work, and God's grace, many Catholic institutions have made important strides forward, but, like Alice in the race in Wonderland, they may be only holding their own. Despite the gains made in the area of capital improvements and operational excellence during the past five years, most Catholic institutions are in a relatively weaker position, as compared with other institutions, than they were in 1965. It is a shattering experience to discover that many of the new state universities (the teachers' colleges of ten years ago or struggling infants of five years ago) have resources in many areas far beyond those dreamed of by Catholic universities.

The recent Jencks-Riesman volume points out that the scholarly ratings of universities do not change much over the years. "Quite aside from their Catholicism or lack of it," is the comment, "currently second-rank institutions are likely to be second-rank a generation hence." Of even more significance is the book's next comment:

> One or two Catholic institutions might break into the charmed circle if the church were able to come up with a master plan concentrating resources on them, but this is unlikely. The pressure to spread resources is as great in the church as elsewhere. Tomorrow's Catholic colleges are therefore likely to occupy much the same position in the academic spectrum as today's."[7]

Catholic higher education has shown its broadest best on the undergraduate level. In fact, a few Catholic liberal arts colleges and undergraduate divisions of Catholic universities are regionally and nationally recognized as among the nation's leaders. A number of other places are moving rapidly in that direction. Almost all Catholic institutions can point to some department or departments where on the undergraduate level they rank reasonably well.

However, when one surveys the total university situation, the Catholic institutions are lagging far behind. Though thirty-eight institutions under Catholic direction characterize themselves as "universities," and a thirty-ninth, Boston College, should, only eighteen offer doctoral programs. From 1960 through 1966, American universities awarded 92,863 doctorates. Among the hundred leading doctorate-granting institutions were the Catholic University (thirty-

[7] Christopher Jencks and David Riesman, *The Academic Revolution* (Garden City, N.Y.: Doubleday & Co., 1968), p. 403.

ninth with 739 degrees), Fordham (sixtieth with 452), Notre Dame (sixty-fourth with 428), St. Louis (seventy-third with 360), Georgetown (eighty-sixth with 267), and Loyola of Chicago (ninety-fourth with 207).

In terms of faculty and student quality, library holdings, research grants, and facilities, how do these schools measure up? The most recent index is the Cartter study of the 106 universities which averaged at least ten doctorates yearly in the 1953–62 period.[8] Unsurprisingly, the study confirmed the reputation of Harvard, California at Berkeley, Yale, Michigan, Columbia, and Stanford as national leaders in graduate education. From the optimist's point of view, the Cartter study established that the Catholic University, Fordham, Georgetown, Notre Dame, and St. Louis have among them fourteen graduate departments, rated as "good" or "adequate" on a six-step scale: (1) *distinguished,* (2) *strong,* (3) *good,* (4) *adequate,* (5) *marginal,* (6) *insufficient* (for doctoral program). Though no Catholic university department is found in the categories of *distinguished* or *strong,* the fact that a number of departments are in the third and fourth categories place some programs among the leading 20 of the 106 institutions surveyed.

There is, however, another point of view. This is simply not good enough. The fulcrum of influence in the contemporary world is the university. Increasingly, government, industry, world trade, diplomacy, the churches, labor, and management are turning, almost by reflex, to the modern university for knowledge and brain power. Had the American Catholic community combined its resources to establish a few centers of eminence in graduate-level work, the picture today would be different. The scramble for support and the parochial rivalries between institutions (even those operated by the same religious order) have fragmentized and dissipated Catholic resources. Moreover, the compulsion of the American bishops to establish and support vast numbers of elementary and secondary schools has meant no "official" support to speak of for Catholic institutions of higher learning. Whether it is now too late to build up four or five great university centers under Catholic inspiration and direction is a moot point. One point is clear, though: if it does not happen soon, it will be too late, and the world will be the poorer for the lack.

[8] *An Assessment of Quality in Education* (Washington, D.C.: American Council on Education, 1966).

*   *   *

One could jokingly say that the trouble with Catholic education began the day that the first lay teacher was hired. Historically the college and the religious community were totally integrated. The administration and operation of the college was simply a continuation of the community structure. The father abbot or rector of the community served likewise as president of the college. College and community finances were pooled, and given the straitened circumstances of their early years, the community supported their college. One should not get the impression that when religious or clerics faculty spoke of "our" school, this was some kind of a self-serving enterprise. Robert Henle has written sensitively on the point:

. . . they were wholly conscious that they were engaged in an apostolic endeavor for the benefit of the students entrusted to them and for the benefit of the church, and their dedication to the children and to the church was deep, sincere, and most effective. Whatever their training may have lacked, for the most part, they have had a tremendous influence on their students and were loved and revered by generations of Catholics.[9]

The problem of recruiting and holding first-grade faculty is formidable for those institutions that are neither tax-supported nor well-endowed—among them most Catholic schools. Since the day is over, even in the smaller colleges, when a Catholic college or university can count on its own religious or priests to assume most of the teaching load, the choice is simply what kind of lay teachers the school is prepared to engage. If they are to be the best available, the institution must recognize that excellence must be appropriately recompensed.

Nor is Mr. Chips the answer. Once upon a less frenzied time, his love of the church or of the Congregation of the Holy Grail or of dear old St. Aelred's itself compensated both for Mr. Chips's modest professional preparation and inadequate stipend. The lingering innocence on the part of some church-related college presidents with reference to this fact of academic life explains in part the mediocrity that will continue to blight their institutions until they pass out of existence. Not that anything has changed the ideal of dedication

[9] "A Report on the American Catholic University," submitted to the International Federation of Catholic Universities, April, 1968.

for which Mr. Chips stands. Rather, some institutions have for too long a time been taking advantage of Mr. Chips.

It is true that the position of the pedagogue has traditionally been considered a kind of special vocation that provides much of its satisfaction in the realm of the intangible. Somehow these rewards have had to compensate in some measure for the lack of cold coin. Teachers and professors do value the more leisurely nine-month working year, the extra holidays and vacations for study and research, the prestige of the professional position, the privilege of membership in the academic community, and the satisfaction of sharing knowledge with colleagues and disciples. On the other hand, the college professor can point to the heavy expenses of his years of advanced degree preparation, often as not with accompanying indebtedness, the heavy outlay for books and periodicals, as well as the memberships and travel associated with his field of specialization, and the cultural level of living expected of him.

In recent years, the teaching profession through its professional organization, the American Association of University Professors (AAUP), has been able to exert strong pressure on college administrations and governing boards to improve salaries. Each year the national office of the AAUP invites all institutions to participate in a study of the economic status of the profession by completing a detailed questionnaire on salary practices.

The first study, in 1959–60, involved 332 institutions. The report published in 1968 contained figures from 1000 colleges and universities. Because of the close attention accorded these reports within the academic profession, administrators and boards of trustees greet their appearance with mixed emotions. These published reports, however, have effectively helped to narrow the gap between the earnings of a college professor and those of other professional classes, to say nothing of truck drivers, plumbers, and electricians.

The AAUP study has set up average and minimum compensation scales according to seven categories—AA through F—for each of the standard academic ranks: professor, associate, assistant, and instructor. In 1967–68, for example, the average salary scale established for a full professor ranged from the AA category of $25,750 to the F category of $7720. In turn, the range for an associate professor began at $15,140 and descended to $7630; for an assistant professor, from $11,610 to $6760; for an instructor from $8710 to

$5950.[10] Though an institution received a rating for each of the four ranks, its overall grade comes from the letter for the lowest-compensated rank—a fact that can, in some instances, distort the picture. Conceivably, St. Borgia's College could be paying A salaries to its associates, assistants, and instructors (the great majority of any faculty), but because its full professors' salaries fall into the D category, the school would receive an overall rating of D.

The names of 120 American Catholic institutions were among the 1000 that figured in the 1967–68 study of salary practices but five have to be left aside because they failed to submit current figures. Thus we speak more accurately of 115 of the nation's 233 Catholic colleges and universities as active participants in the study. Possibly a few of the silent schools regarded the study as an invasion of privacy or lost the questionnaire. Perhaps one or two other schools were simply modest about their achievements in providing for their faculty. But unhappily the unwillingness of 118 Catholic colleges and universities to submit to a professional measurement can only be called myopic.

How did the 115 reporting schools compare with other schools throughout the nation, according to average professional compensation? Some of them were remarkably high in the scale; most of them were an average good; a few were substandard but evidently improving.

No school of any kind attained the rather idealistic AA rating in all four ranks. There were thirty-seven institutions in the single A category and no Catholic school was among them. Boston College, Marquette, Notre Dame, Saint Mary's (California), and Santa Clara, however, just missed because of a B for the rank of full professor. Catholic University, Fordham, Georgetown, Holy Cross, and St. John's (Minnesota) were A or B for all four categories. Another twenty-seven institutions were A or B in three of the four categories, and an additional twenty-one of the total 115 institutions placed twice in either the A or B categories, usually for the lower professional ranks, which means that most of their faculties were receiving better than average recompense.

Are these figures discouraging? Not when compared with the progress made over the past eight years. In the original AAUP study, for the 1959–60 school year, only eleven Catholic institutions took

[10] *American Association of University Professors Bulletin,* June, 1968.

part and two of them did not authorize publication of their salary figures. Only one Catholic school appeared among the sixty-two institutions receiving an overall rank of C or better on the then-average compensation of $7960.

All of this, of course, costs money, and for the Catholic (and most other) private colleges money has to come from tuition. The question is: How far can the spiral ascend before church-related education becomes the prerogative only of the affluent? Today a student's desire for a distinctive religiously oriented college education is very much conditioned by his or her family's ability to meet the price. It once was argued that those who want it badly enough would find the way. It was pointed out that federal loans, part-time work, partial scholarships, etc., are available. This they are, and many collegians take advantage of these opportunities to attend private schools. However, because of the tight money market in recent years the federally guaranteed loan program has fallen woefully short of its promise. In 1967 only 430,000 of an estimated 962,000 students were able to get loans, because the banks found it more profitable to lend money to other borrowers at higher interest than the 6 per cent allowed by law.

On the other hand, it is easy to understand how a youngster, a girl, particularly, hesitates to contract debt and prefers to avoid the burden of outside work, especially—and this is the critical new factor—since relatively inexpensive publicly-supported colleges are springing up everywhere. Taxes are rising to pay for them: why not use them? Last year the states spent over $5 billion on higher education just for operating expenses, triple the sum spent eight years ago and a 43 per cent increase in the past two years alone.

The squeeze on the private colleges is clearly seen in the case of Illinois. Along with $616,000,000 to operate during the 1967–69 biennium, the state's tax-supported universities and colleges asked for an additional $1 billion to cover the construction and operation of new public institutions. Though the private institutions of Illinois in 1966–67 had places for another seventeen thousand students, the executive director of the State Board of Higher Education argued that the increased number of students would be coming largely from families with no history of college-going and would be attending a college simply because one was at hand.

Whether he likes it or not, the president of the typical private college or university today must allot a great deal of time to the task of raising funds from voluntary sources. This job is distasteful and often severely hampers his opportunity to provide leadership on his own campus and in the wider service of society. How successful has his pursuit of the dollar been?

The all-time high was set in 1964–65, with a grand total of better than $1.2 billion.[11] This sum included gifts from alumni and friends, church agencies, foundations, business, and industry. Leading the list were Princeton ($53,000,000) and Harvard ($51,000,000), but another seven universities each reported upward of $20,000,000. An additional eleven institutions each acquired between $10,500,000 and $17,500,000; these included Georgetown, Notre Dame, and St. Louis. In all, 240 colleges and universities each received $1,000,-000 or more.

But that river of gold has been drying up these past few years, and the expense of operating a university is inexorably mounting. To stay in business on a competitive basis with the state universities, the big, private institutions are out, hat in hand, knocking on doors.

Columbia has undertaken a three-year campaign to raise $200,-000,000. Chicago is asking $360,000,000 over a ten-year period, while neighboring Northwestern is going for $180,000,000 on a five-year campaign. Over the next four years Duke seeks $100,000,000 and, aided by a $25,000,000 grant from the Ford Foundation, New York University is nearing completion of its $100,000,000 drive. Yale plans a $100,000,000 campaign for gifts over the next decade.

For the less affluent and less prestigious schools, the situation is moving from grim to desperate. Without massive assistance from government, both federal and state, without enormously increased support from foundations, industry, and other private sources, the deserving institutions will have to sacrifice quality to survive, while many borderline or mediocre ones will most probably not survive. The competition for support prompted Cardinal Cushing's ominous prediction: "The future of higher education is on the state university campus because the charity dollar can no longer compete with the tax dollar."

A ray of sunshine in the darkening sky is that government is beginning to accept the position that it best serves the public interest by helping to maintain a strong system of nonpublic higher education. In turn, acceptance of this principle is blurring the distinc-

[11] Statistics from Council for Financial Aid to Education, Report for 1966.

tion between public and private education. At least as far as funding goes, public institutions are receiving massive support from private sources—foundations, business, industry, friends, and alumni. For their part, some private universities are coming to be heavily subsidized by the state; e.g., one-half of the operating budget for Columbia and Harvard comes from the federal government.

Private higher education sees that it has little choice but to turn to the state and federal governments for financial help. After going through literal bankruptcy, the University of Pittsburgh became a "state-related" institution of the commonwealth of Pennsylvania, which means that over half of its operating budget comes from the state. Temple University in Philadelphia has assumed the same relationship to the commonwealth. Every accredited four-year collegiate institution in New York, except seminaries, qualifies for direct grants by the state for each student enrolled. The size of the grant is determined by the degree level: for a student pursuing a bachelor's or masters's degree the sum is $400, and for the doctor's degree it is $2400. A growing number of states have established college scholarships given on a basis of ability or need, or both, to be used at any accredited institution within that state. Among these states are California, New York, Illinois, and Michigan.

In a historic about-face, the Association of American Universities in June, 1968, issued a joint appeal to the federal government to assume a greater share of the cost of higher education. The appeal by this prestigious forty-two-member organization combined the interests of both public and private education. They were in agreement that while present federal programs for specific purposes like research and residence halls are vital, there is a desperate need for operational subsidy on a regular and continuing basis for private education. They also stated that some national norms will have to be developed for distribution of federal largess that would combine the quantity of service to the community and the quality of the education dispensed. Last August the Carnegie Commission on Higher Education urged that the federal government double its aid to higher education from $4 billion to $8 billion yearly in order to meet urgent national priorities. What will all this mean for Catholic higher education?

Over the past twenty years Catholic institutions of higher learning have been able to grow largely through participation in federal programs that provided loans and grants for housing and educational facilities. It would be disastrous if they could no longer qualify for these government grants and loans as well as for funds for research and equipment, fellowships, and scholarships, just as other institutions do. In June of 1967, however, the Maryland Court of Appeals ruled that a law providing state grants for educational facilities to three church-affiliated colleges was invalid. The attorney general of Maryland then appealed the decision to the U. S. Supreme Court. The Court did not see fit to accept jurisdiction and allowed the lower court decision to stand. Since the eligibility of any sectarian institution for federal grants has already been challenged on grounds of violating the First Amendment, it is predictable that shortly the courts will address themselves to this issue.

Would a restructuring of ownership and control obviate this problem? Some years back, when Loyola University was competing for the New Orleans CBS television outlet, the question of foreign ownership came up. The U. S. Court of Appeals (District of Columbia circuit) upheld Loyola's claim that it was a "domestic" (i.e., American) corporation chartered by the state of Louisiana, despite the fact that final control was then thought to be vested in the Holy See in Rome. The U. S. Supreme Court declined review. Had jurisdiction been accepted, however, and a contrary decision handed down, all Catholic institutions would probably have been barred from federal programs. If the same question arises again, the federal courts may demand complete local autonomy, i.e., separate incorporation of the institution outside the sponsoring religious order, as a condition for participation in federal programs.

The question of public support from the states is more complicated by reason of the restrictions written into most individual state constitutions. Last fall Fordham released a study by Walter Gellhorn and R. Kent Greenawalt of the Columbia University Law School which addressed itself to the question: "What must Fordham do to achieve legal parity with other private independent universities in New York State?" The study was commissioned by Fordham to determine what modifications in its structure and mode of operation might be necessary to become eligible for financial assistance from the state. The so-called Blaine Amendment bars public monies to any school under denominational control. Though almost all the Gellhorn-Greenawalt recommendations for change could be accepted (many had in fact already been planned), several others could not be without sacrificing Fordham's Jesuit sponsorship and Catholic commitments.

It helps clarify the basic question to ask who actually owns the buildings, property, and other assets that make up Georgetown or Santa Clara or St. Catherine's? Technically, ownership is vested in a self-perpetuating board of trustees, comprising three or five or seven or whatever number of members of the religious order, appointed by a provincial. "Ownership" here, however, is used only by analogy. The ownership of a university or college does, of course, in several ways resemble ownership of income-producing property, but in at least two crucial aspects it does not.

The men and women associated in the work of higher education are not simply employees with an exclusively salary relationship to the trustees of the university. The young, highly professional lay teacher resents the "master-servant" idea of his relationship to the university. Any talk of a lay-religious "partnership" in higher education makes little sense until the assets of the college are completely separated from those of the religious community. A number of Catholic institutions have taken, and are taking, this step. If there is any lingering ambiguity on the point of ownership it should be dispelled by the McGrath study, *The Canonical and Civil Law Status of Catholic Institutions in the United States.* One key paragraph states:

Charitable and educational institutions chartered as corporations under American law are not *owned* by the sponsoring body. The legal title to the real and personal property is vested in the corporation. It is the corporation that cares for the sick or grants academic degrees. It is the corporation that buys and sells and borrows money. If anyone *owns* the assets of the charitable or educational institution, it is the general public. Failure to appreciate this fact has led to the mistaken idea that the property of the institution is the property of the sponsoring body.[12]

The ownership of a college or university is not proprietary, but rather a trust with accountability to the various publics the institution serves and with responsibility for attaining the objectives for which it was chartered. By contrast with the misunderstanding in the Catholic sphere, no one regards the civic leaders making up the Harvard board of overseers or the board of trustees of the Uni-

[12] John J. McGrath, *Catholic Institutions in the United States* (Washington, D.C.: Catholic University of America Press, 1968), p. 33.

versity of California as "owners" of these institutions in any literal sense. They are considered public servants who hold a public trust. The college or university, no matter what the sponsorship, is a creature of the natural order and hence is governed by the laws and principles of the natural academic order. It is chartered by the state as a civil corporation for a public purpose, and as such enjoys certain privileges and immunities, e.g., tax exemption, eminent domain, draft deferment of students, and judicial exception. Administrators and trustees of a Catholic college or university are also then stewards of the public trust.

And yet for understandable historical reasons society was not clearly aware of this reality. Without exception the earliest foundations were under church sponsorship and clerical control. The reason is obvious: the churches supported the institutions. Little money was forthcoming from Congress or the state legislatures. The era of princely private benefactions did not dawn until huge personal fortunes became relatively common. Storr notes that "between the Revolutionary and Civil Wars, Harvard received less than a quarter of a million dollars in large gifts, exclusive of funds raised by subscription, although its alumni and friends must have included many of the richest college men in the country."[13]

The Puritans had founded Harvard College in 1636, modeled on Emmanuel College of Cambridge with the mottoes *Christo et Ecclesiae* and *In Christi Gloriam*. The Anglicans undertook William and Mary in 1639 and by the dawn of the American Revolution seven other colleges were organized under religious sponsorship: Yale, Princeton, Washington and Lee, Columbia, Brown, Rutgers, and Dartmouth. An eighth, Pennsylvania, was the only one without direct church affiliation. Ordained or licensed clergymen filled the chief administrative offices and did much of the teaching. Even into the twentieth century, clergymen held the presidency of such institutions as Princeton and Brown.

In fact, American society early became used to the idea that the support and management of higher education were a prime responsibility of the churches which, in turn, used the colleges to prepare their clergy. Colleges sprang up everywhere, many built on the most precarious financial foundation. Taking the Catholic colle-

[13] Richard J. Storr, *The Beginnings of Graduate Education in America* (Chicago: University of Chicago Press, 1953), p. 4.

giate foundations alone, only one out of four founded before 1850 survives today, about one in three founded between 1850 and 1899 are still doing business, and a bare 36 per cent of those opened between 1900 and 1955 are yet with us.[14]

The instinctive reaction of some people to the thought of transferring title of ownership, or even sharing responsibility for ownership with the laity, is that proponents of these ideas are betraying the order's patrimony and surrendering to secular forces. Alongside the fear and insecurity is a legitimate concern. For it is true that the control of property is a basic protection for educational commitment. It would be absurd to set in motion a train of circumstances that would empty Catholic institutions of the very reason for their existence. One can look in any direction today and see great institutions that began with a firm religious commitment—Harvard, Yale, Columbia, Southern California, Chicago, Amherst—and have lost all but symbolic vestiges of their Christian origin. Those who push these examples, however, lack confidence in the kind of machinery that could be established and the kind of trustees that could be assembled to guarantee a perpetuity of the original commitment by the founding group.[15]

It seems incomprehensible that a group of lay trustees would make the superhuman effort to finance and operate a university indistinguishable from its neighboring state-supported or richly-endowed private rivals. Moreover, given a clear definition of the nature and objectives of the institution in its charter, it should not be difficult to select as members of the board persons who are known to be in complete sympathy with the broad objectives that have guided the institution from its inception. If no such laymen can be

---

[14] Edward J. Powers, *A History of Catholic Higher Education in the United States* (Milwaukee: Bruce Publishing Company, 1958), p. 47.

[15] St. Louis and Notre Dame both have made provision for reasonable insurance against an abrupt reversal of basic commitment to the Christian and Catholic tradition embodied in each place, respectively, for 150 and 125 years. At St. Louis a two-thirds vote of the trustees is required for a substantive change in the by-laws or disposal of property. At Notre Dame, two-thirds of the "fellows of the university" (of the twelve fellows, one-half are Holy Cross Fathers) must similarly approve changes in the by-laws. Indeed, this is a common arrangement. At Emory 70 per cent of the board members must belong to the Methodist Church; at American, 60 per cent; at Southern Methodist, 50 per cent. Until relatively recent years Chicago and Southern California reserved places on the board for members of the church.

found among its alumni, friends, and benefactors—that is, men and women, lay and cleric, who are deeply committed to the goals of the institution as the founding religious group—then our Catholic colleges and universities have indeed failed.

*   *   *

In what may well have been the most sweeping innovation in the history of Catholic higher education, during the first six months of 1967 three religious orders that run institutions of higher learning— St. Louis, Notre Dame, and Webster—announced plans to immediately surrender exclusive ownership and their control over policy. While the Society of Jesus, the Congregation of the Holy Cross, and the Sisters of Loretto, respectively, remain the sponsoring group, legal ownership, and final authority over administration and policy have become invested in boards of trustees whose majority is lay. At the same time a score of other Catholic-managed institutions began to invite "outsiders" to serve on their legal governing boards.

Nor was money the primary reason, even though there are Catholic educators who still labor under the illusion that the only problems besetting Catholic higher education are financial. Granted that these problems are enormous and pressing, they are not the critical problems. A blank check on the state treasury or the federal reserve would not solve problems like the dominance of religious orders, reliance on Old World tradition, amateurish administration, shortsighted financial policies, confusion between the pastoral and academic areas, insulation from the main stream of contemporary thought, and lack of definition of purpose. Almost all these are problems that flow from nonrecognition of the character of the work of contemporary higher education.

A university is something that belongs to the natural order, and its operational principles and the virtues of its community are not those of the religious house and its community. The university community functions in a collegiate manner as it discharges its responsibility for the discovery, transmission, and application of truth. Apprentices are admitted to the community to learn from masters and doctors. Competence, experience, and seniority are the coin of the university community. Senior professors and scholars earn the right to enter into the appropriate level of policy-making both directly and through representatives. The Catholic university or college can by no means escape the natural law governing the operation of the academic community. In the university community, religious paternalism is out of place.

Vatican II's "Decree on the Apostolate of the Laity" insists that all the elements making up the temporal order "possess their own intrinsic value," and that this value "has been implanted in them by God, whether they are considered in themselves or as parts of the whole temporal order."[16] Moreover, even though God has united all things, both natural and supernatural, in Christ Jesus, this "not only does not deprive the temporal order of its independence, its proper goals, laws, resources, and significance for human welfare, but rather perfects the temporal order in its own intrinsic strength and excellence and raises it to the level of man's total vocation upon earth."[17]

Moreover, the document argues: "The laity must take on the renewal of the temporal order as their own special obligation. Led by the light of the gospel and the mind of the church, and motivated by Christian love, let them act directly and definitely in the temporal sphere. As citizens they must co-operate with other citizens, using their own particular skills and acting on their own responsibility."[18]

Three important conclusions emerge from these words: (1) the temporal order (including the academic world) enjoys its own God-given autonomy; (2) the presence in time of the historical Christ or of the ecclesiastical Christ does not reduce the independence of things in the temporal sphere (including the academic community); (3) the layman has a special obligation and competence for action in the temporal sphere (including the academic area).

People today expect to find at least the same standards of excellence in Catholic schools that they demand of the best private and state institutions. And the present system of government is simply not improving Catholic institutions rapidly enough. It is questionable whether, even with increased financial resources, it ever can do so. If Christian humanism is worth supporting, lay men and women must assume at least equal, and eventually dominant, responsibility for Catholic higher education. Indeed, many thoughtful observers

---

[16] "Decree on the Apostolate of the Laity," Article 7, *The Documents of Vatican II*, ed. by Walter M. Abbott (New York: The America Press, 1966), p. 497.

[17] *Ibid.*

[18] *Ibid.*, p. 498.

feel that such broader support is contingent upon the orders' abdicating *exclusive* control over their institutions. We are no longer living in the collegiate world of the thirties or forties or fifties. Today's college has its own style and character.

Perhaps the most relevant changes today lie in the composition of student body, faculty, and administration. Imperceptibly, but inexorably, a shift has taken place away from the primary and immediate emphasis in the Catholic collegiate institution. Few, if any, Catholic institutions, would not claim to be at least partially selective in admission of students; few, if any of them, can make provision for large numbers of applicants who are unable to pay their own way. In brief, the desire of the student of 1969 for a distinctive Catholic education is largely conditioned by his academic achievement and potential as well as his ability to pay for it. These schools no longer cater to the "poor but good" boy. Catholic higher education is no longer formally and *immediately* apostolic.

As these institutions expanded in size and complexity, they recruited more and more lay teachers and increasingly opened up administrative posts to them. Among lay faculties of Catholic colleges and universities everywhere, there has developed a growing interest in a larger role in everything that affects the institution's operation. Here then is the clash.

The old monastic and religious-order forms of government are, in the nature of things, authoritarian. Dioceses and monasteries and religious houses, despite the development of the concept of collegiality in the church, are still essentially structured by "line" authority. In other words, authority is given to an appointed or elected superior, who then exercises his office as God's representative. His subjects freely submit their will to his as part of their dedication as religious. Obedience, humility, and docility are Christian virtues and many religious in their following of Christ attempt to practice them. But the monarchical structure of the monastery and the ascetical attitudes of the monk can not be extrapolated bodily from the cloister to the campus. To try it is to introduce serious disorder into both.

In the past it was not unusual for religious subjects to be shuffled from their posts without prior discussion or notice, and while such a practice might have had some justification as part and parcel of a venerable ascetical tradition, in the contemporary college and university—for that matter, in any kind of school—it is self-defeating.

It is arguable, moreover, that the essentially familial quality of religious obedience has been overlooked and underdeveloped. Tenure for religious and priests may not be necessary to protect their income but it is vital to protect their status as teachers and researchers. Arbitrary or unilateral removal upsets the fundamental working conditions of the scholar. Granted that, as part of religious commitment, a person has the right through a promise of obedience to place himself under the direction of a superior or bishop, this action cannot totally obliterate the natural freedoms of the academic world. Or if it must, then priests and religious literally have no business there. Some modified style of tenure for these people must be elaborated which will balance their religious commitment with their academic status, and some realistic recompense must be found commensurate with their professional status.

When we look at the scene today, the obvious question arises: Did the original religious constitutions envisage the modern, largely lay-staffed American Catholic university or university college? Is it not something of an anachronism in 1969 that one man or woman, the superior-president, should function as a corporation sole, with almost no institutionalized checks and balances; that practically absolute power—legislative, executive, judicial—should be concentrated in a single office? Is it not a further anachronism that the chief advisers to the superior-president remain the *religious* house consultors? These are the men or women with whom the president is usually required by the constitutions to discuss the major business of the religious house and, in the absence of any other group, of the university.

This anomalous situation is largely traceable to the failure to appreciate the difference between higher education in the United States and in Europe. The most obvious major difference is an essential one. American Catholic colleges and universities as institutions of higher learning receive their charter not from the Holy See, or their order or the Roman Congregation of Seminaries and Universities, but by the act of the particular state in which they are located. Moreover, the continuance of the charter, to say nothing of extensions or modifications, depends upon the act of the particular state. Accordingly, American priests and religious engaged in college-level education are, as we have seen, "stewards of the public trust."

It follows that the first duty of the college is to serve the community according to its needs and its moral demands. This is the sense of "community" or "society," as interpreted in the *Constitution on the Church in the Modern World* and in the *Declaration on Religious Freedom* of Vatican II. Awareness of this public responsibility does not detract from concomitant service to the church, but at the same time it broadens the service and removes it completely from any narrowly parochial or sectarian understanding. In other words, the Catholic college or university must exist to serve the whole American community in following out the reasonable norms and practices that the American experience in education has evolved. Service and influence, not ownership and control, are the overriding concepts. It is ironic that so many of the religious teaching groups whose founders sought only to serve and to bring Christian influence to bear on society through their pioneer educational ventures are today helplessly bogged down in proprietorship of real estate.

The priests and religious engaged in higher education rightfully look upon the institutions they founded as a powerful witness to Christ, the inspiration and goal of Christian humanism. In varying degrees all those who join in the educational work must recognize this commitment. A professor whose personal philosophy of education is in basic disagreement with that of the institution would feel —and be—out of place. At the same time, if the institution fails to articulate its distinctive commitment, it is risking its own integrity. It is inconceivable that a religiously founded and oriented institution would attract scholars and teachers by de-emphasizing or camouflaging its distinctive *raison d'être*. On the other hand, if the institution is not aware that it possesses a distinctive reason for being, the sooner it passes out of existence or under other control, the better.

There are Catholic college administrators who are feverishly trying to project a lay image. They probably figure that acceptance is in proportion to the number of lay deans or vice-presidents which can be displayed in the roster of government so the "in" thing is to look lay.

There is another opinion that would allow every other kind of sponsorship of higher education except by church or religious groups. But this is crude discrimination. A religious congregation or a diocese has as much right to be in education as any other group. In fact, if they hadn't been historically, many of the greatest institutions of the world would not have seen the light of day. It is necessary, however, to distinguish control from *sponsorship*. Jacqueline Grennan has stated that "the very nature of higher education is opposed to juridical control by the churches." She is right—but sponsorship or inspiration is a college of another color.

*   *   *

The future of the liberal arts college for women has come under close scrutiny, and for those, mostly small, institutions under Catholic sponsorship, there are distinctive problems. Nowhere are pastoral motives and moral objectives in the founding and operating of a school more clearly observable than in this large segment of the Catholic higher education world. The religious congregations and dioceses that have spawned the vast number of institutions of this type were principally motivated by concern for the Catholic upbringing of young ladies as well as for their protection from the evils of secular education. Nor was this concern always ill-founded. At least there would seem to have been more justification for this approach relative to women's colleges than in the case of the Catholic men's colleges or the universities.

In our male-dominated culture the education of women, particularly higher education, has always been a topic of warm debate. Though today we have accepted in theory the educational equality of the sexes, it neither was that way always nor is it in practice consistently honored in contemporary society. There was a time when advanced studies for women were viewed with almost universal suspicion and wide misgivings. Bishop Fénelon's solemn affirmation that contact with learning would be almost as fatal to womanly delicacy as contact with vice was a conviction of the seventeenth century, probably no less widespread than the understanding behind the solemn remark of the German philosopher Lessing in the next century, that the woman who thinks is as ridiculous as the man who puts on rouge.

American society was slow to accept collegiate institutions for women, and only a handful existed anywhere prior to the Civil War. So far as the academic world was concerned, the female seminary or the finishing school was supposedly the limit defining the scholarly talents of the fair sex. Womanly ambition was expected to confine itself to more genteel pursuits than questing for degrees.

Efforts to emancipate the American woman from her kitchen or sewing room were frequently hooted at by commentators of the contemporary scene.[19]

However, as society shifted in its general attitude concerning the role of woman, this change came to be reflected in the structure of education. Originally a collegiate education was simply conceived of as preparation for a profession. Since the ministry, law, medicine, and management were male preserves, it would be the rarest of families that would even think of college for the girl. Then where could she go? The single profession where she did have entree was teaching, and as the drive for universal free education spread over the land, the need for trained teachers led both to the founding of normal schools for women and the opening of existing institutions to them.[20] In 1836 Mary Lyon founded the Mount Holyoke Female Seminary in western Massachusetts. Her stated aim was teacher education, with secondary aims of religious education and health education. During its first forty years, Mount Holyoke sent over 70 per cent of its graduates into teaching.

Almost from its foundation in 1833, Oberlin College in Ohio admitted women students, with the first three lady "bachelors" receiving the A.B. degree in 1840 on equal terms with the male graduates. Another Ohio college, Antioch, founded in 1853 with Horace Mann as first president, was coeducational from its inception. Edward J. Powers speaks of 209 institutions for the higher education of women in existence by 1875 but points out that most were only

[19] When the Kentucky legislature granted a college charter to Van Doren's College for Young Ladies at Lexington, with the right to confer a diploma and honorary degrees of M.P.L. (Mistress of Polite Literature), M.M. (Mistress of Music), and M.I. (Mistress of Instruction), a Southern editor in his account of the action was prompted to some caustic suggestions about additional degrees that might be awarded the ladies. He offered for the consideration of his readers: M.P.M. (Mistress of Pudding Making), M.D.N. (Mistress of the Darning Needle), M.S.B. (Mistress of the Scrubbing Brush), and M.C.S. (Mistress of Common Sense). As honorary degrees he suggested: H.W. (Happy Wife), H.H. (Happy Husband) and finally M.W.R.F. (Mother of a Well-Regulated Family). From an unpublished dissertation, cited in Powers, *op. cit.,* pp. 180–81.

[20] By the 1860's teaching was still the career par excellence for women but precedents were being set in other fields. At the time of the Civil War, there were more than five hundred women doctors and some seventy among the clergy. There were fewer than ten lawyers and the first lady was admitted to the bar in 1869.

academies, with perhaps not more than six of actual college status.[21] The University of Deseret, founded in 1850 (later to become the University of Utah), and the State University of Iowa, launched in 1855, were also begun on a coeducational basis. After the Land-Grant College Act of 1862 and the consequent rise of the state universities, the number of new foundations of women's colleges declined sharply—except among Catholics.[22]

Though late-comers to the field, the religious congregations of women and the bishops zestfully made up for decades lost. The first four-year Catholic college for women, the College of Notre Dame of Maryland in 1896, came out of an older academy for girls, the Institute of Notre Dame. The first college actually founded and chartered as such was Trinity College in Washington in 1900. By 1905 there were five such institutions in existence, and ten years later there were nineteen. Between 1915 and 1930, Catholic women's colleges sprang up like dandelions after a spring shower—by actual count fifty-six, or almost four foundations per year. The listing by Powers gives 119 four-year colleges and an additional twenty-one junior colleges but that was ten years ago; many have been founded since.

Only thirty-two have an enrollment of over 750, which many educators today would consider a bare minimum for academic adequacy and economic viability. There are distinguished exceptions to this rule-of-thumb but one can be pardoned for wondering if all *fifty* of the Catholic liberal arts colleges for women whose enrollment is *below 500* are exceptions. It is fair to inquire how many major degree programs, how varied the course offerings, how deep and well-prepared the faculty, how adequate the library and laboratories, how well-compensated the lay faculty and staff, how qualified the students can be in a four-year collegiate-level institution with fewer than 500 full-time students.

The Ford-Roy study of Catholic colleges and universities published in 1968 lists 142 institutions primarily for laywomen. Of this total thirty-three have opened their doors since 1950. Moreover, it found eighty-four junior colleges (some for men, some coed) new

21 Powers, *op. cit.,* p. 195.

22 Justin Smith Morrill, elected to the U. S. House of Representatives in 1854, championed federal aid programs to education. Morrill introduced the Land-Grant College Act in 1857. Though vetoed by Buchanan, the act was signed into law by Abraham Lincoln in 1862.

on the scene since 1950. In all, it arrived at a total of 139 Catholic collegiate institutions established since 1950, and made the pointed observation that at that writing 115 had not received regional accreditation. Going into 1966 there were 196 collegiate entities not regionally accredited but 107, or 55 per cent, were junior colleges. Of the 196 figure, 145 had fewer than 100 full-time students, and 185, or 94 per cent, had less than 300 full-time students. Some 56 were operated for the training of religious or clergy.

A word of explanation is in order relating to the recent phenomenon of the "sister formation college," in order to better understand some of these newly founded institutions of higher learning. During the 1950's, there was a general awareness that the times called for a more professional approach to the preparation of nun-teachers. In 1953, years before Sputnik, Catholic educational leadership had set up the National Sister Formation Conference. The ideal held up by the conference, even then realized by many congregations of teaching sisters, went beyond the ordinary standards of pre-service and in-service training expected of the contemporary teacher. In the enthusiastic implementation of these ideals, a multitude of colleges sprang up exclusively for nuns. Despite much talk of cooperation and sharing of resources, most congregations "went it alone." Some of these institutions later did admit a number of laywomen in order to generate income.

The result has not been a spectacular success. While there have been a few viable operations from the economic and academic points of view, the bulk of these colleges are almost caricatures of the real thing. The harm is not so much in the modest education which the individual receives, but more, in that the religious women trained in this environment move out into schools and colleges without having been exposed to the best in modern education. To borrow a cliché that still illumines the point, many of these people, despite individual talent and competence, are simply not in the mainstream, so that later when they become teachers and administrators their institutions suffer accordingly. The mischief is almost irreparable when religious women (or men) of high ability and poor training end up in policy-making positions in the congregation or college. They are innocent of the true academic life, ignorant of standard collegiate operation, and conditioned henceforth to judge condescendingly all of "secular" higher education.

On the other hand, there are many other congregations which

from the beginning have had their young sisters do college work side by side with lay students in an already solidly established college, have given them excellent graduate work in secular or Catholic universities, and have brought them back to improve the congregation's own college. It would be assuring to hear that the sisters' congregations will not attempt any more collegiate foundations for their own personnel—but there will be more. Some satisfaction may be taken, however, in the knowledge that the number of new establishments may be more than offset by the total of established sister formation colleges which will merge with more viable collegiate institutions.

How does a small liberal arts college for women know when it is an exception to the standard norms relating to size? If it is serving a distinctive function in a way that is favorably comparable with the best schools in its category and rests on a reasonably firm financial basis, then that college should exist. But it is not sufficient to insert into the catalogue preface that "Our Lady of the Junipers is fully accredited." The general academic accreditation given by the regional accrediting associations is a minimal recognition and in some sections of the country is an extremely modest endorsement. For there is a clubby tolerance among colleges, and generally warnings of particular weaknesses are nicely balanced off with fulsome praise of distinctive strengths. Some associations by policy carry weak sisters year after year as provisionally accredited and it is almost unheard of that an institution would lose its accreditation.

Almost invariably the Catholic women's college was modeled on the Catholic men's college in terms of curriculum, discipline, and ideals. True, there were the obvious gestures to those artistic and domestic skills which society has always consigned to the female, but, in general, the women's colleges got under way blissfully unaware of, or unconcerned with, the experience of the male institutions. The Powers' history makes this well-founded observation:

Following the footsteps of colleges for men, Catholic colleges for women ignored the compelling prescription: one cannot give what he does not have or teach what he does not know—and allowed their academies to become colleges before a faculty of college quality was assembled. It was not unusual to find among the faculty teachers who themselves had never had the opportunity to attend a college and it was, in fact, extraordinary to find faculty members who had attended any college other than the one in which they were teaching. Lay teachers

—never numerous in the early women's college—were regularly recruited from the previous year's graduating class. Whatever excellence may be claimed for the moral training offered at such schools, it is questionable, indeed, whether there was quality opportunity available for intellectual development.[23]

If the Catholic community was tardy in making formal provision for the higher education of women in separate colleges, they were even more slow in getting into the field of coeducation on the collegiate level. In fact, the beginning was pretty much of an accident. In 1909, twenty-eight years after its first college-level instruction and two years after its change in nomenclature from college to university, Marquette of Milwaukee decided to establish a summer session of eight weeks' duration to enable teaching sisters to take some college courses. One can easily imagine the clucking of tongues among the Jesuit black robes at the prospect of this feminine invasion, and clerical nervousness must have greatly increased when some laywomen happened to present themselves along with the nuns for admission to the special courses. Perhaps no one at the admissions office that memorable first registration day could think up a reasonable excuse for refusing them but, in any event, they were duly admitted. That the Jesuit community was nonplused is evident from the belated suggestion of the father provincial that, in view of the school's embarrassment, all summer school classes should be canceled. However, whether through academic grace or economic concern, the ladies were allowed to continue through that summer as well as the summer sessions of 1910 and 1911 while higher authorities in Rome weighed the situation. It was only in 1912 that the Jesuit general sent a favorable reply: Marquette could admit both lay and religious women to all its summer sessions.

But then came another crisis. As summer credits piled up and degree requirements were fulfilled, some of the ladies (who also had acquired credits elsewhere) applied for a Marquette degree. Clerical brows once again were crinkled and new pondering was called for. Nothing in the documents told how a Jesuit college for men could award a bachelor's degree to a woman. Perhaps the general was wise enough to know when to break off battle, for the pioneer Marquette coeds did get their degrees as they have continued to do in increasing numbers there for the past sixty years. Full and equal

[23] Powers, *op. cit.,* p. 195.

coeducation, however, took a few more years. In 1914 DePaul of Chicago became the first Catholic school to admit women on an equal basis with men for all the regular academic sessions. That same year Sisters College was founded at the Catholic University of America. Today sixty-five collegiate institutions under Catholic direction identify themselves as coeducational.

What is the future of the separate liberal arts college for women? That the idea retains much vigor, at least among Catholics, is obvious from the great number of foundations even since 1950, so that now approximately one-half of the women's colleges in America are under Catholic direction. On the other hand, there has been hardly a single college of this type chartered by other groups since 1930, and what few have been established belong to a complexus of institutions. We see here another manifestation of the educational lag between the Protestant and Catholic educational enterprise. While the movement to sponsor women's colleges among Protestant circles drew to a close more than thirty years ago, the intervening period marks the greatest growth in the number of foundations among Catholics.

A good part of the explanation for the separatist approach to higher education and the late acceptance of coeducation by Catholics derives from the traditional European attitude toward the commingling of the sexes, and the fact that Catholic higher education was so extensively entrusted to the religious congregations. Because of their own celibate state and life by rule more or less removed from general society, these consecrated men and women deliberately restricted their dealings with the opposite sex. Obviously sisters would best take care of the girls, and priests or brothers would best take care of the men.

But over and beyond these factors there is a deeper philosophical issue: should a woman be educated differently from a man? Are those feminine characteristics which seem to call for modifications in the educational process innate or acquired? Are they biologically determined or the result of massive psychological conditioning? Among others, Ashley Montagu has remarked that the behavior of women in our culture has in large part been in response to the behavior of the male toward them, while the redoubtable feminist, Simone de Beauvoir, laments that a woman's physical processes have consigned her to a slave's fate, leaving men free to do the important things of the world.

The fact that men have always acted as if they were the superior beings and that women *de facto* have always accepted a somewhat inferior status in major areas, like the pursuit of a livelihood or politics or war, is used to prove both sides of the argument. There are those who argue that the masculine-dominated culture has oppressed and degraded woman, treating her basically as an object of sex. They make the point that the greater physical strength of the male, which was used to subordinate the woman of primitive culture, is not a biological reason for female subservience today but a cultural outcome. What they seem to be saying is that, just as smaller men are not necessarily intimidated by larger men except in the brute physical order, so in modern culture a woman is not naturally subject to man. In fact, they mention that women now are more resistant to disease, more capable of bearing pain, and longer-lived than their male counterparts.

Plato may not have had access to the mountains of statistics furnished us by the Metropolitan Life Insurance Company or the U. S. Bureau of the Census but he stated some sound ideas about the education of women, that for his day were revolutionary indeed. In discussing the education of the guardian class in his *Republic,* he has Socrates saying:

If, then, we find that either the male sex or the female is specially qualified for any particular form of occupation, then that occupation, we shall say, ought to be assigned to one sex or the other. But if the only difference appears to be that the male begets and the female brings forth, we shall conclude that no difference between man and woman has yet been produced that is relevant to our purpose. We shall continue to think it proper for our guardians and their wives to share in the same pursuits.[24]

He further argues that natural qualities make the potential guardian and that certain women may possess these as well as certain men: "So for the purpose of keeping watch over the commonwealth, woman has the same nature as man, save in so far as she is weaker," and he concludes by saying, "Now for the purpose of producing a woman fit to be a guardian, we shall not have one education for men and another for women, precisely because the nature to be taken in hand is the same."[25]

[24] *Republic* of Plato, Bk. IV, chap. 15 (Cornford Translation, p. 152).
[25] *Ibid.,* p. 154.

Plato's great disciple, Aristotle, and, in turn, the Stagirite's great-est commentator, Thomas Aquinas, must have had serious reserva-tions here, for both settled the status of woman by describing her as an underdeveloped human being.[26] Of course modern feminists emphatically reject this ancient philosophical garbage. They hold that the clear intellectual and emotional distinctions between the sexes are based simply upon differences in metabolism, in hormones, in fat distribution, and in bony structure. In *The Art of Loving,* Erich Fromm speaks for an articulate group that insists that there is a masculinity and a femininity in character as well as in sexual function.[27] Some distinctive qualities that he finds predominate in the feminine character are: productive receptiveness, protection, realism, endurance, and motherliness. Certain masculine qualities are: penetration, guidance, activity, discipline, and adventuresome-ness. Not that Fromm assigns these qualities exclusively to one or other sex. Rather he explains that both sets of characteristics are to be found in a distinctive blend in each individual but the feminine blend can be distinguished from the normal masculine blend. Then there is Betty Friedan who, after countless interviews with women throughout the United States, discovered a feminine "mystique."[28] She argues persuasively that for fulfillment as a person a woman must have an education and involve herself in something mean-ingful outside her home. And so the argument goes back and forth.

Any meaningful discussion of the future of the separate collegiate institution for women must be alert to the rapid revolution in our contemporary society about the role of women, which has resulted in a certain dislocation and even chaos. Certainly the concept of the separate women's college cannot be dismissed out of hand before a number of critical factors are carefully scrutinized. Admittedly, it is difficult to lay down an aprioristic limitation to the concept of equality between the sexes. Perish the thought that woman and man will ever have to compete in any arena where the contest con-sists in matching muscle, sinew, or physical strength. Happily, the mind they both possess is the human mind anchored in a human personality which admits of delightful and mysterious differences.

[26] St. Thomas Aquinas, *Summa Theologica,* III A and Supplement, Ques-tions 27–34.

[27] New York: Bantam Books, Inc., 1956, pp. 30–31.

[28] *The Feminine Mystique* (New York: W. W. Norton and Co. Inc., 1963), pp. 325–26.

Hopefully, we are leaving behind the era wherein one-half of the race's brain power is left lying fallow, while the world cries out for more scholars, scientists, engineers, doctors, and philosophers—whose ranks happen by tradition to be pretty well limited to the male sex.

At long last American society has theoretically decreed the equality of the sexes as far as the opportunity for higher education goes. Maybe it is a necessity that theory precede practice, for in this case the practice is lagging sadly behind. The American Council on Education reports that from among the women who finished high school only one-fourth were actually entering college. In fact, a smaller proportion of women are in college today than in 1920.[29]

Economic equality also is still a long way off. Every third married woman works on a job outside her home and, in fact, the ratio of adult working women to men is one to two. However, thoroughly competent young and middle-aged women are holding positions today in business and industry but a dual standard of recompense still prevails. Someone has well remarked that it has proved much easier to weaken and destroy the old roles that women traditionally filled than to create new ones. We often hear the assertion that women must be something more than wives and mothers but we are still waiting for a convincing explanation of what this something ought to be.

The ambitious and intelligent college girl confronts obstacles in our contemporary coeducational institutions. The prevailing attitude of the male-dominated faculty is that "you simply can't depend on them." What is meant is that the chances of the highly intelligent and academically ambitious female persevering, not simply through her undergraduate degree program but on into and through graduate school or professional school, are quite slender, relative to the male student. Freud wisely wrote that the woman in love or the woman in pregnancy is beyond formal education. Here we see the most re-

[29] "In recent years the most disappointing development, to those most concerned with the higher education of women, is the failure of women to keep pace with men in college enrollments. In 1920 there were almost as many women as men students in our institutions of higher learning and while the proportion of young women who go to college has increased substantially in the past forty years, it has fallen so far behind the increase in the numbers of young men who go to college that there are now nearly two men for every woman enrolled." Mabel Newcomer, *A Century of Higher Education for American Women* (New York: Harper & Brothers, 1959).

peated pattern of conflict between the biological and the scholarly roles lying before a young female. In many cases, a fear of spinsterhood propels many a nineteen-year-old girl into an early marriage, often with later regrets. The male is generally incapable of grasping what takes place in the mind of young women torn between the awareness of her intellectual prowess and the immediacy of a wedding ring.

There are advocates of the philosophy that women can successfully combine a career with marriage by simultaneously working, or by continuously interrupting her career for childbirth, or by beginning (or resuming) her career after the children are started in school. The words of O. Meredith Wilson on this point are worth reflection. In urging that men and women be educated together in appreciating and becoming familiar with life, he says:

The place for modifying programs of the education of women is neither in the nature of the materials nor of their content; it is in recognizing that there is a tentativeness about someone's commitments to intellectual life during the time they are twenty to twenty-five years old. The tentativeness becomes actual detachment for a period following marriage. The need is for counseling and guidance in the period prior to this time of tentativeness and detachment that will make more certain a late return to the world of inquiry and academic life.[30]

At his own institution, the University of Minnesota, President Wilson can point to the "Minnesota Plan" begun in 1960. It is neither a college nor a curriculum. It is a coordinating agency that tries to explore, exploit, and explain the resources of the university to women. The first assumption is that the needs of the mature woman are not those of an eighteen-year-old coed fresh out of high school. Counselors abound to update the woman returnee's degree program, indicate new study directions, provide short cuts, etc. Self-study and self-propulsion are insisted upon. A number of other universities and colleges have established similar programs for mature married women. Perhaps here is a new field for some of our strategically located Catholic colleges for women. The almost total absence of Catholic institutions from this increasingly important field is surprising. Loyola University of Chicago with its well-developed Home

[30] "A Woman Is a Woman Is a Woman . . . ," *Education and a Woman's Life,* ed. by Lawrence E. Dennis (Washington, D.C.: American Council on Education 1963), p. 7.

Study Division has at least made some moves in this direction by providing the opportunity for correspondence courses toward a degree.

There are a number of advantages accruing to the separate liberal arts college for women. It can set its own priority of educational goals. It can be less specialized and more liberal in its curriculum. The atmosphere does more easily lend itself to feminine things, for example, the type of residence hall equipped with large kitchens, sewing rooms, and "homey" parlors. Preparation in the traditional career fields of teaching or nursing or office work can be emphasized. Basic cultural areas like the fine arts and the history of music and art can be stressed. Side by side with pre-career science there can be more general approaches to science concepts. Most particularly, perhaps there can be closer student-faculty rapport, in marked contrast to the crowded campuses of the educational giants. The scramble for grades need not be so mad nor the compulsion to qualify for graduate and professional work so strong.

In sum, there is a special atmosphere or personality about a women's liberal arts college that easily distinguishes it from other types of collegiate institution. Counselors seem pretty well agreed that for certain girls this is the best kind of college and for other girls it would not be.

Though the debate about separate colleges for women goes on and on, a significant number of these institutions have undertaken cooperative moves on varying levels with neighboring schools. The future of a significant number of small Catholic colleges for women —the same thing must be said concerning colleges for men—seems to hinge on their pooling resources and sharing facilities either among themselves or as coordinate colleges of larger institutions. History cannot be unscrambled, but the incredible myopia that has led to the founding of four, five, and even six Catholic colleges in the same city is happily lifting. We can hope that this prodigal proliferation, so long the scandal of the academic world, is over. Indeed, there are many bright signs signaling a saner future.

Two Louisville institutions, Ursuline College for women and Bellarmine College for men, have already combined their offices of academic and student affairs and are moving toward eventual financial merger. The College of St. Benedict and St. John's University, Collegeville, Minnesota, have accepted the recommendation of an outside study group that they work toward full merger. They have publicly spoken of the possibility of corporate merger by 1971. The College of St. Francis in Joliet and Lewis College in nearby Lockport, Illinois, have announced their intention to work toward academic coalescence. Despite unanticipated obstacles caused by the Los Angeles Archdiocesan Chancery, Immaculate Heart College is determined to pursue its announced intent of joining the Claremont Colleges complexus before 1970. Marymount College, also of Los Angeles, is relocating its campus at Loyola University of Los Angeles.

There are of course any number of kinds and degrees of "coalescence" or "collaboration" or even "merger." How do they work in practice? One excellent example is the St. Mary's College-University of Notre Dame "coexchange" program. Over the years the two institutions have had close cooperation in extracurricular activities and in social affairs. In 1965 "coex" began and extended cooperation to the academic area. The schools have adopted almost identical calendars and grading systems, thus facilitating the exchange of students and professors between campuses. After freshman year, St. Mary's girls may register for any Notre Dame course not offered at St. Mary's. They are able to major in Russian, government, physics, and psychology by taking their upper-division courses at the university but their degree is still from St. Mary's. The girls may also enter Notre Dame's professional schools, such as architecture, business, and engineering. Highly qualified girls may register for graduate courses in their major. The speech and drama departments of the two schools have merged, and there are a number of joint appointments between them. In turn, Notre Dame students may register for any St. Mary's course not taught at Notre Dame. All undergraduate education courses are taken at St. Mary's. Each institution, however, has retained—and intends to retain—its own identity and independent administration.

Nor should coordination take place only among colleges of the same religious coloring. The nature of higher education cries out for the kind of enrichment brought by association with different cultural traditions and patterns. In a very authentic sense, an understanding of ecumenism by Catholic colleges may well be the most important ingredient in the formula for survival. It will be a happy day, indeed, when the scandal of four Catholic women's colleges in the same city blithely going their independent way to mediocrity will be replaced by the closest of collaboration among themselves and with neighboring private and public institutions.

It goes without saying that the same ecumenical spirit of openness must mark the Catholic university. The active presence by persons who are not Catholics in the Catholic university community is both desirable and necessary to bring authentic universality to the Catholic university itself. Those of other views, whether students, faculty, or administrators, bring rich contributions from their own traditions. They likewise ensure by their active participation the seriousness and integrity of the search for understanding and commitment.

*   *   *

Some of the leading liberal arts colleges and universities under Catholic sponsorship are already largely declericalized. But when the process has run its inevitable course, what *is* the institution? Philip Gleason phrases it this way:

In what sense is a Catholic university Catholic if it is composed predominantly of lay professors who employ, in their teaching and research, the same methods and norms as their counterparts in secular universities, and who are engaged in the pursuit of knowledge in autonomous spheres that are in no way dependent upon any over-all "Catholic position"? What, in short is the reason for being of the *Catholic* college or university?[31]

On what is the title "Catholic" based? Juridical recognition by the church or sponsorship by a Catholic religious institute are today more than ever tenuous. Even the fact that the bulk of the teachers and students might happen to have a Catholic religious affiliation hardly makes an institution of higher learning "Catholic." Somehow, the valid base must be found in a distinctive conception of man and the universe, not in precise dogmatic or scholastic formulas, but in a contemporary kind of inspiration which created so much of Western culture and civilization.

For the past several years, study groups of the International Federation of Catholic Universities have grappled with the problem, trying to articulate a contemporary philosophy for the Catholic university. At Land O'Lakes, Wisconsin, during the summer of 1967, a group of educators of the North American Region of the Federation drafted a statement on the nature and role of the contemporary Catholic

[31] "A Historical Perspective," *The Shape of Catholic Higher Education*, p. 52.

university which many critics hailed as the first significant document on the subject in years.[32] Their statement did not pretend to present a full and detailed philosophy or description of the Catholic university nor of all of Catholic higher education. It did, though, describe in detail the centrality of theology in and the need for genuine autonomy for the Catholic university.

Many graduates of Catholic collegiate institutions past the age of thirty might wrinkle their noses at mention of theology, which, with philosophy, is not ordinarily regarded as the most rewarding of their college study memories. There has been, yes, a sterility about and an overreliance on traditional scholastic philosophy and theology. There has been an unexamined premise operative in the Catholic college that somehow these two subjects are coextensive with Christian humanism. If anything, the history of the teaching of philosophy and theology is the best refutation of the assumption, or else, until fairly recent years, Catholic colleges were communicating Christian humanism in the minutest of doses. Despite the rhetoric of the catalogue, the quality and professional preparation of the staff assigned to teach in these areas has been often an occasion of chagrin. But an exciting change has taken place. The new generation of pedagogues in the best Catholic places are making these subjects as challenging as any other academic discipline. Where competently presented, philosophy and theology are powerful integrating disciplines without which humanism is *manqué*.

Some institutions have found that by offering a richer variety of philosophy and theology courses which reflect other traditions and by making the courses optional, student enthusiasm mounts.

George Bernard Shaw said it first but a long series of heavy-handed repressive actions by church authorities has given wide credence to his dictum that the words "Catholic university" are a contradiction in terms. Shaw's point was that, since by nature a university is dedicated to the pursuit of truth, and Catholics maintain that they already have "The Truth in uppercase splendor," Catholic universities function solely to transmit this Truth from one generation to another. Therefore, the university in Catholic hands is reduced to "a propaganda mill, a purveyor of dogma, where alien ideas are forbidden and honest open-ended consideration of other

[32] "The Idea of a Catholic University" (Notre Dame: University of Notre Dame Press, 1967). The document appears as Appendix B to this volume.

than the accepted philosophy, the approved theology, and frozen tradition is outlawed."[33]

The touchstone of honest academic freedom is theology both because of its distinctive nature and because it has long been esteemed a clerical preserve. However, if the premises set forth in this chapter and in the Land O'Lakes statement regarding the nature of higher education are valid, then it must follow that the privileges and responsibilities of scholarship belong to each discipline within the university structure. The discipline of theology cannot be an exception. The Catholic university must arm its professors of theology with the same academic freedom that is accorded its historians, physicists, and sociologists. There is no more academic justification for the entry by a local bishop or provincial into the university discipline of theology, than there is for the local mayor or governor to intrude into the field of political science.

It is the prerogative and duty of the scholar to put forth the fruits of his scholarship into the academic marketplace to be examined, tested, modified, accepted, or rejected by his peer group. This body alone can appropriately challenge or approve because it has earned authority and competence in the same field of learning. The very justification for the science of theology in the curriculum as an academic discipline is precisely that it is not catechesis and, therefore, not directly subject to the magisterium or teaching authority of the church. On the level of higher learning, the church's official magisterium has only an indirect influence, that is, the teaching church speaks authoritatively to the consciences of its members in the academic community, just as it does to the consciences of its members holding elective office in political society. Its influence in both spheres is indirect, not direct. The teaching office of the bishop is charismatic and hence his authority is always exercised outside the formal structure of the university.

Advance and development of theological thought can never take place unless responsible theologians are able to present the results of their investigations with the same liberty as responsible scholars in other fields. Whatever vigilance must be exercised over the orthodoxy of Christian doctrine taught in parochial schools or pulpits, a theological faculty of a Catholic university is in another category.

[33] John Cogley, "Catholic Universities: The Future of an Illusion," *Commonweal*, June, 1967.

The Catholic university is not "the church writ small," nor is it a church nor even the teaching arm of the church.

Admittedly there are risks involved in freedom. There are occasions where pastors and parents are dismayed over certain "progressive" ideas that their young people pick up in a theology course. Allowing that this concern is often enough based on pastoral or parental ignorance of perfectly orthodox concepts emerging from the ferment of the theological world, there still are instances which justify protest. Intelligent analysis and responsible discussion of Catholic dogma and official pronouncements of the Holy See on issues of faith and morals should always be encouraged in the college classroom.

However, part of the responsibility of the professor is to be aware of the background and level of maturity of his auditors, so that opinions which call in question principles of Catholic faith and morals are to be presented with the same careful balance that is expected in the presentation of delicate and controversial questions in other academic disciplines. Moreover, despite personal differences and disagreements with any given doctrine, a teacher of college-level theology is failing in his task if he does not present fairly and completely what the church has officially pronounced or taught in matters of faith and morals. Serious and consistent departure from these norms by a lay or clerical faculty member would indicate lack of competence and should be dealt with in the same way as would a case of serious incompetence in any other department of the institution. The principle here, however, is that the institution has jurisdiction in such matters, not the chancery.

Looking at the frailty of the church of the last century, one of the great modern historians wrote of the grave loss resulting from the disappearance of the universities, which had been Catholic and often papal in their founding. In all of them there had been a faculty of theology, and "round this mistress science their whole intellectual life had turned." When restored they came back as universities under the state, dedicated to natural truth alone. His poignant summation continues:

Education, the formation of the Catholic mind in the new Catholic Europe, would suffer immeasurably, and religious formation be to its intellectual development an extra something added on. There would be the further mischievous effect that henceforth not universities but seminaries would set the tone of theological life. The leaders of Catholic thought would not be the professional thinkers whom a university produces, but technicians, those to whom the important work of training the future clergy is committed and who, among other things, teach them theology. The effect of this destruction of the faculties of theology in the universities of Catholic Europe, the disappearance of the old Salamanca, Alcala, Coimbra, Bologna, Douai, Louvain, and Paris, is a theme that still awaits its historian. Louvain was indeed restored in 1834, but the healthy interplay of the theological intellects of half a score of Catholic universities, the nineteenth century was never, alas, to know.[34]

We have been talking only of Catholic higher education. For whatever consolation it may offer, the current malaise in the university world is affecting institutions everywhere—from Mexico City to Rome to the Sorbonne to Columbia to Berkeley. One might further reflect that the university is the only social institution which has never had a Protestant Reformation, never a French Revolution, never an industrial revolution, in fact, not even a Vatican II.

The university of the twelfth and thirteenth centuries was a child of the church, and Christianity gave it vigor and vitality even as it, in turn, was ennobled and enriched. In its current struggle to remake itself the modern university will still need to borrow inspiration and strength from the Christian tradition and will continue to enhance it.

The Catholic community must face the question most recently asked by the Jencks-Riesman study, not whether a small number of Catholic universities will prove capable of competing with Harvard and Berkeley (and widening the query—a reasonable number of Catholic colleges able to compete with Swarthmore or Vassar) on the latter's terms, "but whether Catholicism can provide an ideology or personnel for developing alternatives to the Harvard-Berkeley model of excellence."[35]

There are solid grounds for a firm "yes."

[34] Philip Hughes, *A Popular History of the Catholic Church* (New York: The Macmillan Company, 1947), pp. 238–39.

[35] Jencks-Riesman, p. 405.

CHAPTER EIGHT

The Future: Modes, Moods, and Models

The mercy of sleep is that it suspends concern and responsibility for the unknown that tomorrow always brings. Our seers and prophets have already limned a broad outline of tomorrow with challenges and opportunities which now demand our best imagination and courage. The future belongs to the wide-awake and the bold.

For anyone past forty-five it may prove startling to realize that the babies born today will be living most of their lives in the twenty-first century. By next year, over half of the nation will be twenty-five years young or younger. By 1970 the overwhelming majority of the entire globe will be nonwhite and hungry, and every fourth inhabitant will be Chinese. In 1910 every third American lived on a farm, while in 1969 the total is about six in a hundred. Today 70 per cent of the nation resides on 1 per cent of the land. By the year 2000 there will be an estimated 312,000,000 Americans.[1]

We talk casually about the explosion of knowledge but the implications are staggering. The first doubling of man's knowledge from the beginning of recorded history took place in 1750. The second came in 1900, the third in 1950, and the fourth in 1960. Where will it all stop? How do we educate for it? What kind of a school can cope with it? The engineer and the technologist and the research scientist are swelling the sum total of human knowledge fantastically. Most medical operations could not have been performed and most medical prescriptions could not have been written even a dozen years ago. Some 70 per cent of the skilled trades in use in American industry in 1900 are no longer in existence. It is predictable that before the close of the present century the bulk of the technical processes now considered essential in the fields of business and engineering by which men earn their living will have become as obsolete as the trade of the cooper or blacksmith. We are informed

[1] Study by the Urban Land Institute for the Ford Foundation.

that 90 per cent of the scientists of all time are alive today, and that most of the scientific literature of the world has been published within the last dozen years.

The technological revolution, which has already turned the world upside down, is really only getting under way. As Robert M. Hutchins has shrewdly observed, it will not end until we are blown up or until we have returned to that workless paradise from which Adam and Eve were forcibly ejected some time ago. Forty years ago, John Maynard Keynes predicted that work in the countries of the West would be unnecessary by the year 2030 A.D. Were he alive today, he would have to revise his estimate downward.

In the past few years, automation has accounted for the vacating of millions of jobs while creating millions of more sophisticated ways of making a living. Some prophets predict that within twenty years the average workweek will be approaching twenty hours. In mastering the energy of nature, in automating the machine process, in annihilating space and time, in achieving instant communication, in refashioning his environment, man has just about made obsolete the traditional school in which we grew up. With more and more students to educate, for a longer and longer period, to master more and more subject matter, at a higher and higher cost, to prepare for an increasingly complex and sophisticated mode of living—have we even begun to plan for the kind or kinds of vehicles required?

For most of us the terms "schooling" and "education" are synonymous, and we think of schooling as formal instruction in some sort of institution exclusively dedicated to that purpose. Like going to a restaurant to get a meal, one "gets" an education by "going to school." Moreover, we have always blindly assumed that the way to improve education is simply to improve the school. Yet there have always been other ways of getting meals, and, as a matter of history, other times and other civilizations have transmitted a way of life through agencies other than the schools. One wonders, for instance, what would have happened to the Hellenic idea and ethos if the Athenians had had to rely on makeshift classrooms rather than the assembly and amphitheater.

More than anything else, in our planning for the future we need to free ourselves of the models, methods, and mentality of the past. It makes little sense to bog our thought down in profitless quarrels over separation of church and state or government's role in education when the entire context has shifted—or will be shifting—into a twenty-first-century setting. True, the next thirty years will be a period of transition and some parts of the country will be able to adapt more readily than others. It would be unwise to talk about dismantling what we now have while dreaming of what might happen in the twenty-first century. In addition, we bear a responsibility for the Christian formation and education of the present generation. Yet there must be dreams and brave experiments geared to the technological revolution all around us.

Perhaps technology will have steered us by the eighties back to the home for much of formal education. Bringing young people together in a school has important social values, but no one any longer argues that group learning is the most efficient way of educating. Because the readiness level and the attention span vary so widely among pupils, the precise moment of learning is expectedly different among twenty-five or thirty learners. We have never been rich enough to put every pupil on a log with a Mark Hopkins on the other end, but it is easy to conceive of every child before too long with a computer tutor. Far from depersonalizing teaching the machine may decidedly enhance the personal element in the process. As Stanford philosopher Patrick Suppes has pointed out, computer-assisted instruction (CAI) potentially bestows upon every learner a personal Aristotle. So often the teacher must teach to the middle half of the class. "The machines," Suppes says, "offer a chance to do much better teaching on an individual basis for the top 25 per cent and for the bottom 25 per cent."[2]

With its battery of teletypewriters and typewriters tied by phone to a central computer and its taped "voice," CAI now shepherds pupils using light pens and cathode-ray tubes through math, spelling, and what have you, displaying a patience and thoroughness no human teacher can rival. Of added value is the computer's careful remembrance of every action of each student—the time and rhythm of progress factors, for instance. The resulting data permit the staff to re-program a course and to tailor it more precisely to individual weaknesses and strengths.

Technical advances will make the present school a museum. One day individual learners and small neighborhood groups will be able to dial into central banks of learning programs for much of their instruction. One can visualize a high-school program in Euro-

[2] "Future of the Computer Tutor," *Educom*, September, 1967, p. 5.

pean history, in which the general topics will be programmed for all students alike, but with complementary and supplementary programs treating of a specific Lutheran or Catholic contribution to the period (prepared and paid for by the sponsoring group) accessible through another whirl of the dial. The bulk of school library holdings will be on microfilm or video tape available to everyone through dialing.

Pupils will be able to bring home packaged programs to plug into the home TV set. At least one Catholic university is already working along these lines in its center for educational technology. It is forseeable that itinerant teachers will be visiting homes and block centers for individual instruction, and that students may need be at the school itself every other day for not more than two or three hours. The two-way visual telephone will multiply the presence of the finest teachers in combination with the television set of 1980, which will bear about the same resemblance to the present set as the Thunderbird does to a Model-T Ford, and will make every home an extension of the classroom or seminar room.

Admittedly it is difficult to shake one's self out of the hypnosis of the present. Creatures of time and space that we are, we instinctively embrace the actual moment of the fleeting *now*. Ideas are revolutionary and tend to upset the established order, but almost invariably after a new idea has taken over, in time it, too, becomes institutionalized, part of the establishment, and a defender of the *status quo*. Yet, one of the distinctive characteristics of Christ's church is that it be *catholic* or universal, not simply in space but *in time*. In other words, the response of the Christian community in its institutions to the social needs of its people must faithfully reflect the insights and collective wisdom of each generation. Any other less flexible stance is a denial of the nature of Christ's church. Openness to the ever changing reality around us is an essential note of the Christian. Because the church is an organic body with a truly temporal dimension, it lives by adaptation to ongoing history which is its daily response to God's ever-revealing Spirit. The church may not be of the world but it must be in the center of it to be true to the mission of its Founder.

The first and basic outcome of Christian education is to prepare the initiates for life in the contemporary community. When this is not done, education is out of step with the times. An older voice, a century ago, brooded and wrote forcefully on this point. Here are his words:

They who are educated in our schools seem misplaced and mistimed in the world, as if born and educated for a world that has ceased to exist. They come out ignorant of contemporary ideas, contemporary habits of mind, contemporary intelligence and tendencies, and large numbers of them sink into obscurity, and do nothing for their religion or their country; or what is worse, abandon their religion, turn their backs on the church, and waste all their energies in seeking pleasure, or in accumulating worldly wealth.[3]

The worst result of this kind of education, said Brownson, was that it failed to produce living men, "active, thinking men, great men, men of commanding genius, of generous aims, and high and noble aspirations; and hence it also fails to enable the church to take possession of humanity, and to inspire and direct its movements."[4] In facing the needs of tomorrow we may have to abandon or radically change certain cherished forms. The risks are simply those of the man of faith who realizes that the Spirit of God still hovers over our never completely illumined world.

It could be argued from the mere fact that we can raise the question of justifying the existence of the Catholic school, that we are falling short of the goal. Given the exalted goal, absolute achievement would have been an impossibility. Yet the same goal is the goal of the family, the parish, and the whole Christian community. We must keep reminding ourselves that the crisis rocking the Catholic educational world today is the same crisis that is revolutionizing our total society. Catholics have expected too much of their schools just as America generally has overtrusted the public school. Perhaps the nation will be more realistic in planning future patterns.

However, the talk of the wholesale closing down of Catholic schools is foolishness. While we can talk about the school of tomorrow, we must not forget the school of today and while it is vital that we plan for the school children of 1980 and 1990, we have a very real responsibility for the youngsters of 1970. The financial burden is not a valid reason alone for shutting down a Catholic school—not

[3] Orestes A. Brownson, "Catholic Schools and Education," *Brownson's Quarterly Review*, January, 1862, pp. 66–84. Reprinted in Neil G. McCluskey, ed., *Catholic Education in America* (New York: Teachers College Bureau of Publications, 1964), p. 103.

[4] *Ibid.*

for the people of the most affluent nation in history, who spend hardly 7 per cent of the gross national product on education.

Catholic education in the decades ahead is going to have to make some choices: each diocese, each congregation or order will have to examine its resources and look at local needs—and then determine how best service can be rendered. The approach must be innovative and courageous. In spite of risks experiments must be undertaken. There will be no single pattern covering the entire United States of America.

In some areas with a concentrated Catholic population with a tradition of solid support for good Catholic schooling, the schools should continue with the adaptations and adjustments needed to make them viable for the future. Some of the patterns we shall discuss in this final chapter. In areas where there exists the equivalent of a second public-school system, the new cooperative programs of ESEA and other federal programs yet to come will inevitably bring the Catholic and public systems closer together.

In other dioceses or parts of a diocese, the Catholic schools, especially at the secondary level, can continue strong because of community understanding that will allow a pattern of dual enrollment to flourish. There are limitations, which we can later discuss, but in towns or cities where proximity of the partner schools makes dual enrollment practical, thousands of youngsters will be enabled to divide their day between a public and a Catholic school. Some dioceses may be well advised to revise drastically their commitment to separate schools and make use of their resources and personnel in new ways. In any event, no matter what form it may take, the Catholic school remains a legitimate and desirable entity "wherever it is sociologically possible, pastorally desirable, and positively wanted by parents." Where it is not, there are—as we shall see—valid substitutes. No longer can the Catholic school be considered the exclusive teacher of religion in the Catholic Church.

With their eyes to the future, several dioceses—among them Saginaw, St. Louis, Baltimore, New York, and Boston—have already completed or are undergoing thorough self-studies by outside agencies to plan their educational tomorrow. A model study is that done in 1967–68 for the Archdiocese of Denver by the Office for Educational Research of the University of Notre Dame.

Many observers of the current scene feel that the enrollment in the Catholic elementary and secondary schools has peaked and will stay on a plateau for the foreseeable future. Certainly one no longer hears talk of "every Catholic child in a Catholic school." As a matter of record, the proportion of the nation's Catholic children that could be accommodated in these schools has not varied greatly over a forty-year period. About one-half of the elementary-school-age group and about one-third of the secondary-school-age group have attended Catholic schools, which conversely means that historically the majority of American Catholic youngsters have always been in the state schools.

The challenges of the future require some basic retooling of the existing structure of Catholic education. Two major modifications concern administration and finance. The parochial school as an independent, parish-controlled, and parish-financed operation is an anachronism. For the greater good all parochial schools should serve several parishes or districts as diocesan schools. This will mean, of course, that pastors will have to surrender control of their schools to the diocese. Five or ten years ago such a proposal would have been dismissed as monstrous. Canon law firmly vests authority over the parochial school in the pastor. However, a growing number of today's pastors would readily give over the school to other control.[5]

We speak loosely of a Catholic school "system" but only a few dioceses have begun to approach education systematically. The diocesan school board and superintendent's office should henceforth allocate schools and priorities in building, pass on additions, consolidations, and suppressions of schools. They should have the authority to designate special schools to be located at strategic points in the diocese. In these schools exceptional children would at long last get their full due. There should be special schools and staffs for the mentally retarded and physically handicapped. There should be a special diocesan provision for transporting those handicapped pupils who attend regular schools. College preparatory schools, terminal schools, preprofessional schools, and technical schools should likewise be designated for patronage by youngsters of an entire area or district of a diocese.

We may wince at the charge, but unhappily there is a basis for the accusation that Catholic schools, especially the high schools,

[5] Surveys of pastors' attitudes in the dioceses of Rochester, Portland (Ore.), Ogdensburg (N.Y.), and Galveston-Houston made by Notre Dame's Graduate Department of Education are the basis of this statement.

make a practice of using the public schools as a "dumping ground" for "problem" children and difficult learners. Until we reorganize our schools systematically, and catch up in the counseling business, this charge will not down.

Let us turn to the teacher. Henceforth, all teacher contracts would be arranged by the diocesan office. Salary scales, assignments, transfers, replacements, promotions would be handled on a diocesan level by a central office. Health benefits, tenure, retirement, sick leave, and pensions would be provided for in the same way.[6]

Curriculum planning and experimentation, teacher accreditation, standards for promotion, advanced placement, selection of textbooks, enforcement of library standards, etc.—all these important items would now come under the diocesan administration and school board. Should ten schools in the diocese offer Russian-language courses in the sixth grade? Can Latin or French be started in this particular school at the fourth-grade level? Is there profit in accepting a long-term loan for science equipment under provisions of the National Defense Education Act or ESEA? These would all become routine matters for the diocesan superintendent's office. The diocesan superintendent would be assisted by an active school board, equally composed of clerical and lay members, which meets regularly and works closely with him in evolving policy and practice for the diocese.[7] In sum, the office of the diocesan superintendent of schools becomes a position of authority over and leadership of the Catholic school *system*. In turn, the superintendent is aided and advised by the diocesan school board, to which he is accountable.

Finance comes next. Tuition is now abolished. In its place there is a school tax levied on every adult member of the diocese. The present system of financing Catholic school education is unbelievably archaic, obsolete, and inefficient. In this matter we are a good one hundred years behind the public-school system, whose architects long ago argued successfully that the burden of support for the

[6] In 1960 the present writer spoke of these things to a largely unconvinced, national meeting of the Catholic school superintendents. Six years later at their Cincinnati gathering, the Association of Catholic School Superintendents, NCWC, the following proposition was presented for formal debate: "We propose that centralized financing of Catholic education, particularly in the area of teachers' salaries is essential to the survival of the Catholic school system."

[7] At their Cincinnati meeting the superintendents discussed this proposition: "We propose that each diocese in the United States establish a policy-making school board, the membership of which will include laymen and laywomen.

commonly-used public school was a total community responsibility because of its important benefit to society. The token tuition collected by the parochial school today is usually supplemented by regular "throw-it-in-the-Sunday-basket" appeals to parish generosity. How much fairer and more practical to share the tax burden and to concentrate during certain periods of the year on whatever all-diocesan drives for supplementary funds prove necessary. Henceforth, let the education of the youngsters in the rich suburban parish and the declining downtown parish be paid for out of the same central fund. And if private schools directed by religious orders want to be supported in this way, it is only proper that they become an integral part of the diocesan system.

Once a central control comes over the parish schools, intelligent planning for expansion can take place. Economy can become the keynote. Facilities can be shared as much as possible. Several neighboring schools can make use of expensive facilities like auditoriums, gymnasiums, home economics departments, and industrial arts wings. If needed, school buses can be used to bring pupils to these centrally located facilities.

One eminently practical suggestion for the seventies is that the best of the contemporary convent facilities be shared among several religious teaching groups. The price of a station wagon or a minibus is modest compared with the operating cost of a convent built for twenty sisters in which seven of the stalwarts rattle around. In fact, certain convents might well be converted to housing for single women teachers as a form of supplementary non-cash income.

It is no secret that the percentage of family income contributed to the church does not rise as that income increases. In fact, studies made by the Office for Educational Research at Notre Dame show that the average family giving as a percentage of average family income actually falls as the income levels increase. The average contribution for the five lowest-income parishes in one Midwest diocese is .0363 of family income. The portion of family income given in the middle-income parishes is .0216. In the upper-middle-income parishes the share falls to .0203, and in the upper-income parishes the share is .0099. In this average-sized diocese the intra-parish finance picture reflects a dismal understanding of economic equity. Nor is the picture brighter when inter-parish finance is considered. Low-income parishes are generally left to fend for themselves, and any transfer of funds from a wealthy parish is rare indeed. The result is that in order to provide parochial schooling a significantly larger percentage of family income must go to the church in low-income parishes than in high-income parishes.

In one diocese the current annual expenditure per pupil in the Catholic or elementary schools is approximately $140. It is estimated that within five years all school costs will increase by at least 25 per cent. It is the opinion of all the major superiors of the congregations which staff the schools of this diocese that within five years there will be a 50 per cent reduction in the number of religious available for teaching. This reduction in contributed services will automatically raise the per pupil outlay by $100. As Catholic lay teachers form bargaining groups and succeed in ameliorating their salaries and professional benefits, there will be a further reduction in their "contributed" services. In fact, the religious and clerical teachers will not be far behind them in their need for improved salaries and fringe benefits. Therefore, a conservative estimate of the per pupil cost of educating a child in a Catholic elementary school in this diocese in 1973 is $350 or an increase of 250 per cent over the 1967–68 expenditure.

*   *   *

The antiquated structure of governance and finance in Catholic education frustrates efforts by the religious orders and congregations "to continue, improve, and strengthen" the Catholic school. One Conference of Major Superiors of Women Religious described their own helplessness to effect improvement on a large scale because each parish continues to guard the autonomy of its parish school. After viewing the shortage of sisters and the poverty of the small parish school, the provincial superior may judge that cooperation, even consolidation, with neighboring schools is vital for a school's survival. She can do nothing, however, due to the order's contract with an individual pastor. The sisters hesitate to walk away but, increasingly, this drastic step may be the only way that the sisters themselves can be professionally saved for the larger educational needs of the church. By now it should be obvious that poor working conditions and lack of professional growth are common reasons why many nuns leave the convent.

The words of this group of major superiors command attention:

In a structure which inhibits innovation, [a sister's] students cannot receive the benefit of her training and competence. In a structure composed to some extent of self-contained classrooms, she senses keenly her inability to be an expert in all fields, yet is very aware of the injustice to the child if any single subject is not given full recognition. In a structure where, because of financial limitations, unprepared teachers are employed, she lacks professional stimulation. In a structure which subtly excludes the poor and underprivileged, she finds attitudes of social justice difficult to foster. In a structure where little imagination is used to open the riches of the liturgy to the parish, she fruitlessly endeavors to make religion vital in her classroom. In a structure which isolates education from liturgical life and social action, she questions whether the ideal of Christian education can be realized. And in a structure which ignores her individual abilities and differences, she struggles, "filling a slot" instead of fulfilling a call.[8]

Some bishops and pastors, to say nothing of the backward-looking Catholic layman, seem to think that the only change that has taken place among the sisters is in the tailoring of their religious habits. Despite the outrageous interference by a few prelates in the sisterhood's efforts to undertake programs of deep and ongoing renewal, most of these groups are already well along the way to the renovation called for by Vatican II. "Freed from living behind a wall which separates the 'profane' from the 'holy,'" religious women are rediscovering Christ through His redeemed world. In establishing their relevance to this world, they are replacing an autocratic authority with one that is open to participation and dialogue. They are discerning their vocations as a call to be in and for the church so that, in the words of Paul VI's encyclical *Lumen Gentium,* they can "give an increasingly clearer revelation of Christ."

The sister-teacher of the future can no longer be treated as a pious demi-child, trained to docility and secluded in anonymity. The new nun expects to find the same openness, dialogue, truth-searching, and respect for person which she is now finding in her own community. Paternalism is out. No longer can she be expected to tolerate the situation in which her own professional authority as a teacher or administrator is crudely ignored or thwarted by an authority derived from merely ecclesiastical structure, or the situation in which her conscientious effort to stimulate thought and to

[8] Statement, March 1, 1968, in response to a request from Archbishop Cousins of Milwaukee for comment on *A Statement on Catholic Schools,* issued by the American hierarchy in November, 1967.

form the responsible Christian student is hindered at times "by the over-zealous concern of clergy and parents for the student's protection from the very problems which she will later meet."

If some dioceses are forced to abandon a section of formal Catholic schooling, in the fallible opinion of this writer, it ought to be the first six grades. To achieve maximum results Catholic education should start with the seventh grade of junior high school and continue through senior high school. Some junior colleges under diocesan and religious-order directions would mean that many tens of thousands of Catholic young men and women, at a critical stage of intellectual maturation, would be exposed to philosophy, theology, Christian humanism, and Catholic social thought. This is no small gain. A number of Catholic colleges presently struggling to survive as four-year institutions might find their own salvation while making an invaluable contribution to society by becoming first-rate junior colleges.

There are people who advocate that the Catholic school of the future should be an elitist school, not in the sense of a high-tuition or strict-entrance-requirement institution, but rather as a school engaged in a specialized task. One kind of preparatory school could function as a leadership center both for the young men and women from whom would come many of the priests, sisters, and brothers of tomorrow and for other youngsters who would be prepared to assume greater leadership roles as members of the laity. In the past, Catholic high schools have been a considerable source of vocations. Over the ten-year period, 1954–64, for example, 344 of the 386 priests ordained in the San Francisco archdiocese had attended Catholic schools.

Another type of school could be a boarding institution run for children from deprived areas which then might qualify for federal and state subsidy. It could offer the living and educational experience whose absence often means failure for ambitious young people trapped in a ghetto slum. In such an educational community ideal witness could be given to the reality of the Christian mystery. In its most perfect setting the symbolic and ritualistic expression of that mystery, the Eucharist, could be better celebrated and the pre-eminently social implications of the mysterium, love for and service to the brethren, could be better emphasized.

The time has come for the affluent parishes of suburbia to take on sponsorship of schools in the inner city, even where the bulk of the children served belong to no Christian congregation. It is even conceivable that some parochial schools should be completely turned over to the public-school system as an immediate answer to the staff turnover, overcrowding, inadequate funds, and community torpor which have stifled education in the ghetto. Perhaps this is the kind of thing to be done cooperatively with other church groups, in the finest meaning of ecumenism.

The past decade has seen a widening acceptance of an intriguing approach to the school issue—"shared time" or more precisely "dual enrollment." In substance the proposal is simply to share the school time of children between the state-supported public school, which provides general education in a denominationally neutral context, and the church-supported school, which offers certain academic subjects and school activities within its own atmosphere. This is the description of the idea by Harry L. Stearns, a former superintendent of schools and later chairman of the division of education for the United Presbyterian Church, one of the first to publicize "shared time."

The idea is of fairly recent origin and represents a confluence of thinking on the subject by several people.

In 1958 John C. Bennett of Union Theological Seminary asked, "Is it impossible to think of the construction of part-time parochial schools?"[9] In a later article, Claud D. Nelson said:

In my pamphlet "Church and State" (National Council of Churches, 1953, p. 33), I suggest experiments pointing toward a community resolution of the educational problem; I developed the idea further in a Methodist seminar in 1959. In an earlier session of the same seminar, Father McCluskey mentioned as one of the seemingly possible choices in dealing with this conflict situation "modification of the present structure of the public school, so that broader Catholic participation could become both possible and desirable" (Research Consultation on the Church and State," Second Assembly, April 16–18, 1959, p. 9). In the discussion of Father McCluskey's address, Harry Stearns of New Jersey said that he would be perfectly willing, as a school superintendent, to enter into conversations to work out such an arrangement—provided always that public and parochial schools were separately administered and financed.[10]

[9] *Christians and the State* (New York: Charles Scribner's Sons, 1958).
[10] "Proposal on the School-Aid Impasse," *The Christian Century*, April 12, 1961, p. 448.

In any event, dozens of communities have welcomed the idea as a partial solution to their school problem. Over three hundred public-school systems now report shared-time programs and several hundred more have been discussing the idea. Michigan, Ohio, Illinois, and Wisconsin in the Midwest along with Pennsylvania have the greatest number of programs but some shared-time programs have been placed in all but a handful of states.[11] The only state where the courts have made a negative ruling is Missouri. There the wording of the state constitution states specifically that a pupil must be in full-time attendance at one school if that school is to qualify for state reimbursement for the pupil.

The first high school to be built on the shared-time principle is St. Paul's in Chicago. Now in its fourth year, St. Paul's 500 students have the option of taking a substantive share of their courses and activities at nearby Kennedy High School with 2000 students. It is still too early to evaluate this experiment but public-school and Catholic-school officials are planning a complete evaluation.

Of course there are many problems still unresolved in dual enrollment. The first, undoubtedly, is acceptance. Most Catholic families still prefer to send their children to a "full" Catholic school. It has been found in the St. Paul-Kennedy experiment that feeder schools provide a potential incoming freshman class of eight hundred. About one-half want only St. Paul courses; about one-quarter choose only Kennedy; and only one-quarter want shared time between the two schools. The tense racial situation in southwest Chicago may be a seriously complicating factor in the family preference for the Catholic school with its whiter student body.

Some observers raised the legitimate question of whether *dual* enrollment will for the student become *duel* enrollment. How big a problem is divided loyalty for an adolescent living in a situation where the public school is larger, has established traditions, many more extracurricular activities, and a rich variety of sports programs? Moreover, is it possible that the "Catholic" half of the dual enrollment situation would evolve into a predominantly girls' school since athletics play such a large part in the life of a boy? On the other hand, knowledgeable administrators in both the public and Catholic sectors are evolving expertise to cope with these "selling" problems.

---

[11] Shared time data in: James E. Gibbs, *Dual Enrollment in Public and Non-Public Schools,* U. S. Office of Education Circular No. 772. Anna Fay Friedlander, *Shared Time Strategy* (St. Louis, Mo.: Concordia Press, 1966).

Nor is dual enrollment a one-way street. Already there are examples of science and language teachers from a Catholic high school moving into public schools where shortages or sudden shifts may have depleted a department. If Catholic schools, for instance, make their skilled science and Latin teachers available, shared time will mean a real *sharing*. Much of the reluctance by public-school administrators to get involved in these programs is their concern that they would simply be servicing gratis, pupils for whom they have no official responsibility. Despite these difficulties, dual enrollment holds significant possibilities for many areas in the country. Above all it exemplifies the concern spoken of by John XXIII. As he wrote in *Pacem in Terris:* "Since men are social by nature, they are meant to live with others and to work for one another's welfare. A well-ordered human society . . . demands that each contribute generously to the establishment of a civic order in which rights and duties are progressively more sincerely and effectively acknowledged and fulfilled. . . . It also requires that they collaborate together in the many enterprises that modern civilization either allows or encourages or even demands." Shared time is the kind of thing Pope John was referring to when he expressed the hope that it would be possible "for all the citizens to share as far as they are able in their country's cultural advantages."

Another innovative idea, the "educational park," also lends itself to dual enrollment. Both Pittsburgh and Chicago have made feasibility studies of the plan, which calls for clusters of schools surrounding the cities. Eventually these parks would replace most of the old inner-city high schools. Within the complex would be terminal schools, vocational schools, college prep schools, and experimental schools. The Pittsburgh Catholic schools are planning to participate.

The town of Swanton in Vermont is the site of what may be the prototype educational park. The U. S. Office of Education showed its interest in the project by making a study-grant under Title III of the Elementary and Secondary Education Act. The proposed institution would combine in a single facility the public-high-school and Catholic high school students from Swanton, Highgate, and Franklin —towns respectively of 4000, 2000, and 1000 population. The three communities voted in September of 1967 to raise a $3,000,000 bond issue to finance the new school. Its design will be a radical departure from traditional school buildings with the classrooms grouped in circular segments about a central "trunk." One circle will contain the "religious" school and an interfaith chapel. The concept is that the public and parochial functions will operate independently but under the same roof.

Some communities might experiment with cosponsorship of a junior or senior high school with non-Catholic religious groups. Elsewhere ecumenical cooperation could take the form of a common school of Christian faith activities with a thoroughly competent staff drawn from different church groups. This would become a replacement for the Confraternity of Christian Doctrine and released-time classes. This "school of Christian life" would have classrooms and seminar stations, lounges, recreation basement, chapel, counseling offices, etc. Young people from both public and nonpublic schools would be able to utilize such a facility, to say nothing of parent groups, young-married-couple clubs, etc.

In fact, some communities already have this type of center built on property adjacent to the public high school. An operating example is the Holy Rosary Educational Center in Flint, Michigan. The center comprises eight classrooms and a library; a combination auditorium-cafeteria with kitchen facilities; lounges; work and counseling rooms; a chapel; and even a small clinic. Flint authorities report that the total cost was less than $500,000, including the twenty-three acres of land, building construction and furnishing, along with the roadway and landscaping. In the center are offered programs in religious education to elementary and secondary school pupils, parents, senior citizens, and college students from non-Catholic campuses. Community recreational and cultural activities are likewise centered here.

In the words of Eugene Borowitz, "The critical issue concerning ecumenical education is not whether it shall be but only what kind it shall be." He points out that our contemporary culture is forcing men in a dozen different ways to confront their neighbors. If our choice is not to educate our neighbors to the reality of other religions, they will not remain blissfully ignorant—"our society in its mindless mixture of exploitation and change will teach them what we might have hoped to channel through responsive purposefulness."[12]

Authoritative voices in the American church have joined in pleading for an awareness that a poverty exists in the Christian community

[12] "A Call for Ecumenical Polemics," an address to the national convention of the Religious Education Association, November 21, 1966. Printed in *Religious Education*, LXII (March–April, 1967), 107–12.

"because of our tragic separation." Our separation creates a "poverty" in the world since we deny it our full witness to Christ by our divisions. The same body stated:

Ecumenism also demands a knowledge of and respect for the beliefs and practices of other confessions and religions. Educators should prepare themselves to teach these traditions accurately and sympathetically by going to the sources. Where possible, teachers from these other traditions should present this material; this is especially true at secondary and higher levels of education.[13]

* * *

Certainly of equal significance is the new attitude in official Washington on the part of both governmental and professional education offices toward the Catholic school. Anyone in the past who has worked on the national level of Catholic education has at times felt discomfited, almost like a foreigner, in dealing with certain of these organizations. On occasion the U. S. Office of Education and the National Education Association seemed to operate as if their mandate was limited by law to public education. This is changing. While occupying the office, Dr. Howe repeatedly stated that he considered himself the U. S. Commissioner of Education and not merely the U. S. Commissioner of *Public* Education. Even that sturdy defender of public education, the National Education Association, with its historic antagonisms toward parochial schools, has been undergoing a gentle thaw. Several important components of the NEA have moved far in working with the NCEA. For the past several years the National Association of Secondary School Principals has cosponsored workshops, invited participation in many of its professional programs, and in general evinced a genuine concern for the pulling together of all secondary schooling in the United States. The research department of the NEA is taking the first steps to ensure cooperation in such areas as statistics and data. The NEA field service has offered its considerable resources to any group of private-school teachers or administrators. All of these straws augur well for the future harmony of American education.

However, each of these gestures should be at least matched by

[13] Committee on Education for Ecumenism of the Bishops' Commission for Ecumenical Affairs (1966).

corresponding overtures from the Catholic side. In the past, Catholic educators and school people generally have evinced small interest and concern over the problems of public education in their own involvement in Catholic schooling. Happily, as was discussed earlier in the book, the old "parochial" attitude is rapidly disappearing. As far as the U. S. Office of Education goes, Catholic schools should act as if they *are* part of the total enterprise and welcome the concern and expertise of the office. One proposal deserves consideration: the creation of the office of Assistant Commissioner for Private Education with special responsibility for the nonpublic schools. Relative to the NEA and the particular state education associations, as well as the professional teacher organizations, Catholic school boards and administrators ought to encourage teachers and staff to join and to be active members.

What the church might well do to come to a final resolution of its century-and-one-half-old dilemma over where its schools fit in the American context has already been talked about in detail. An immediately-called-for final step would be to renounce the Catholic kind of "no communication" philosophy, which we deprecated in the philosophy behind the *Everson* and *McCollum* court decisions. The *Code of Canon Law* now states:

> Catholic children may not attend non-Catholic, neutral or mixed schools, that is, those which are open also to non-Catholics. It is for the local bishop to decide, in accordance with the instructions of the Holy See, under what circumstances and with what precautions against the danger of perversion, attendance at such schools may be allowed.[14]

With a more mature understanding of the nature of the secular and with a formal declaration by Vatican II of the need for openness and exchange among men of good will, the necessity of Canon 1374 is no more. It should be quietly left behind along with other vestiges of the nineteenth-century-siege mentality of the Catholic Church.

Such a move would more readily come about if the American public-school world would formally make these acknowledgments:

1. That value formation is an important goal of schooling and not just a private matter to be cared for at home and in the church.

---

[14] Canon 1374. Translated from the Latin in *Catholic Education in America*, p. 176.

2. That as now constituted the public school cannot honestly by itself undertake value formation.
3. That those agencies which are competent by nature to inculcate values in the young are needed to complement the work of the public school in secular education.
4. That the states and federal government should continue to find feasible ways to make cooperation between public and private schools work.

Industry and the universities have moved much more rapidly into automated techniques and video tape—they have more money—than have the secondary and elementary schools, where the need to update processes is just as great. It might help relieve the mind of anyone still skittish over separation or domination to reflect that this is a fresh new field without the scars of past battles between public and nonpublic schools. Sharing is two-directional, and the nonpublic schools may have something important to give here. As C. Albert Koob, executive secretary of the NCEA, said at the University of Notre Dame's summer session last year:

> With the acceptance of team teaching, itinerant teachers, specialized technicians, and purchased services of every kind, private schools *can* contribute something. I see every reason to hope that some day in the future, we will put together outstanding teams of specialists in each of the disciplines and each of the specialized service areas who will then be used to go from one school to the next to improve the quality of education and in many instances do the actual instructing.[15]

The absence of communication has in the past prevented the two sectors of American education from developing patterns of cooperation like those sketched by Father Koob. We can confidently predict that the shape of things to come will be different.

If the secular nature of the public school is accepted in a positive sense—as opposed to a nihilist or negative sense—the public school can invite outside agencies to work with it in planning and carrying out activities from which it is directly barred by constitutional prohibition or social wisdom. The two areas that merit some detailed comment are the residual religious items still within the public school and the teaching "about" religious values. Let us take each category in turn.

[15] "Practices and Potentialities for Public-Private School Cooperation," July 1, 1968.

Pageants and Plays of a Semireligious Nature. The public school should not be prevented from re-enacting historical events which are part of community tradition. The arrival of the Mormons has given a distinctive coloring to communities in Utah and southern Idaho, as has the founding of the California missions in California. Every community has roots, some of which largely involve religious men and religious ideals. When the public school joins in the commemoration of the arrival of the Mormons in Salt Lake or the work of the Franciscan padres in the Santa Clara Valley, it should be allowed within reason to follow the record. The Christmas play or Easter pageant or Hanukkah tableau are more sensitive points. If these are presented primarily as cultural and educational offerings, there should be little objection. In fact, some understanding by students of these things has real value for our pluralistic society.

Religious Displays and Symbols. Where such activities enjoy long-standing community sanction, there is usually no need to yield to pressure groups seeking to effect a change. Where the introduction of this sort of activity has not been prepared for or would exacerbate community tensions, it would seem more Christian and more prudent not to push for, e.g., the Christmas crèche. On the other hand, Christians have every right to protest the secularist policy which would erase the Noel, the shepherds, and the star of Bethlehem from classroom decorations and school programs, provided the primary emphasis and intent is to present them as part of our culture.

Observance of Religious Holidays. To arrange vacation schedules and school holidays with an eye to major religious festivals of the year is an elementary form of cooperation between school and church authorities. Though teachers and pupils have a right to be excused from school to make their required religious observances, these arrangements should be made with consideration for the school administrator's problems. For an example of what mischief can happen, state and federal matching funds are generally computed on average daily attendance, so, unless he is advised sufficiently in advance, the public-school superintendent or principal might run into annoying bookkeeping difficulties. Some Catholic leaders have proposed another approach: that we cease to observe holy days of obligation as holidays in our schools. The holiday no longer serves any useful purpose, they argue, but it does much to promote tensions in regards to transportation, state aid, and the development of a uniform school calendar for all of the schools in the state.

Student Absence for Retreat. Most Catholic superintendents seem to think that hard feelings can be avoided if the pastors schedule retreats after school hours or on holidays. Where these times are not feasible, any possible clash can be avoided by planning far enough in advance and by consulting public-school officials.

Religious Emphasis Days or Weeks. These practices would seem to indicate a sincere desire on the part of public-school administrators to make up for the absence of formal religious teaching in the schools. Even though of questionable value in their usual form, they have a place and, where well planned, they might even be encouraged. A series of talks on moral and spiritual topics seems perfectly acceptable, though this should be planned in a cooperative manner by participants. The slight risk of indifferentism for Catholic students must be weighed against the positive values derived by the religiously unchurched student. It might also be kept in mind that these activities will often be scheduled without him if the priest declines to participate. His absence proves nothing; his presence continues to enrich the contemporary ecumenical spirit.

Church-Affiliated Clubs. Because of its professedly neutral character, the Hi-Y Club (high-school YMCA and YWCA) has long had entry into the public school. The Masonic youth affiliates, the DeMolay and the Rainbow Girls, have also had ready access to high-school students in the public school. Perhaps the time is now come for urging that the same privilege be extended to the CYO and similar Catholic-sponsored youth clubs. In a few cities junior Newman Clubs have been organized in the public schools, currently numbering well over 100,000 members. New York, where the first club was started over thirty-five years ago, has enjoyed success in junior Newman Club work. Perhaps greater efforts in this direction would help other cities to better reach Catholic youngsters in the public school.

The Library. The present policy of denying or limiting important books in the field of religion as well as leading church-sponsored magazines and journals to high-school libraries is due for re-examination. Neutrality here defeats the educational purpose of the school. If needed, a multi-faith advisory committee could be asked to work out an equitable formula for the school board that would make significant thought in print available to students. If necessary, separate shelves with appropriate labels could identify the offerings. A criterion that would help in choosing periodicals would be whether they are indexed in the *Readers' Guide to Periodical Literature.*

Textbooks and Teaching Materials. On occasion a course in social studies will discuss sensitive issues in the areas of sex, marriage, and family life without proper balance and in ways derogatory to the traditional moral teaching of the Christian churches. Granted that many traditional ideas of human relationships are shifting because of new insights and understanding of man and his condition, junior and senior public high school are perhaps not the most appropriate places to sell the "new" morality. Questions relating to sex and marriage, family planning, therapeutic abortion, criminal sterilization, euthanasia, etc., should be approached with delicacy. Public-school administrators are anxious to avoid the unseemly controversy and ensuing publicity which crude treatment of these flammable issues invariably brings. This is another natural field where the school could enlist the competence of skilled clergymen or counselors.

Pressure to have sex instruction included in courses in social studies is on the increase. Many films about human growth and reproduction present the matter with delicacy and discretion. Others do not. The quarrel is not with the knowledge these films bring but rather with the circumstances of their showing. At least, it was formerly questioned by many people whether these films should be shown to mixed groups or whether even showing a film on feminine hygiene or general sex instruction to an all-girl audience is appropriate. Responsible educators, including some Catholic superintendents, argue that the alarming results of widespread ignorance of sex matters require the school to step in and assume responsibility because of parental failure. In San Francisco and in New York, to cite only two instances, the Catholic school office has led in preparing instructional material on sex now used among all types of schools.

Religious Counselors and Chaplains in the Schools. With the rise of counseling and guidance services in the public schools, it seems strange that so little has been done to enlist the help of clergymen for these programs. Commonly a good counselor will recognize his inadequacy to deal with problems which have a medical or psychiatric basis, and so call for qualified assistance from a doctor or a psychiatrist. It would seem to be the part of common sense to follow a similar policy relative to those student problems which are basically moral or religious. A number of municipalities, e.g., Detroit, have successfully engaged the services of trained priests as full-time marriage counselors working in the city courts. Similarly priests and religious are counseling in the juvenile courts as full employees. Even if for some reason the school district cannot reimburse them, the diocese should be ready to pay for counselors or chaplains in the public schools. The wearing of "people" clothes rather than clerical or religious garb in most places no longer presents an impediment. Nor should it anywhere.

Religious Census. Questions on official forms about religious affiliation of the student, even on an optional basis, have been protested as a religious "test." Secularist and Jewish groups, moreover, have succeeded with regularity in keeping such questions off the decennial census. In the school, however, this information can be important. In case of a serious accident a Catholic pupil has the right to be taken to a Catholic hospital and to have a priest summoned. Almost any conceivable program to provide spiritual counseling or sacramental opportunities for Catholics in the public school depends upon the ability to identify them.

A wide consensus exists as to the worth of supplementing courses in social studies for older pupils with at least a schematic acquaintance with American religious values. Such a supplement would have to be carefully prepared by a multi-faith group and taught by experienced teachers. There still remains in many parts of the Protestant world an appalling ignorance of things Catholic. It must be admitted that the general Catholic knowledge of the non-Catholic world is hardly better. Shouldn't Catholic-high-school students have a truer understanding of pivotal figures in Protestant history, like Luther, Henry VIII, and Calvin than the simple caricature which so many of them used to acquire? American society would be the gainer if non-Catholic youngsters knew what the Mass meant in Catholic belief, and if young Christians appreciated the meaning of the Torah for the Jewish people. The alternative to some imaginative planning here is to prolong our contrived ignorance of the sources of America's spiritual greatness.

At times Catholic opinion is sought about a likely-to-be controversial book for the public-school library. In one city the Catholic superintendent asks his reviewing committee to appreciate that the book is not likely to represent a 100 per cent Catholic viewpoint and, therefore, cannot be submitted to the same standards established for books and texts to be used in Catholic schools. It is usually enough if the book does not have false or slanted statements. Public-school teachers themselves are told not to allow discussions of controverted doctrinal or moral points but to urge pupils to discuss these things with their parents or clergyman. This is not just an easy way out. The immaturity of the students and their large ignorance does not qualify them to handle such subjects calmly and profitably. But since the 1962–63 "No Prayer-No Bible" decisions of the U. S. Supreme Court, educators are increasingly urging courses "about" religion and religious history.

Some significant beginnings in teaching about religion have already been made. The Florida State University at Tallahassee has a two-year project under way to prepare a religion curriculum for social studies courses in public high schools. During 1969 and 1970, some sixty teachers will be trained in special summer institutes and will test religion units for high-school social studies courses. Present plans call for the Florida State Department of Education to publish a curriculum guide for use throughout Florida.

Indiana has likewise taken leadership in this field. Many public high schools in the state provide carefully planned optional courses in biblical literature. The Religious Instruction Association is, in fact, based in Fort Wayne.[16] This is an incorporated organization founded to promote "the significant, legal, and proper uses of religion and religious literature, including the Bible, in public schools."

Even before the 1963 Bible-reading and prayer negative decisions, there was a total of sixty-eight high schools in seventeen states offering courses with such titles as "The Literature of the Bible," "Bible History," and simply "The Bible."[17] The number of high

---

[16] Address: Religious Instruction Association, 4001 Fairfield Ave., Fort Wayne, Ind. 46807. The executive secretary of the association and his assistant have published a valuable compendium of everything being done in this field. James V. Panoch and David L. Barr, *Religion Goes to School: A Practical Handbook for Teachers* (New York: Harper & Row, Publishers, 1968).

[17] A study reported in the *English Journal* ranks the Bible along with Greek mythology and the *Iliad* of Homer as one of the three richest sources of allusions in the literature generally presented in American public-school English classes. The new awareness of this fact and the removal of all doubt as to its legality have hastened the building of units on "The Bible as Literature" by curriculum study centers in several states. Packets of material are now available on biblical subjects from the Religious Instruction Association and other national offices.

schools presently providing such courses has snowballed during the past five years.

*   *   *

Perhaps the greatest irony in the contemporary discussion of the future of the Catholic schools is the naïve assumption among some Catholics that if these schools are phased out, in the long run the Catholic parent will save money by having his youngster in the state-supported school. Studies done by Notre Dame's Office for Educational Research have pinpointed some of the fallacies behind this thinking. If American society lets pluralism in education die, the price will indeed be dear. Much of the cost of parochial-school education has hitherto been absorbed in such fiscal categories as "contributed services" and "convent foundation." With the shrinkage in the number of religious teachers occupying convent residences, the rental figure per occupant rises grotesquely. What once might have been an extremely economical housing arrangement, becomes a luxury. Closing and consolidating schools will take up some of the slack, but many more fully-salaried lay teachers will have to be brought in. Better central organization will produce more efficient schools, hopefully, but new sources of subsidy must also be found.

It is almost paradoxical that business and industry have been so slow to assist in the financing of the nonpublic schools. Their alertness and sensitivity to the encroachment of government in every other area of human activity is a byword. Every reason they publish for keeping the state out of their affairs has validity in the field of education. Yet with a few notable exceptions, business and industry have not been generous in their support of the nonpublic schools. Here and there, however, things are changing. One Illinois diocese has been partially successful in persuading the heavy taxpayers in its area to contribute yearly one hundred dollars for each of the twenty-thousand-odd high-school youngsters in the Catholic schools.

The immediate crisis in Catholic education may be financial, but it is not really the root one, just as a man's immediate trouble can be the blister on his left heel but his deep-down problem is cancer of the liver. We repeat, if the Catholic community were truly convinced that the separate Catholic school system is the necessary way to pass on the faith to the next generation, then they would find the money. If Catholics were convinced that the school was the one best way, the clergy and laity would be terribly derelict in their duty for not having made provision from the beginning that every Catholic child be in a Catholic school. In a nation which spends $25 billion for tobacco and liquor and $26 billion to operate its public elementary and secondary schools, money cannot honestly be the principal problem. At least not yet.

On the other hand, it would be foolish to underestimate the financial factor, which is inexorably going to become more crucial. Some relief is forthcoming from various auxiliary service or child-benefit enactments; some substantial assistance may be forthcoming if the recently passed Pennsylvania law governing "purchase of services" is sustained by the courts and is then imitated by other states. A final look should be taken at both categories.

Among the most valuable pupil benefits is use of the school bus. Denial of equal busing service to pupils in Catholic elementary and secondary schools in the name of separation of church and state is about as self-defeating and benighted a policy as has survived into the last third of the twentieth century, yet in one-half the states the school bus still does not roll for pupils in Catholic schools. Children attending parochial schools have every right to the same kind of publicly provided transportation as have pupils in the public schools. It is no longer merely a question of the state's choosing to accommodate parochial-school pupils or of allowing them to profit by such a service along established routes for public-school children. Every school district should provide home-to-school-and-return conveyance for *all* school children. At present only a handful of states provide this equal service.

Much of the emotion and controversy over the issue would disappear if the state department of education went out of the bus business. Since operating a transportation is per se a noneducational activity, it would more naturally fit into a more appropriate department. The "wall of separation" would appear less formidable if the state highway commission or the department of highways or the vehicle licensing department or the state motor police were supervising the buses rather than school districts or state departments of education. These groups only receive the franchise through delegation from the state itself. It is the state which possesses the police power, which in all other instances it delegates to the political subdivisions of the state. There is nothing intrinsically educational about the inspection of the tires on a school bus, or the establishment of qualifications to drive one.

Teaching materials and textbooks are other important benefits which, if provided from public funds, would ease the financial squeeze on parochial schools. Last June's U. S. Supreme Court decision in the New York textbook case has opened the way for other states to provide a similar benefit for nonpublic-school pupils. There are some sticky administrative procedures to be worked out here but the effort has to be made. Sectarian-sponsored schools cannot expect the state to supply instructional material that is obviously colored by denominational principles or beliefs. Nor by "denominational" is here meant what Justice Douglas means—any reference to God as Creator or to man's supernatural destiny. On the other hand, perhaps the time has come to rethink the question of "special" textbooks. If additional material is called for to supplement or complement what the subject educationally calls for, let the interested parties supply it. Restraint and tact should be exercised by all those concerned. What must be avoided is the kind of pressure that forces a school to drop *The Merchant of Venice* as a piece of anti-Semitic literature, or of *Uncle Tom's Cabin* as defamatory of the Negro character. The use of advisory bodies would serve to lessen problems here.

The Elementary and Secondary Education Act and the National Defense Education Act have already established norms and policies to govern areas like the allocation of audio-visual machines and material and the sharing in remedial and special category programs. Where restrictive measures in any state constitution or its strict interpretation bar parochial-school youngsters from receiving these benefits through the state office of education, the federal government should continue to establish channels to see that the purpose of these educational measures is not thwarted.

As part of its normal function the contemporary elementary and secondary school is expected to provide tests and materials administered by qualified personnel to assist pupils in special ways. If there is a physical handicap which impairs vision or hearing, or there is a mental deficiency or a speech problem, special help is expected to be available. It should be routine for the government to provide the needed facilities, preferably within the nonpublic school but at least in some accessible place, for parochial-school youngsters.

In the contemporary high school the guidance program is as much a fixture as team sports. Almost from the opening week of freshman year, students are pointed toward college and vocation. The skilled counselor knows how to motivate, how to get to the root of personal or family problems that may be an impediment to scholastic success. No other generation seems to have needed this extra solicitude more than the current pressure-prone and tension-ridden "revolting" generation.

The "purchase of secular services" from sectarian-sponsored institutions is a concept which has been regularly upheld by the courts in special areas.[18] Many states have turned to these private institutions for care of abandoned children, orphans, the physically and mentally handicapped, juvenile delinquents, and the indigent aged and infirm. The national Medicare legislation is the most recent widespread application of the principle that the state may utilize any existing facility to ease the burden of medical costs and hospitalization for its citizens. The fact that the home or the hospital is conducted by Christian Brothers or Sisters of Charity is irrelevant to the state's purpose.

In January of 1968, the state of Ohio began to purchase $15,000,-000 of supplemental educational services from the nonpublic schools of the state. The money is distributed at the rate of twenty-five dollars per pupil per school year, and its chief beneficiaries among Ohio's 390,000 nonpublic-school children are those enrolled in the Catholic schools. The secular services that may be purchased include testing and counseling; programs for the deaf, blind, emotionally disturbed, crippled, and physically handicapped; audio-visual aids; speech and hearing programs; remedial reading; and educational TV services. No funds may be expended for religious instruction or materials. No money is handled by the nonpublic institutions or offices, but all requests are made through public-school superintendents in the districts in which the nonpublic schools are located.

Last June, the commonwealth of Pennsylvania took a historic advance which, if sustained by the courts, may help set a national pattern for the future and bring all aspects of American education closer together. Because of its critical import, the Pennsylvania situation and the new law deserve careful consideration.[19]

---

[18] The 1899 *Bradfield* v. *Roberts* decision of the U. S. Supreme Court allowed aid to a sisters' hospital for a secular purpose—the care of the indigent poor.

[19] The full text of the Pennsylvania law may be consulted in Appendix A

In Chapter Five we discussed in general terms the financial problems of American education. The Quaker State is typical of those heavily populated states whose creaky financial structure for supporting public education could topple at any time. Quite unintentionally and innocently the Catholic schools of the state could become the demolition agent of the antiquated structure. How? Last year these five conclusions were presented to the voters and legislators of Pennsylvania.

1. That nonpublic education—embracing 23 per cent of all elementary- and secondary-school pupils in the commonwealth and effecting vast tax savings to the total public—is a factor of basic importance to the economy and the educational future of the state.
2. That any substantial reduction in numbers of the nonpublic-school population spells severe economic hardship to Pennsylvania and grave disturbance for her public schools.
3. That nonpublic education in Pennsylvania, which for eleven decades has borne the burden of immense service to the total public, cannot much longer meet the cost of continuing this service in spite of any desires or sacrifices on the part of its supporters.
4. That many public-school districts of the commonwealth are today faced with too severe financial difficulties to permit their accommodating substantial additional population resulting from reduction in nonpublic-school population.
5. That the solution of Pennsylvania's educational crisis is to afford nonpublic education a measure of support, within strict constitutional limitations, sufficient to enable it to continue to render its public service.

During the year that the bill was discussed, passed, and signed into law, Pennsylvanians spent $1.546 billion on elementary and secondary education. Of this total the state supplied $561,000,000, local taxpayers paid $635,000,000, and $350,000,000 represented the value of the contribution of citizens who sent their youngsters to the nonpublic schools. The burden, difficult as it might be spread across the state, would become crushing in the urban centers—today

which follows this chapter. The data on this and the next page are taken from a study prepared by the Pennsylvania Catholic Conference, 212 State Street, Harrisburg, Pa.

the least well off of school districts so far as the tax basis goes. Philadelphia is spending $190,000,000 for its present public-school population, but to absorb the Catholic-school children would require an additional $85,500,000. Pittsburgh, now spending $49,-600,000, would have to put out an additional $22,300,000. These figures are simply for operating costs. Capital outlay is another and bigger headache—which during 1968 came to haunt the sleep of many public-school administrators in Pennsylvania.

On the conservative estimate that it is possible to erect a school for something like $2000 per student, you simply multiply that sum by the 600,000-plus pupils in the nonpublic schools to reach a rough figure of $1.2 *billion!* Philadelphia would immediately pay $313,000,000 and Pittsburgh $75,500,000 for new school buildings. Add to this nightmare the fact that in most urban areas land shortages are severe, and if eminent domain is exercised to appropriate property, the tax-paying basis of support is shrunk even more. If more garish colors are needed to embellish the scene, one need but think of other consequences—the administrative anarchy, the acute shortage of qualified teachers and staff, and worst of all, the effects on the children.

Even given the grimness of the Pennsylvania situation, the purchase-of-services bill did not have an easy passage through the legislature. To the credit of their social awareness, a comfortable majority of both houses of the Pennsylvania General Assembly and the governor voted for the future. The bill was written with punctilious respect for the constitutional guidelines that have emerged from U. S. Supreme Court and Pennsylvania State Supreme Court decisions in this field. The subjects of secular hue which the state may purchase from nonpublic schools are limited to the following four: mathematics, modern foreign languages, physical science, and physical education. The state superintendent of public instruction's office administers the program, establishes rules and regulations, and makes the specific contracts. Maybe Pennsylvania has come up with only the partial answer, and maybe the courts will knock it out. But if purchase-of-services does not get a fair trial, nightmares may just become the normal sleeping fare for executives, legislators, and public-school administrators everywhere in these United States.

* * *

In an earlier chapter we tried to analyze the distinctive nature of "Christian" education. Perhaps all attempts to define it or to limit it by description are foredoomed to only partial success. In pressing for precision here there is danger of resembling the pedantic pharisees, who wanted of Christ a propositional distillation of His message in order to refute or institutionalize it. At least we can agree, in closing, that as an educational institution every Christian or Catholic school should concretely give witness to the reality of the Christian mystery. The details of witness may vary from situation to situation and from epoch to epoch but a universal component remains. The Christianity-oriented school is established to facilitate growth in charity by creating an atmosphere or perceptual field based on charity. Its basis is the reality of God the Father and of the mission of His Son Jesus, who became the Son of Man to re-establish the order of charity among men and between mankind and God.

The examination of conscience that the Christian communities engaged in separate religious education must make, begins with an understanding of the nature of the church and its mission to men.

Is the church's primary concern to preserve uncontaminated what it already has, or go out for more? The church is witness, teacher, and servant to man on every age-level in his needs as man. Has the church placed a disproportionate emphasis on teaching those who are "safely" at the center of the church, thereby endangering its role as witness and servant?[20] In other words, do the Catholic schools preferentially serve those young people who are already receiving a good training in Christian life and worship at home, and if so, is this leading to the neglect of young people from marginal or lapsed homes?

In the recent past, the church has been regarded as a monolithic, stable, and compact institution whose mandate was to influence society by eventually bringing all men across its threshold through formal conversion to one true faith in Christ. Today the church is seen as a movement which in varying degrees inspires and influences man as Christ's sacrament in time and space. Didier Piveteau, F.S.C., likens the process to a man swimming in a current throughout his lifetime, wherein he is under the influence of salvation often without

---

[20] Ronald L. Johnstone, *The Effectiveness of Lutheran Elementary and Secondary Schools as Agencies of Christian Education* (St. Louis, Mo.: Concordia Seminary, 1966), p. 144.

being aware of it. In the past the child and the classroom were the focus of ecclesiastical concern. Those children outside the Catholic school, and the adult world were given a modicum of attention. The church's principal instrument for the religious education of over half the Catholic children in America, the Confraternity of Christian Doctrine, still exists "on a hope and a dream."[21]

In varying degrees the Carnegie-Notre Dame, Greeley and Rossi, and Lutheran studies quoted in chapter four conclude that the parochial schools have not done an outstanding job in religious education. So much time and energy are expended raising funds to keep the schools solvent that few resources have been put to grappling with new methods of teaching religion or creating awareness of the Christian community. Somewhat tardily have we begun to prepare media to reflect the new theological and scriptural insights, as well as the better psychological understanding of the teaching-learning relationship. The difficulty of the task should only challenge to more intense effort.

The re-examination of the Catholic school in the past seven or eight years has made it clear that the Catholic sponsorship of a school on any level does not guarantee its success as a school nor as an incubator of dedicated Catholics. Neither the Greeley and Rossi nor the Lutheran study could find more than a few marks that differentiate the parochial-school product from the young Catholic or Lutheran from the public school if both came from relatively sound Christian homes. The Lutheran study asks:

Is this perhaps because for a youth to grow at all noticeably in his Christian faith and life, such growth must come for interaction and encounter with other ideas, other beliefs, other behavior patterns that come only from getting out into the ebb and flow of the world around him? Is there not potentially great value in a public school education for our youth, provided we work closely with them in additional challenging programs (weekday programs, released time, shared time, and programs yet to come) that stimulate them and help them grow in the environment in which they must eventually earn their living?[22]

[21] A survey of CCD directors unearthed a bewildering confusion of goals, general ineffectiveness, and frustration. One-half of the diocesan directors responding to the survey described themselves as not professionally trained, and two of every three doubted the effectiveness of their diocesan offices. (*Ave Maria*, May, 1968).

[22] Johnstone, *op. cit.*, p. 146.

Obviously these are serious questions and admit of neither a simple nor a general answer.

There are Catholic leaders who agree that the most effective way of applying the principle which incessantly seeks to combine educational reality and Christian life is within the public-school system. They insist that it is in the public school that the church must find the possibility of proclaiming and developing the faith with a system of religious teaching given *in* the school, though not *by* the school. They want Catholics—teachers and students—in the public schools without any ambiguity or sense of inferiority. In future years this may well be the case for even more Catholic school children. The parochial school as we have known it may not be achieving its original objectives. Some of these objectives have been assumed by the public school or no longer exist, such as: providing a school in a frontier community where there was no school, preserving a particular language and culture, protecting the faith of Catholic children from Protestant proselytism.

The key issue is not simply to have or not to have parochial schools. It is Christian education. The dioceses and parishes must rigorously evaluate their efforts on behalf of all their people—children, youth, adults. Again, it must be stated that there is no blueprint which will prove applicable everywhere. To repeat, traditions, conditions, and resources vary widely among the 156 dioceses and 18,604 parishes into which is divided the Catholic Church, U.S.A., 1969. Prayer and thought must be applied to each situation. The question in its simplest form becomes: How perceptive are we, how well do we envisage the needs of God's people and the means of translating, reshaping, and discarding forms that have the dust of centuries upon them, while creating fresh forms that bear the spirit of Christianity and provide new relevance to an ancient message?

Despite the many unresolved problems that the future holds, it is predictable that the new approach of the Catholic community to its own schools, as well as to the public schools, will be more akin to the progressive attitude of the 1890's. It is not impossible that by the 1990's both the present public-school system and the Catholic system will be replaced by one comprehensive school system, publicly supported, within which the educational objectives of the religious groups can also be realized.

In its evolutionary path into the future, the Catholic school still has a vital role to play in American society. It will be boldly contemporary, educationally superlative, distinctively Christian, and increasingly ecumenical. It will be a bridge to "further the dialogue between the church and the family of man to their mutual benefit." Because of its Vatican II–inspired openness, it will no longer seem to be one of the hierarchical church's instruments of conquest, and though under church control, it will not necessarily be administered by it. Because it can then truly *serve* society, it will be supported by society. In this perspective the Catholic school can find a place, instead of being "as it is today, a sign of contradiction, even among Catholics, between its partisans and its adversaries."[23]

Catholic education is trembling on the brink of a new era of greatness. But we need the courageous vision of the kind argued for by John Henry Newman in asking us to accept the truth that "in a higher world it is otherwise, but here below to live is to change, and to be perfect is to have changed often."

[23] Jean Sinclair, "L'Éducation Chrétienne au Concile," *Études,* March, 1966, p. 391.

Appendix A

PENNSYLVANIA NONPUBLIC ELEMENTARY AND SECONDARY EDUCATION ACT

Introduced as H. 2170 December 12, 1967.
Amended by Senate June 11, 1968.
Signed into law June 19, 1968

AN ACT

To promote the welfare of the people of the Commonwealth of Pennsylvania; to promote the secular education of children of the Commonwealth of Pennsylvania attending nonpublic schools; creating a Nonpublic Elementary and Secondary Education Fund to finance the purchase of secular educational services from nonpublic schools located within the Commonwealth of Pennsylvania for the benefit of residents of the Commonwealth of Pennsylvania; authorizing the Superintendent of Public Instruction to enter into contracts to carry out the intent and purposes of this act, and to establish such rules and regulations as are necessary; providing for the payment of administrative costs incident to the operation of the act; providing procedures for reimbursement in payment for the rendering of secular educational service; and designating a portion of revenues of the State Harness Racing Fund and of the State Horse Racing Fund as the sources of funds.

The General Assembly of the Commonwealth of Pennsylvania hereby enacts as follows:

Section 1. Short Title.—This act shall be known and may be cited as the "Nonpublic Elementary and Secondary Education Act."

Section 2. Legislative Finding; Declaration of Policy.—It is hereby determined and declared as a matter of legislative finding—

(1) That a crisis in elementary and secondary education exists in the Nation and in the Commonwealth involving (i) the new recognition of our intellectual and cultural resources as prime national assets and of

the national imperative now to spur the maximum educational development of every young American's capacity; (ii) rapidly increasing costs occasioned by the rise in school population, consequent demands for more teachers and facilities, new but costly demands, in the endeavour for excellence, upon education generally; the general impact of inflation upon the economy; and the struggle of the Commonwealth commonly with many other states, to find sources by which to finance education, while also attempting to bear the mounting financial burden of the many other areas of modern State governmental responsibility;

(2) That nonpublic education in the Commonwealth today, as during past recent decades, bears the burden of educating more than twenty per cent of all elementary and secondary school pupils in Pennsylvania; that the requirements of the compulsory school attendance laws of the Commonwealth are fulfilled through nonpublic education;

(3) That the elementary and secondary education of children is today recognized as a public welfare purpose; that nonpublic education, through providing instruction in secular subjects, makes an important contribution to the achieving of such public welfare purpose; that the governmental duty to support the achieving of public welfare purposes in education may be in part fulfilled through government's support of those purely secular educational objectives achieved through nonpublic education;

(4) That freedom to choose nonpublic education, meeting reasonable State standards, for a child is a fundamental parental liberty and a basic right;

(5) That the Commonwealth has the right and freedom, in the fulfillment of its duties, to enter into contracts for the purchase of needed services with persons or institutions whether public or nonpublic, sectarian or nonsectarian;

(6) That, should a majority of parents of the present nonpublic school population desire to remove their children to the public schools of the Commonwealth, an intolerable added financial burden to the public would result, as well as school stoppages and long term derangement and impairment of education in Pennsylvania; that such hazard to the education of children may be substantially reduced and all education in the Commonwealth improved through the purchase herein provided of secular educational services from Pennsylvania nonpublic schools.

Section 3. Definitions.—The following terms whenever used or referred to in this act shall have the following meanings, except in those instances where the context clearly indicates otherwise:

(1) "Nonpublic Elementary and Secondary Education Fund" shall mean the fund created by this act.

(2) "Secular educational service" shall mean the providing of instruction in a secular subject.

(3) "Secular subject" shall mean any course which is presented in the curricula of the public schools of the Commonwealth and shall not include any subject matter expressing religious teaching, or the morals or forms of worship of any sect.

(4) "Nonpublic school" shall mean any school, other than a public school, within the Commonwealth of Pennsylvania, wherein a resident of the Commonwealth may legally fulfill the compulsory school attendance requirements of law.

(5) "Purchase secular educational service" shall mean the purchase by the Superintendent of Public Instruction from a nonpublic school, pursuant to contract, of secular educational service at the reasonable cost thereof.

(6) "Reasonable cost" shall mean the actual cost to a nonpublic school of providing a secular educational service and shall be deemed to include solely the cost pertaining thereto of teachers' salaries, textbooks and instructional materials.

Section 4. Nonpublic Elementary and Secondary Education Fund.— There is hereby created for the special purpose of this act a Nonpublic Elementary and Secondary Education Fund dedicated to the particular use of purchasing secular educational service consisting of courses solely in the following subjects: mathematics, modern foreign languages, physical science, and physical education, provided, however, that as a condition for payment by the Superintendent of Public Instruction for secular educational service rendered hereunder, the Superintendent of Public Instruction shall establish that (i) solely textbooks and other instructional materials approved by the Superintendent of Public Instruction shall have been employed in the instruction rendered; (ii) a satisfactory level of pupil performance in standardized tests approved by the Superintendent of Public Instruction, shall have been attained; (iii) after five years following the effective date of this act, the secular educational service for which reimbursement is sought was rendered by teachers holding certification approved by the Department of Public Instruction as equal to the standards of this Commonwealth for teachers in the public schools: Provided, however, That any such service rendered by a teacher who, at the effective date of this act, was a full time teacher in a nonpublic school, shall be deemed to meet this condition.

Section 5. Administration.—The administration of this act shall be under the direction of the Superintendent of Public Instruction, who shall establish rules and regulations pertaining thereto, make contracts of every name and number, and execute all instruments necessary or convenient for the purchase of secular educational service hereunder. All expenses incurred in connection with the administration of this act shall be paid solely out of the Nonpublic Elementary and Secondary Education Fund and no money raised for the support of the public schools of the Commonwealth shall be used in connection with the administration of this act.

Section 6. Moneys for Fund.—(a) Permanent moneys. Into the Nonpublic Elementary and Secondary Education Fund shall be paid each year:

(1) All proceeds from horse racing up to the first ten million dollars ($10,000,000) realized by the State Horse Racing Fund established by the act of December 11, 1967 (Act No. 331), remaining after, and not required for, payment of all the items of administrative cost set forth in subsection (b) of Section 18 of that act, plus

(2) One-half of all such horse racing proceeds in excess of the sum of ten million dollars ($10,000,000), the remaining half thereof to be paid into the General Fund.

(b) Temporary Moneys. Until the time that proceeds in the amount of ten million dollars ($10,000,000) shall, in a given fiscal year, have been paid into the Nonpublic Elementary and Secondary Education Fund as provided for under subsection (a) of Section 6 hereof, three-fourths of the proceeds from harness racing realized by the State Harness Racing Fund established by the act of December 22, 1959 (P.L. 1978), as amended, remaining after and not required for, the payments provided for in subsections (b) and (d) of Section 16 of that act, shall be paid into the Nonpublic Elementary and Secondary Education Fund according to the following formula:

(1) The entire three-fourths of the harness racing proceeds for any fiscal year shall be paid into the Nonpublic Elementary and Secondary Education Fund until such year as the horse racing proceeds designated by this section for the said fund are of such amount that, combined with the harness racing proceeds, the sum of ten million dollars ($10,000,000) shall have been realized by the Nonpublic Elementary and Secondary Education Fund.

(2) Proceeds from harness racing shall cease to be paid into the Nonpublic Elementary and Secondary Education Fund for any fiscal year in which proceeds from horse racing, designated by this section for the Nonpublic Elementary and Secondary Education Fund, shall equal ten million dollars ($10,000,000).

Moneys in the Nonpublic Elementary and Secondary Education Fund are hereby appropriated to the Department of Public Instruction to be used by the Superintendent of Public Instruction solely for the purchase of secular educational service hereunder and administrative expenses pertaining thereto as provided for in Section 5 of this act.

Section 7. Reimbursement Procedures.—(a) Request for reimbursement in payment for the purchase of secular educational service hereunder shall be made on such forms and under such conditions as the Superintendent of Public Instruction shall prescribe. Any nonpublic school seeking such reimbursement shall maintain such accounting procedures, including maintenance of separate funds and accounts pertaining to the cost of secular educational service, as to establish that it actually expended in support of such service an amount of money equal to the amount of money sought in reimbursement. Such accounts shall be subject to audit by the Auditor General. Reimbursement payments shall be made by the Superintendent of Public Instruction in four equal installments payable on the first day of September, December, March and June of the school term following the school term in which the secular educational service was rendered.

(b) Reimbursements for any fiscal year for the purchase of secular educational service hereunder shall not exceed the total amount of the moneys which were actually paid into the Nonpublic Elementary and Secondary Educational Fund in that fiscal year.

(c) In the event that, in any fiscal year, the total amount of moneys which were actually paid into the Nonpublic Elementary and Secondary Education Fund shall be insufficient to pay the total amount of validated requests hereunder in reimbursement for that year, reimbursements shall be made in that proportion which the total amount of such requests bears to the total amount of moneys in the Nonpublic Elementary and Secondary Education Fund.

(d) The Budget Secretary shall, by July fifteenth of each year, certify to the Superintendent of Public Instruction, the total amount of money in the Nonpublic Elementary and Secondary Education Fund.

Section 8. Effective Date.—This act shall take effect July 1, 1968.

Section 9. Severability.—If a part of this act is invalid, all valid parts that are severable from the invalid part remain in effect. If a part of this act is invalid in one or more of its applications, the part remains in effect in all valid applications that are severable from the invalid applications.

Appendix B

STATEMENT ON THE NATURE OF THE CONTEMPORARY CATHOLIC UNIVERSITY

1. *The Catholic University: A True University with Distinctive Characteristics.*

The Catholic university today must be a university in the full modern sense of the word, with a strong commitment to and concern for academic excellence. To perform its teaching and research functions effectively the Catholic university must have a true autonomy and academic freedom in the face of authority of whatever kind, lay or clerical, external to the academic community itself. To say this is simply to assert that institutional autonomy and academic freedom are essential conditions of life and growth and indeed of survival for Catholic universities as for all universities.

The Catholic university participates in the total university life of our time, has the same functions as all other true universities and, in general, offers the same services to society. The Catholic university adds to the basic idea of a modern university distinctive characteristics which round out and fulfill that idea. Distinctively, then, the Catholic university must be an institution, a community of learners or a community of scholars, in which Catholicism is perceptibly present and effectively operative.

2. *The Theological Disciplines.*

In the Catholic university this operative presence is effectively achieved first of all and distinctively by the presence of a group of scholars in all branches of theology. The disciplines represented by this theological group are recognized in the Catholic university, not only as legitimate intellectual disciplines, but as ones essential to the integrity of a university. Since the pursuit of the theological sciences is therefore a high priority for a Catholic university, academic excellence in these disciplines becomes a double obligation in a Catholic university.

3. *The Primary Task of the Theological Faculty.*

The theological faculty must engage directly in exploring the depths of Christian tradition and the total religious heritage of the world, in order to come to the best possible intellectual understanding of religion and revelation, of man in all his varied relationships to God. Particularly important today is the theological exploration of all human relations and the elaboration of a Christian anthropology. Furthermore, theological investigation today must serve the ecumenical goals of collaboration and unity.

4. *Interdisciplinary Dialogue in the Catholic University.*

To carry out this primary task properly there must be a constant discussion within the university community in which theology confronts all the rest of modern culture and all the areas of intellectual study which it includes.

Theology needs this dialogue in order:

a) to enrich itself from the other disciplines;

b) to bring its own insights to bear upon the problems of modern culture;

c) to stimulate the internal development of the disciplines themselves.

In a Catholic university all recognized university areas of study are frankly and fully accepted and their internal autonomy affirmed and guaranteed. There must be no theological or philosophical imperialism; all scientific and disciplinary methods, and methodologies, must be given due honor and respect. However, there will necessarily result from the interdisciplinary discussions an awareness that there is a philosophical and theological dimension to most intellectual subjects when they are pursued far enough. Hence, in a Catholic university there will be a special interest in interdisciplinary problems and relationships.

This total dialogue can be eminently successful:

a) if the Catholic university has a broad range of basic university disciplines;

b) if the university has achieved considerable strength in these disciplines;

c) if there are present in many or most of the non-theological areas Christian scholars who are not only interested in and competent in their own fields, but also have a personal interest in the cross-disciplinary confrontation.

This creative dialogue will involve the entire university community, will inevitably influence and enliven classroom activities, and will be reflected in curriculum and in academic programs.

5. *The Catholic University as the Critical Reflective Intelligence of the Church.*

Every university, Catholic or not, serves as the critical reflective intelligence of its society. In keeping with this general function, the Catholic university has the added obligation of performing this same service for the church. Hence, the university should carry on a continual examination of all aspects and all activities of the church and should objectively evaluate them. The church would thus have the benefit of continual counsel from Catholic universities. Catholic universities in the recent past have hardly played this role at all. It may well be one of the most important functions of the Catholic university of the future.

6. *The Catholic University and Research.*

The Catholic university will, of course, maintain and support broad programs of research. It will promote basic research in all university fields, but, in addition, it will be prepared to undertake by preference, though not exclusively, such research as will deal with problems of greater human urgency or of greater Christian concern.

7. *The Catholic University and Public Service.*

In common with other universities, and in accordance with given circumstances, the Catholic university is prepared to serve society and all its parts, e.g., the Federal Government, the inner city, et cetera. However, it will have an added special obligation to carry on similar activities, appropriate to a university, in order to serve the Church and its component parts.

8. *Some Characteristics of Undergraduate Education.*

The effective intellectual presence of the theological disciplines will affect the education and life of the students in ways distinctive of a Catholic university.

With regard to the undergraduate—the university should endeavor to present a collegiate education that is truly geared to modern society. The student must come to a basic understanding of the actual world in which he lives today. This means that the intellectual campus of a Catholic university has no boundaries and no barriers. It draws knowledge and understanding from all the traditions of mankind; it explores the insights and achievements of the great men of every age; it looks to the current frontiers of advancing knowledge and brings all the results to bear relevantly on man's life today. The whole world of knowledge and ideas must be open to the student; there must be no outlawed books or subjects. Thus the student will be able to develop his own capabilities and to fulfill himself by using the intellectual resources presented to him.

Along with this and integrated into it should be a competent presentation of relevant, living, Catholic thought.

This dual presentation is characterized by the following emphases:

a) a concern with ultimate questions; hence a concern with theological and philosophical questions;

b) a concern for the full human and spiritual development of the student; hence a humanistic and personalistic orientation with special emphasis on the interpersonal relationships within the community of learners;

c) a concern with the particularly pressing problems of our era, e.g., civil rights, international development and peace, poverty, et cetera.

9. *Some Special Social Characteristics of the Catholic Community of Learners.*

As a community of learners, the Catholic university has a social existence and an organizational form.

Within the university community the student should be able not simply to study theology and Christianity, but should find himself in a social situation in which he can express his Christianity in a variety of ways and live it experientially and experimentally. The students and faculty can explore together new forms of Christian living, of Christian witness, and of Christian service.

The students will be able to participate in and contribute to a variety of liturgical functions, at best, creatively contemporary and experimental. They will find the meaning of the sacraments for themselves by joining theoretical understanding to the lived experience of them. Thus the students will find and indeed create extraordinary opportunities for a full, meaningful liturgical and sacramental life.

The students will individually and in small groups carry on a warm personal dialogue with themselves and with faculty, both priests and laymen.

The students will experiment further in Christian service by undertaking activities embodying the Christian interest in all human problems —inner-city, social action, personal aid to the educationally disadvantaged, and so forth.

Thus will arise within the Catholic university a self-developing and self-deepening society of students and faculty in which the consequences of Christian truth are taken seriously in person-to-person relationships, where the importance of religious commitment is accepted and constantly witnessed to, and where the students can learn by personal experience to consecrate their talent and learning to worthy social purposes.

All of this will display itself on the Catholic campus as a distinctive style of living, a perceptible quality in the university's life.

10. *Characteristics of Organization and Administration.*

The total organization should reflect this same Christian spirit. The social organization should be such as to emphasize the university's concern for persons as individuals and for appropriate participation by all members of the community of learners in university decisions. University decisions and administrative actions should be appropriately guided by Christian ideas and ideals and should eminently display the respect and concern for persons.

The evolving nature of the Catholic university will necessitate basic reorganizations of structure in order not only to achieve a greater internal cooperation and participation, but also to share the responsibility of direction more broadly and to enlist wider support. A great deal of study and experimentation will be necessary to carry out these changes, but changes of this kind are essential for the future of the Catholic university.

In fine, the Catholic university of the future will be a true modern university but specifically Catholic in profound and creative ways for the service of society and the people of God.

Land O'Lakes, Wisconsin
July 23, 1967

Index